JOHNS HOPKINS UNIVERSITY STUDIES

IN

HISTORICAL AND POLITICAL SCIENCE

———

EXTRA VOLUMES   NEW SERIES, No. 12

THE ANGLO-JAPANESE
ALLIANCE

THE ANGLO-JAPANESE ALLIANCE

BY

CHUNG-FU CHANG, Ph. D.

BALTIMORE: THE JOHNS HOPKINS PRESS
LONDON: HUMPHREY MILFORD
OXFORD UNIVERSITY PRESS

1931

The Lord Baltimore Press
BALTIMORE, MD., U. S. A.

PREFACE

There is no doubt that the most important single factor in the international relations in the Far East in the first two decades of the twentieth century was the Anglo-Japanese Alliance. During its life the Alliance affected directly the interests of four nations, namely: Japan, Great Britain, China, and Korea; and indirectly the interests of the United States, Russia, Germany, and even France. The fact that the Alliance was not abrogated until a Four-Power Pact was consummated at the Washington Conference indicates the important position the Alliance occupied in the relations between the Powers having interests in the Pacific.

Almost six years had elapsed since the termination of the Alliance in August, 1923, when ratifications of the Four-Power Pact were deposited with the United States Government. Since then, rumors of a renewal of the Alliance have appeared at least twice in the world press, first in the summer of 1927, and again in the winter of 1928. On both occasions world-wide interest was aroused. This gives evidence that, even now, the Alliance is of more than historical interest.

On this subject two books have been written: *China, the United States and the Anglo-Japanese Alliance,* by Mr. G. Zay Wood, and *The Anglo-Japanese Alliance,* by Professor Alfred P. Dennis. The

v

first book is *une livre d'heure*. The second is a more
scholarly treatise. However, since the appearance
of that work much additional material has been made
available.

Since the ending of the World War several governments in Europe have opened their archives, in
whole or in part. Based upon these documents his-
torians have endeavored to reconstruct the diplomatic history of Europe. But they have largely
neglected those of these documents which involve
the Far East. On the subject of the Anglo-Japanese
Alliance not even such widely used documents as the
British Parliamentary Papers, the British Parliamentary Debates, and the Foreign Relations of the
United States have been thoroughly and systemati-
cally consulted.

In view of the above fact, the author decided to
make a new study of the subject. In preparing this
monograph the author has used Chinese and Japanese materials. It is regrettable, however, that the
diplomatic documents in the archives of the Tokio
Government have not yet been opened to the public.

The writer sent to Japanese book stores for
memoirs of Prince Ito, Count Mutsu and other Japanese statesmen, but these memoirs are out of print.
This explains why in this monograph only a few
Japanese sources have been used. Nevertheless, it
is the belief of the author that, even if these Japanese sources were accessible, the result of the study
in its general outline in this monograph would not

be affected, because, in fact, a large number of the communications of the Japanese Government have appeared in other foreign documents.

In preparing this monograph the author has been greatly indebted to Professor Westel W. Willoughby and to Professor James Hart. Without their encouragement and kind help, extended to the author in many ways, this monograph might not have been prepared. The author is also greatly indebted to Professor Tyler Dennett, Mr. Frank E. Ross, Mr. Thomas D. McCormick, and Mr. Henry P. Chiu for their part in reading either a part or the whole of the manuscript and in making various valuable suggestions.

C. F. C.

CONTENTS

CHAPTER I

The Origin of the Alliance

" Look at those two island kingdoms, Great Britain and Japan. Are they not like the two eyes in the face? If they could only see together! " said a Japanese gentleman who was looking at a map of the world with Lord Redesdale some sixty years ago.[1] No one at that time dreamed that this was destined to be a prophecy. Great Britain was then one of the strongest European powers, while Japan was then only beginning to emerge out of feudalism. Yet, within the short period of thirty-five years, this wish was realized so far as the two governments were concerned. Fundamental changes had occurred during this interval, which, while weakening Great Britain, had added much to the power and prestige of Japan. In 1902, when the alliance was signed, Great Britain was still the dominant European power, while Japan's complete independence had only been recognized a few years before, Great Britain giving the first real encouragement to Japan's national ambitions by taking the lead in treaty revision in 1894. In view of this fact, it is no wonder that the Anglo-Japanese Alliance of 1902

[1] Lord Algernon Bertram F. Redesdale, *The Garter Mission to Japan,* London, 1906, p. 29.

1

came to the world as something of a shock.[2] That Great Britain, the strongest power in Europe, with a traditional policy of " splendid isolation," should ally herself with a small Oriental nation, the strength of which as a first-rate power was not yet tested, and to which racial equality has never even to this day been accorded, was seemingly past comprehension.

When we examine this matter more carefully, however, we find that this was only a natural outcome of the political events of the preceding years in the Far East, as well as in the rest of the civilized world. Nations do not make or refrain from making alliances merely from sentimental reasons; they do only what their interests require.

The fundamental purpose of British foreign policy has always been the safeguarding of her overseas possessions, above all of India, the jewel of them all. The continued advance of Russia from the north, and of Great Britain from the South, brought these two great powers, rivals for the control of central Asia, ever closer together, until only Afghanistan lay between their spheres of influence. Fearing that the ulterior aim of the forward movement of Russia was an approach to India through the mountains, thus enabling her to strike at the root of their Em-

[2] G. P. Gooch in his *British Foreign Policy in the Twentieth Century* says: " Its conclusion [The Anglo-Japanese Alliance] was hardly less of a surprise to the British Empire than to the rest of the world." G. P. Gooch and J. H. B. Masterman, *A Century of British Foreign Policy,* London, 1917, p. 45.

pire, British statesmen in India were unanimous in
their feeling of anxiety as to the danger menacing them on the northwestern frontier, with Afghanistan the weakest link in their chain of defenses.[3]
The situation was even more perplexing, as there
were no exact frontiers, for these changed continu-
ally with the fortunes of war. Ever since 1868,
British statesmen had labored to effect an understanding with Russia as to the limits within which
the spheres of influence of the two countries should
extend, in order to avoid a war, which, according to
Sir John Lawrence, would involve the two contend-
ing nations in every part of the world.

Russia never hesitated to give the fullest possible
assurances as to her pacific intentions, while continu-
ing to push forward; and, where she went, there she
remained. After her humiliation in Europe at the
hands of Great Britain, she determined on reprisals
in central Asia. The subjugation of the Téké Turko-
mans in 1880-81, and the occupation of Merv and
Sarakhs in 1884 caused no small anxiety in Great
Britain. Certain alarmists already professed to believe that the fate of Herat itself hung in the balance.
More and more the British statesmen were convinced
that there could be no certainty of any check to the
Russian advance until the question of frontier zones
was definitely settled by means of a convention with

[3] For details, see A. W. Ward and G. P. Gooch, *The Cambridge
History of British Foreign Policy, 1783 to 1919,* Cambridge, 1922-23,
III, 72-91, 187-193.

Russia. This was attained in July, 1887, only after a war had been averted, in March, 1885, by the caution of British statesmen, who had remained calm throughout the crisis. Nevertheless, the northeastern frontier of Afghanistan was not defined until March 11, 1895, when an agreement was concluded between the two powers. Nor was the anxiety caused by the border tribes in the East appeased until the last years of the century. From 1878 to 1898 the wars and military operations on or just beyond the borders of British India in which the Indian Government had been engaged were calculated to be no less than sixty-four in number.

These events, testing tremendously as they did the troubled nerves of the British statesmen, were not all. For, at the same time, trouble arose on another frontier of the Indian Empire.[4] After the Franco-Prussian War, France turned to the project of building a colonial empire to recoup her losses in Europe. From 1872 onward, French intrigue became increasingly active in Burma. Deciding to end this situation, Lord Dufferin proclaimed the annexation of the country in January, 1886, after a successful invasion conducted in the winter of the preceding year. This brought the British possessions up to the border of Siam, beyond which lay French Indo-China. Siam, being a country lying between these two rival empires, its independence was of vital importance to India. In May, 1893, France, after de-

4 For details, see Ward and Gooch, III, 193-200.

manding that the territory occupied by Siam on the Annam side of the river should be abandoned, and, after rejecting Siam's proposals of arbitration, without either warning or offer of conditions of peace, attacked Siam and war followed. Peace was not concluded until the 3d of October. Siam promised to concede to France important rights and to renounce to her forever the islands in the river and any claim to territory on the left bank of the Mekong. A claim which demanded the cession of territory, 100,000 square miles in extent, was only withdrawn under the moderating pressure firmly exercised by Lord Rosebery.

In 1891, Russia concluded a secret alliance with France.[5] Although this treaty was wholly concerned with Europe, the friendship thus established naturally extended to all parts of the world. This was highly detrimental to the British interests. Thereafter, it was not France and Russia separately, but the great Franco-Russian combination that Great Britain had to face. To meet this situation, in Europe, Great Britain endeavored to work more or less in harmony with the Central Powers.[6] In the Mediterranean and in the Near East, she had the friendship of Italy and Austria,[7] but in central Asia and in the Far East, in facing the Franco-Russian menace, she stood alone. Naturally, she desired to have some

---

[5] George P. Gooch, *History of Modern Europe,* London, 1878-1919, pp. 174 ff.

[6] Ibid., pp. 142-145, 205-206.

[7] This arrangement was formed with the encouragement of Bismarck. Spain adhered to the second one. Ibid., pp. 150-152.

ally in that part of the world to check the joint advance of France and Russia, and to protect British interests in both India and the Far East. Italy and Austria were useless in those quarters. Germany had as yet very little interest there.[8] Japan was too small for consideration. The only possible candidate, rich and strong enough to meet the need, was China.

Before the Sino-Japanese War, though critics were not lacking in England in depicting the weakness of China as a military power, " the most thoughtful of English newspapers " was still of the opinion that:[9] " We believe that the weight of opinion is on the side of those who hold, as we do, that China could, if hard put to it, organize a most formidable fighting force."

Not only did the British public still have confidence in the potential power of China, but also their interests seemed to be the same. The successive advances made by Russia at China's expense, had taught her to regard that power as her real enemy. Chinese statesmen had time and again expressed that fear.[10] It was Russia who threatened her fron-

---

[8] Germany was not yet a Far-Eastern power, although she possessed several small Pacific islands. She encouraged, rather than checked, the Russian advance in the Far East.

[9] George N. Curzon, *Problems of the Far East,* Westminster, 1896, p. viii.

[10] As early as during the Opium War, Commissioner Lin said: " We do not need to fear those powers beyond the sea; in my opinion the real danger to China in the future will be Russia." The Statesmen of the Ching Dynasty (Kuo Chou Min Chen Yen Hsin Lou), XX, 6. Also see ibid., XXII, 3.

tiers in Chinese Turkestan and on the Pamirs; Russia, who had evil designs in Tibet and Manchuria; Russia, whose shadow overhung Korea; Russia, who was building a great transcontinental railway that was to enable her to pour troops into China at any point along 3,500 miles of continuous border. Thus, writing in 1896, Lord Curzon said:

The very conditions that render Russia the natural enemy of China would appear to constitute Great Britain her natural friend. China desires, or should desire, to keep the Russian Army out of Korea, and the Russian Navy away from the Yellow Sea. We are similarly interested in both objects China wants, or should want, to retain Yoarkund and Kashgar, and therefore requires a defensible and defended frontier on the Pamirs. We are also anxious to avoid Russian contiguity with ourselves at the Hindu Kush or the Karakoram. China attaches, or should attach, a high value to her suzerainty over Tibet, which Russia notoriously covets. England does not quarrel with the former, but could hardly welcome the latter status. If the Trans-Siberian railway will be a menace to Chinese territorial integrity, it will also generate a sharp competition with British Asiatic trade. Farther to the south, the recent apparition of France as an aggressive factor upon the confines of Siam and Burma has been a source of no slight annoyance to China, already exasperated by the theft of Tongking. It is not more acceptable to ourselves, who have no desire for France as a next-door neighbor on the borders of our Indian Empire. There are, therefore, the strongest *a priori* reasons in favor of a close and sympathetic understanding between China and Great Britain in the Far East. Nor, though Chinese armaments are, in their present state, a delusion, and Chinese military strength a farce, and though the full extent of the imposture has been relent-

2

lessly exposed during the recent war, can any one deny that the prodigious numbers of China, her vast extent, her obstinate and tenacious character, and her calculating diplomacy, render her a coadjutor in Central and Eastern Asia of no mean value; just as it would appear that the prestige and power of Great Britain in the same regions might be of corresponding and even greater service to her.[11]

If a British statesman, who believed that the Chinese are " very unwarlike people," and had no confidence at all in the military power of China, even potentially, after the war of 1894-95 had exposed the weakness of the Chinese Empire, still held the conviction that China could be " a co-adjutor in Central and Eastern Asia of no mean value," there can be no difficulty in understanding the British attitude toward that country in the years preceding the Sino-Japanese War. It has been the British policy, for more than a century, to make alliances with Oriental states, in order to secure British safety, power, and final expansion in India. It was chiefly by such means that the foundation of British rule in India had been laid.[12] Now, the Indian Empire was facing a danger from both north and south which, perhaps, ever since the British settlement in India, had never before been so serious. This explains why, in those years, Great Britain was so anxious for the friendship of China.

[11] Curzon, pp. 279-280.
[12] Alfred L. P. Dennis, *The Anglo-Japanese Alliance*, Berkeley, California, 1923, p. 18. C. U. Aitchison, *A Collection of Treaties, Engagements and Sanads relating to India and Neighboring Countries* (Calcutta, 1892), *passim,* but note, in particular, VIII, 280; IX, 433; X, 37, 48; XI, 54.

This desire rose to its height in the early part of 1885, when war between Russia and Great Britain in Afghanistan was seriously threatening. Mr. Colquhoun, the *Times* special correspondent, writing on the probabilities and the advantages of such an alliance, said:

Now I am in a position to state that an Anglo-Chinese alliance is one which not only will commend itself most strongly to the Chinese, and which is feasible and efficacious, but that in the event of war it may be looked upon as almost a certainty.

As regards China, the motive would be, first, the protection of Korea; secondly, the protection of Kashgar, Kuldja, and the north-west of China; thirdly, the recovery of the Amoor Provinces, filched from China by Ignatiev in 1858 under cover of the Anglo-French guns. . . . . And with an English alliance, this could be accomplished with great ease. China has already a large body of good troops . . . . posted at positions which are strongly fortified along the north-eastern frontier. . . . . China has now in Yunnan, Kwangsi, and Kwangtung some 130,000 men available, besides another force in Central China, who could be transported by sea in a few weeks and landed at Port Lazarev or other convenient points in Korea near the Russian frontier, England meanwhile keeping command of the sea. With good leading by English officers the northern Chinese army, augumented by these southern forces, could be hurled against the Russian posts and simply overwhelm the feeble forces which Russia could bring against them. Vladivostok, Nocolievsk, and Possiette, could be taken from the seaboard, and the whole of the Amoor provinces reconquered from Russia, while serious troubles could be raised for her in central Asia from Kashgar and Kuldja. China would eagerly jump at an alliance with England against Russia, to take effect on the occurrence of either of the following events: . . . . Threatening or violating the frontier (1) of Afghanistan, (2) of Kashgar-Kuldja, (3) of Korea. Either of these, to be a *casus belli* for England and China. The Chinese would engage to move an army immediately against the Amoor provinces, and England to guarantee the Chinese Coast and provide transport.

In conclusion, he said:

Russia could thus be rolled back beyond the Amoor, and such a spirit would be aroused in China, especially now that she has the nucleus of a real fighting force ready made, as would keep Russia in check for a generation to come. Do what she will, Russia can never have very large forces in those regions, and China can always crush her by numbers, if only her troops are decently directed and handled, as they would be by even the merest handful of English officers.

There is no one object China would fight for and make sacrifice for like this. That is an absolute certainty. . . . . Russia is the nightmare of all Chinese statesmen—as well may she be—and a burning ineradicable sore in the breast of Manchus. China to a man would hail with ardor an English alliance against Russia. Such an alliance, I need hardly say, would give England the virtual control of the Chinese military and naval forces, and assist her to maintain her position in the Extreme East with comparatively small cost and responsibility, while giving her paramount influence in the commercial development of China.

Japan already favors the arrangement strongly, and it is probable that the following combination will spring into existence, should war be declared between England and Russia. The combination is: (a) Anglo-Chinese as far as Afghanistan, Kashgar-Kuldja, and Korea are concerned; and (b) Anglo-Chino-Japanese for the protection of Korea alone.

In view of the development of the power and commerce of China and Japan, and of the prospective importance of commercial as well as other advantages, such a close relation to these two powers would be of the utmost value to England.

Such an alliance would be based on common and permanent interests, and would be a natural and therefore durable and beneficial alliance. Nothing so advantageous for the future of England in the East could be conceived.[13]

Nor was the British Government slow to appreciate the situation. Lord Granville, then British Secretary of State for Foreign Affairs, in April, 1895, taking the opportunity of the Chinese protest against the British occupation of Port Hamilton, made overtures to the Chinese minister at London.[14] Thereafter the British Government constantly kept in view the winning of Chinese friendship.[15] In 1893, when Siam was at war with France, another opportunity was presented. Not failing to take this opportunity, Great Britain definitely asked of China, through her minister at Peking, Mr. McDonald, a treaty for the protection of Siam against French aggression.[16] In the winter, when Great Britain was negotiating with Russia to define the northeastern frontier of Afghanistan, Chinese cooperation was

[13] Archibald R. Colquhoun, *English Policy in the Far East,* being the *Times* Special Correspondence, London, 1885, pp. 24-26.

[14] Hsieuh Foo-Chen, *The Diary of a Diplomat* (Chu Shih Er Chi), II, 46; *British Foreign and State Papers,* LXXVIII, 143.

[15] Hsieuh, III, 19.

[16] Chinese Minister at London to the Chinese Government, 20th day 9th moon of the 19th year of Kwang Shu (October, 1893); 5th day 10th moon; 9th day 10th moon; Chinese Government to the Chinese Minister at London, 24th day 9th moon; 4th day 10th moon. *The Correspondences of Li Hung Chang* (Li Wen Chung K'ung Chuan Soo), "Telegrams," XV, 5-6.

again asked for.[17] For this, Great Britain was even willing to give certain territorial concessions to China.[18] China at this time was afraid of France and Russia, and did not want to make any entangling alliances. The offer was therefore refused.[19]

[17] Chinese Government to the Chinese Minister at St. Petersburg, 23d day 11th moon of the 19th year of Kwang Shu (December, 1893); Chinese Government to the Chinese Minister at London, 24th day 11th moon; Li to the Peking Government, 14th day 12th moon; Li to the Chinese Minister at London, 15th day 12th moon. Li, "Telegrams," XV, 10-13.

[18] On the borders of Siam and Afghanistan. Li to the Peking Government, 29th day 10th moon of the 19th year of Kwang Shu (November, 1893), Li, "Telegrams," XV, 7; 14th day 12th moon, XV, 12; 17th day 12th moon, XV, 13; Peking Government to the Viceroy of Yunnan, 19th day 11th moon, XV, 9; Peking Government to the Chinese Minister at London, 25th day 10th moon, XV, 7; Li to the Chinese Minister at London, 15th day 12th moon, XV, 13.

[19] Chinese Government on the 4th of the 10th moon (October, 1893), cabled to the Chinese Minister at London: ". . . . The British Minister, Mr. McDonald, suggested that China and Great Britain should enter into a treaty, in view of the French intrigue (in Siam), to safeguard the integrity of Siam. He said that if France knows that there is such a treaty between China and Great Britain, France will certainly not dare to continue the intrigue. The British Government believes that to safeguard the integrity of Siam is to protect her interest in Burma. For this reason she asks for our help. If we make a treaty with Great Britain we will be hated by France. In case France is not to be bluffed and still continues her intrigue in Siam, we will get into trouble. The best way to safeguard the integrity of Siam is, as in the case of Belgium, by making an international agreement between China, Great Britain and France. Please discuss with the British Government and think of some other way to protect Siam. If the British Government asks you about what Mr. McDonald said, kindly tell them that China has never concluded any secret alliance with any power, but she is willing to offer friendly mediation." Li, "Telegrams," XV, 6. Mr. Tang Shao Yi in an interview with a special correspondent of the New York Tribune, published in that paper under Shanghai date, June 12, 1920, said: "The

Then came the Sino-Japanese War. British interests in the Far East demanded peace and the
maintenance of the *status quo* in Korea and upon
the Chinese borders.[20] The central aim of the British
policy in the Far East was to check the Russian advance. A war between China and Japan would not
only involve the British commercial position, but
endanger large general interests of Great Britain.[21]
From the beginning of the controversy, it was these
" large general interests " that British statesmen
took pains to protect. They wished to maintain
peace, and thus to mediate,[22] but they preferred to
allow events to take their own course, if Russia
could reap any advantage from the peace negotiations. Thus, when the Russian proposal was made

---

Anglo-Japanese Alliance would have been an Anglo-Chinese alliance,
if China had won the Sino-Japanese War. Great Britain made overtures to China shortly before the Sino-Japanese War, through her
Minister to Peking, Mr. McDonald. He asked China to enter into
an understanding with Great Britain. China at that time was afraid
of Russia and the Peking Government did not wish to make any
entangling alliances."

[20] See the opinion of Lord G. N. Curzon and Herr von Brandt,
London *Times*, August 9, 1894, and August 29, 1894, p. 3, respectively.

[21] London *Times*, August 1, 1894, p. 9. Observations of Sir Edward
Grey in the Commons on July 30, 1894, *Par. Deb.*, 4th Series, XXVII,
1354.

[22] Reply of Sir Edward Grey in the Commons on July 26, 1894,
Par. Deb., 4th Series, XXVII, 1027. Observations of Sir Edward
Grey in the Commons on July 30, 1894, *Par. Deb.*, 4th Series, XXVII,
1354. Li to the Peking Government, 17th day 5th moon of the 20th
year of Kwang Shu (June, 1894), Li, " Telegrams," XV, 47; 22d
day 5th moon, XV, 52; The Peking Government to Li, 29th day 5th
moon, XV, 60-61; 2d day 5th moon, XVI, 3; Li to the Chinese
Minister at Paris, 3d day 6th moon, XVI, 4.

known at Peking that a convention should be held at
Peking by the three neighboring powers (China,
Japan and Russia) to deliberate over the Korean
question,[23] Great Britain immediately protested and
suggested, instead, an international convention to be
attended by all the interested powers.[24] Neither of
these proposals suited the other powers; their mutual
jealousy prevented them from doing so.[25] The result was that they stood aloof and decided on watch-
ful waiting.

At the beginning and the early stages of the war,
British sympathy was clearly on the side of the
Celestial Empire.[26] It was true that Great Britain
had proclaimed a " strict neutrality " [27] towards the
belligerents, as soon as the war was declared, but
this did not prevent the admiral in command of the
British squadron in Far Eastern waters from demon-
stratively showing his preference for the Chinese,
and he was even suspected of having on some occa-

[23] Li to the Peking Government, 27th day 5th moon (June, 1894),
Li, " Telegrams," XV, 56; Peking Government to Li, 6th day 6th
moon, XVI, 9.

[24] Vice-Minister Chang to Li, 27th day 5th moon (June, 1894), Li,
" Telegrams," XV, 58.

[25] Vice-Minister Chang to Li, 28th day 5th moon of the 20th year
of Kwang Shu (June, 1894), Li, " Telegrams," XV, 59; Li to the
Peking Government, 29th day 5th moon, XV, 61; 7th day 6th moon,
XVI, 10-11; 7th day 6th moon, XVI, 12; 16th day 6th moon, XVI,
24; Li to the Chinese Minister at Paris, 3d day 6th moon, XVI, 4;
Peking Government to Li, 2nd day 6th moon, XVI, 3; Li to the
Chinese Resident in Korea, 8th day 6th moon, XVI, 13; Li to the
Chinese Minister at London, 17th day 6th moon, XVI, 25.

[26] London *Times,* August 1, 1894, p. 9; August 6, p. 6.

[27] State Papers, LXXXVI, 141 ff.; London *Times,* August 7, 1894.

sion endeavored to warn by signal the Chinese admiral of the approach of the Japanese fleet.[28] The *Kowshing* incident which started the war, in which a British transport ship carrying Chinese soldiers was destroyed by the Japanese, certainly could not be expected to enlist any British sympathy for Japan. Commenting on this incident, the *Times* observed on October 1, 1894:

Such explanations as those which the Japanese Government continues to put forth are certainly not of a kind either to diminish the indignation of China or to gain for Japan the sympathies of indifferent powers. . . . . No satisfactory explanation whatever is given as to why the Japanese Commander fired upon the Chinese ships. . . . . The Japanese may have some real excuses for the action of their sailors, but if they have it is high time they produce them. The world is getting anxious to know what they are. . . . .

Perhaps the fact that we are now yielding to her earnest desires on points of great concern to her and of great interest to many of our fellow-subjects may remind her before it is too late, how high the value of the good opinion of other peoples is, and may save her in time from the risk which she now runs of forfeiting the esteem she has earned at home by an unjust policy of aggression and adventure abroad.[29]

Two days later the same paper observed:

Nothing, however, can alter the fact that the sinking of the transport was a horrible business. . . . . And one thing comes out more clearly than ever from the officers' affidavits; namely, that the excuse put forward by the Japanese Govern-

[28] Baron Ramon R. Rosen, *Forty Years of Diplomacy*, New York, 1922, I, 136.
[29] London *Times*, August 1, 1894, p. 9.

ment—that the Japanese commander did not know that the *Kowshing* was a British ship—is absolutely unsupported. . . . . The captain fired his torpedoes well knowing that the ship which was carrying the soldiers whom he regarded as enemies, was a British ship.[30]

But soon the great battles of Ping-Yang (September 15 and 16) and Yalu (September 17) were fought, and in both the Chinese were badly defeated. British public opinion, so far as represented by the *Times,* immediately underwent a change. As soon as this news reached England, the *Times* in a leading article declared:

It is matter for satisfaction that, in this country we did not wait to acknowledge the claims of Japan until Japan had given practical proof that she was no longer a power to be treated as on a level with half-barbarous states. By the treaty which has been ratified, we have shown that we were prepared to recognize her title to the same rights as other civilized powers, independently of the success or failure of her arms. We have removed all reasonable grounds of grievances against us, and we have done so at a time which makes misconstruction as to our motive very difficult. . . . . Great Britain and Japan have no interests which are obviously in conflict with each other. There are some interests which may prove of the highest importance that are common to both nations.[31]

The reason for this change was not hard to find. China, who had been expected for years by Great Britain to defend British interests in the Far East, had now shown herself incapable of protecting even

[30] Ibid., August 3, 1894, p. 7.
[31] Ibid., September 24, 1894, p. 7.

her own interests, to say nothing of those of the British people, who had now to find some other ally for this purpose. Rumors being already rife abroad of diplomatic intervention at the close of the campaign, it was seen that it might be wise for Great Britain, in order to protect her interests in the Far East, to court the friendship of the newly rising power. This idea was expressed by the *Times* itself in the same article:

Despite her pledge to China not to occupy Korea, Russia still hankers after the possession of a secure and open harbor on the Pacific. . . . . But neither Great Britain nor Japan could look upon its fulfillment without concern. To Japan's future development as a maritime state, no more dangerous blow could be inflicted. To ourselves it would be a cause of considerable cost and anxiety. Rumors are already abroad of diplomatic intervention at the close of the campaign, whatever the issue of that campaign may prove to be. Should such intervention take place, it would be strange if the representatives of Great Britain and Japan are not found, at least on some important points, standing side by side.[32]

After the total collapse of the Chinese forces, the about-face of the *Times* was complete. Its selfish purpose cannot be better expressed than by its own words:

It can hardly be any longer supposed . . . . that China is a country whose friendship is worth cultivating by feeble concessions to her pretensions and pride. The myth about her latent power, and the dream about her awakening, have been completely dissipated by the war. . . . . China is a huge inert mass, which will be organized and energized from the outside

[32] Ibid., September 24, 1894, p. 7.

if at all. We shall have to see to it that this process is not carried out by others to our detriment. . . . .[33]

If British public opinion had been favorable to China at the beginning and during the early stages of the war, even more so was the opinion of the British Government.[34] For years Great Britain had nursed China to be her ally in the Far East.[35] Although an offer to become such had been twice refused, the replies of the Chinese Government were so cordial that the project could not be set aside as entirely hopeless. Besides this, Great Britain had still another reason to retain the Chinese good will: the Chinese were her best customers. Already, Great Britain had a preponderating commercial interest in the Celestial Empire, whose vast extent of territory, if entirely opened, would afford an unlimited field for British trade. As mentioned above, British interests in the Far East demanded peace. Japan was this time the aggressor and was thus acting against the British interests.[36] Furthermore, the pivot of British Far Eastern policy, Russia, was sus-

[33] Ibid., September 30, 1895, p. 9.

[34] Li to the Peking Government, 20th day 6th moon of the 20th year to Kwang Shu (July, 1894), Li, " Telegrams," XVI, 29. Li to the Chinese Minister at London, 20th day 6th moon, XVI, 29; Peking Government to Li, 23d day 6th moon, XVI, 30; The Chinese Minister at London to Li, 27th day 6th moon, XVI, 25.

[35] Since April, 1895. See above.

[36] The fact that Japan was this time the aggressor was not unknown. See London *Times,* July 26, 1894, pp. 8, 9; August 1, p. 9; August 6, pp. 6, 7; August 29, p. 3; September 3, p. 4; September 17, p. 4. Li to the Peking Government, 15th day 6th moon of the 20th year of Kwang Shu (July, 1894), Li, " Telegrams," XVI, 24.

pected of being on the Japanese side.[37] Finally, a
defeat of the Chinese Empire would strengthen the
Russian position on the Asiatic continent, and, consequently, weaken that of Great Britain, which
power made it clear to Japan that, if Japan would
not listen to her advice and make peace, she would be
held responsible for the consequences.[38] Perhaps the
reason why Great Britain did not support China and
exert a strong pressure on Japan for peace, was that
she believed, if China were left alone, she would come
out victorious,[39] and above all, that Russia would side
with Japan if she showed too much favor for China.
But soon came the unexpected defeat of China in the
great battles of Ping-Yang and Yalu. At the request
of Li Hung-Chang,[40] Great Britain again urged the
powers to intervene, and suggested for its basis " an

[37] Rosen, I, 135-136.

[38] Li to the Peking Government, 20th day 6th moon of the 20th
year of Kwang Shu (July, 1894), Li, " Telegrams," XVI, 29; Li to
the Chinese Minister at London, 20th day 6th moon, XVI, 29; The
Chinese Minister at London to Li, 27th day 6th moon, XVI, 35.

[39] Captain Lang, R. N., an officer under whom some of the principal Chinese forts were constructed, and who was for many years
the principal European in the Chinese navy, in an interview said:
" in the end there is no doubt that the Japanese must be utterly
crushed. If the Chinese liked they could keep a war going for a
century. She is a self-supporting country, and is quite content to
wait for a desired result. . . . . There is the making of anything in
the Chinese. They are well trained and excellent marksmen, and
the discipline is very good. . . . . The Chinese ships are very good.
. . . . In my opinion Wei-hai-hai is impregnable, and no Japanese
fleet dare approach it." London Times, August 8, 1894, p. 3.

[40] Li to the Chinese Minister at London, 13th day 10th moon of
the 20th year of Kwang Shu, Li, " Telegrams," XVIII, 40.

indemnity to Japan for the expenses of the war and the independence of Korea, to be guaranteed by the Powers.'' [41] But the German refusal prevented this from being realized,[42] and the German arguments were so convincing that even the Prime Minister, Lord Rosebery, was willing to drop the matter, temporarily at least.[43] Foreign powers were already by this time alert to take advantage of the offered opportunities.[44] If rumors were to be believed, China and Japan certainly would not be left alone to deal with each other in the coming peace negotiations. The designs of these would-be-intervening powers were yet unknown. As to the Japanese demands, the British Government was equally in the dark.[45] The English press had already condemned the actions of the Government as hasty and unwise.[46] Thereafter, the British statesmen became very cautious; they tried to come to agreements with the foreign powers beforehand.[47] When, the next spring, Li Hung-Chang again asked for intervention,[48] England moved

[41] *Die Grosse Politik der Europäischen Kabinette 1871-1914* (1924) IX, 243.

[42] Ibid., IX, 243-244.

[43] Ibid., IX, 244 und Fussn.

[44] Ibid., IX, 251.

[45] Ibid., IX, 251.

[46] London *Times,* November 7, 1894, p. 9; November 13, p. 9.

[47] *Die Grosse Politik,* IX, 251, 257.

[48] Li to Chinese Ministers at London and St. Petersburg, 1st day 2nd moon of the 21st year of Kwang Shu (Feb. 1895), Li, "Telegrams," XX, 18.

slowly and refused to say anything before the Japanese terms of peace were known.[49]

When the Japanese terms were known, and England was invited to join the Triple Entente in the Far East,[50] she had to consider the whole question again in its broader aspects. Hitherto, China had been the Far Eastern power, and Great Britain had counted upon her friendship against Russia and to maintain the British position in the Far East. Now China was badly defeated, and, not only that, she would not be able to play the important rôle in Far Eastern matters that she had before, while her weakness would, in the future, constitute a constant danger and a constant temptation. The practical question confronting the British statesmen was how to safeguard England's position as the dominant power in the Extreme East, and how to keep British trade interests from being prejudiced.[51] The cession of Port Arthur meant in fact a Japanese control over North China.[52] In the war Japan had shown herself to be an aggressive power. With such a strategic point in her hands, no one could predict with assurance that British interests in China would not be endangered. Furthermore, a cession of part of the Chinese mainland might lead to similar acts upon

[49] Chinese Minister at London to Li, 2d day 2d moon of the 21st year of Kwang Shu (Feb., 1895), Li, "Telegrams," XX, 18-19; Chinese Minister at St. Petersburg to Li, 6th day 2d moon, XX, 20.

[50] *Die Grosse Politik,* IX, 272.

[51] Cf. the opinion of Herr von Brandt, London *Times,* April 13, 1895, p. 3.

[52] *Die Grosse Politik,* IX, 262.

the part of the other powers, the result of which
would be a dismemberment, or a partial dismemberment, of the Chinese Empire, whose integrity England was anxious to preserve.[53]

By the war Japan demonstrated her position as a
strong power in the Far East and that she could no
longer be thrust aside as a negligible factor. To join
in the intervention would arouse bitter resentment
among the Japanese against England, who, having
the largest commercial interests in the Far East,
would suffer more than any other power from such
a state of things.[54] Great Britain, hated by Russia
on one side, and by Japan on the other, would have
an untenable position in the Far East. Already,
Japan had shown a conciliatory attitude toward
England, and had shown marked consideration for
British interests. Right after the *Kowshing* incident, she promised to pay the necessary compensation. During the war, paying respect to British commercial interests, Japan had abstained from undertaking warlike operations against Shanghai and its
approaches.[55] In the peace negotiations, she made it
clearly known that she would not attempt to secure
any special privileges for Japanese commerce, and
that whatever commercial advantages Japan might
acquire under the treaty with China would be ex-

[53] Ibid., IX, 247, 254.
[54] London *Times,* April 23, 1895, p. 9.
[55] Reply of Sir Edward Grey in the Commons, *Par. Deb.,* 4th
Series, XXVIII, 144.

tended, by the operation of the most-favored-nation clause, to all foreign powers, including England.[56]

After all, the British interests were chiefly concentrated in and around Shanghai,[57] and were not so seriously and directly menaced as those of Russia. After the defeat of China, Korea could not be saved from Russian aggression. With the Liao-tung Peninsula in the hands of Japan, Korea might thus be protected.[58] So, British interests were not in any way threatened, as they might have seemed to be by this stipulation; while, by the economic terms of the peace, they might possibly be advanced.[59] To join in an intervention which was chiefly for Russian interests could not be acceptable to the British public, whose clearly expressed opinion could hardly be misunderstood.[60]

Nor did the British statesmen fail to realize that, by standing aloof, Great Britain had to run the risk of isolation.[61] In view of the fact, however, that the interests of the intervening powers were by no means identical, who could tell that they would maintain harmony throughout their intervention? Any rupture of the triple entente in the Far East would afford Great Britain an opportunity to come to an agreement with one or the other of these states.[62]

[56] London *Times,* April 23, 1895, p. 9.
[57] *Die Grosse Politik,* IX, 264.
[58] Ibid., IX, p. 260.
[59] London *Times,* April 8, 1895, p. 9.
[60] *Die Grosse Politik,* IX, 272, 273.
[61] Ibid., IX, 271, 272, 273.
[62] Ibid., IX, 273.

Even should their unanimity remain unbroken
throughout, Great Britain had still reserved to herself entire freedom of action.[63] The result of such
considerations was that " the interests of England
in East Asia were not sufficiently injured by the
Japanese terms of peace, in order to justify an intervention, which probably could be accomplished
only by force." [64] The English cabinet decided not
to intervene,[65] and, of course, at the same time, not
to take any steps against the powers.[66] Therefore,
she advised Japan to yield.[67] But, on the question of
Formosa, she strongly resented the French attitude
and let the Japanese know that she sympathized
with their occupation rather than with the desires of
France.[68]

Before the Sino-Japanese war, Japan had no particular political preference for either England or
Russia. When England occupied Port Hamilton, in
1885, Japan considered it as even more detrimental
to her interests than to those of China.[69] It was true
that England was the first country to surrender the

[63] Ibid., IX, 273, 274.

[64] Ibid., IX, 266.

[65] Ibid., IX, 268.

[66] Ibid., IX, 273.

[67] Summary of articles in *Jiji Shimpo* published in June and July,
1895. *The Secret Memoirs of Count Tadasu Hayashi,* ed. by Andrew
M. Pooley, 1915, p. 113. London *Times,* May 6, 1895, p. 5.

[68] *The Secret Memoirs of Count Tadasu Hayashi,* ed. by A. M.
Pooley, London, 1915, pp. 113-114.

[69] Li to the Peking Government, 7th day 3d moon of the 11th
year of Kwang Shu, Li, " Telegrams," V, 38. *State Papers,* LXXVIII,
144. *Parl. P.,* China, No. 1 (1887), Nos. 2 and 8.

treaty rights which had deprived Japan of all power over foreign residents and had prevented her from raising her tariff, but this concession was relinquished with the greatest reluctance.[70] If Japan did not consider England as her friend, she had no more reason to consider Russia as being so. As a neighboring power, Russia had more interests in conflict with Japan than had England. For years, Russia and Japan had been engaged in a dispute as to the possession of Saghalin.[71] This was only settled in 1875, after prolonged negotiations, by an agreement according to which Russia was to have this island, while Japan was to have complete sovereignty over the whole of the Kurile group.[72] In 1861, Russian marines landed on the Japanese islands of Tsu-Shima in the Korean straits, and took virtual possession of them. Her withdrawal was only effected at the instance of the British Minister.[73] In 1860, Russia became a neighbor of Korea, when, after the treaty of Aigon (May 16, 1858), Mraviov ordered the occupation of Vladivostok and Possiet Bay. Ever since then Russian surveying parties had been active on the eastern coast of the peninsula. This gave rise

[70] Count Shigenobu Okuma, *Fifty Years of New Japan* (Kaikoku Gojanenshi), English version, ed. by Marcus B. Huish, 2d ed., London, 1910, I, 101 ff.

[71] Ibid., I, 98-100.

[72] April 25, 1875, *State Papers*, LXVI, 218 ff. Stanley K. Hornbeck, *Contemporary Politics in the Far East*, New York, 1919, p. 197. Vladimir (pseud. for Zenone Volpicelli), *Russia on the Pacific and the Siberian Railway*, London, 1899, p. 324.

[73] Kanichi Asakawa, *The Russo-Japanese Conflict*, Boston and New York, 1904, p. 7.

to the suspicion that Russia was aiming at the occupation of some Korean port, which might thus endanger the safety of Japan.[74]

But, when the war broke out between China and Japan, the actions of Great Britain and Russia had to be determined by their larger interests on the continent, as a result of which, in the beginning of the war, the impression in Japan was that, " Russia would be inclined to side with Japan,"[75] and that " Great Britain might have a secret agreement with China, and in the event of war breaking out with Japan, she might render China some aid."[76] The brilliant military successes of Japan, her determination to humble China, but, above all, the prudent secrecy maintained regarding the conditions of peace, aroused the watchfulness of Russia. When the conditions of the peace imposed at Shimonoseki became known, Russia, after a careful consideration, made the momentous decision to side with China.[77] She decided to interfere and to take the necessary steps to insist on the withdrawal of Japan from Southern Manchuria and Port Arthur.

There were many reasons to suggest this action.[78] She had to guard the interests of her great future

[74] Vladimir (pseud.), p. 320.

[75] Rosen, I, 135.

[76] Hayashi, p. 78.

[77] The decision was reached by " a special Commission under the presidency of the Grand Duke Alexis, the head of the Navy, and composed of all the Ministers of State." Rosen, p. 136.

[78] Cf. Rosen, I, 136; Asakawa, p. 71; Vladimir, p. 352; " Novoe Vremya " reported in London *Times,* April 22, 1895, p. 5; *Die Grosse Politik,* IX, 270.

railway and to secure a convenient terminus on the Pacific. The future Siberian railway, if flanked by the continental possessions of Japan, would lose much of its importance, and would be deprived of a short route to the sea. Japan was at that time already in virtual possession of Korea. The occupation of such a strategic position as the Liao-tung Peninsula, a key at once to Peking, Manchuria, and Korea, would render the independence of Korea an illusion and make Japan the dominant power in the eastern part of the Asiatic continent. This would in turn constitute a grave danger to the entire future of the Eastern policy of Russia, who would suffer severely " in the material interest and in the prestige of a great power." [79] Furthermore, the Japanese could not be allowed to gain a foothold on the continent, because they would unavoidably have a tendency to spread like " a drop of oil on a sheet of blotting-paper," [80] as Prince Lobanov expressed it. On the other hand, the intervention would establish claims for compensation from China.

It was almost impossible for Russia alone to approach victorious Japan with a demand so deeply wounding to the susceptibilities of a proud nation. Had it not been for the ready and active cooperation of France and Germany, Russia would have hesitated to act. [81] Previous to the intervention and during the war, both France and Germany were

[79] London *Times,* April 22, 1895, p. 5.
[80] Rosen, I, 136.
[81] Rosen, I, 137; Asakawa, p. 71; *Die Grosse Politik,* IX, 265-266.

friendly to Japan, a feeling which was recipro-
cated.[82] This was particularly true with regard to
the latter power. Without her help, Japan could not
have concluded the new treaty with England which
was signed just a few months before the war.[83] During the conflict, Germany had twice refused to consider an intervention that would stay Japan's hand
in Korea and prevent her from humiliating China
completely.[84] Finally, on March 8, 1895, before the
Chinese envoy Li Hung-Chang left the Chinese
shores, the German Government, through her Minister at Tokio, had warned the Japanese Foreign
Office that European powers had been asked by
China to interfere, that some of these powers had
already agreed in principle, and that, according to
the latest report, a " Japanese demand for a cession
of territory on the mainland would be particularly
susceptible to provoke intervention." [85]

In France, since the war, Japan had grown considerably in the opinion of the French public.[86] In
fact, the startling victories of the small Island Kingdom, with a population of about 40,000,000, that had
swept away the opposition of a vast Empire having
a size thirty-five times that of Japan and whose
population was numbered in hundreds of millions,
captured the imagination of the people of Europe.

---

[82] Hayashi, pp. 77, 81. *Die Grosse Politik,* IX, 329.
[83] *Die Grosse Politik,* IX, 329.
[84] Ibid., IX, 241; 243-245.
[85] Ibid., IX, 253.
[86] London *Times,* September 22, 1894, p. 5.

After the battles of Ping-Yang and Yalu, the special correspondent of the London *Times* was able to report that " from the present moment they may do what they will, they may act with the greatest freedom imaginable, they may invade territories, indulge in what are called encroachments, act, in a word, like any other people possessing a sense of force, it will never enter the head of any European power to call them to account for their acts, or even for their fancies." [87]

But a judgment, based as this was upon purely sentimental reasons, could hardly be right. It was soon found that the success of Japan aroused jealousy of nearly all the powers; even Spain was reported to have taken measures in the Philippine Islands in view of " contingencies which might result from the great triumph of Japan over China." [88] However, mere jealousy was not enough to draw France and Germany into the imbroglio. They both had more vital reasons. France believed [89] that Japan's predominance over China, as the result of the taking of the Laio-Tung Peninsula, was " a constant menace for the interests of Europe, and a serious blow dealt at the rights of the immediate adja-

[87] Ibid., September 22, 1894, p. 5.

[88] Observations of M. Sone, the Japanese Minister at Paris, London *Times,* April 23, 1895, p. 5.

[89] Cf. Article in *Débats,* reported in the London *Times,* April 11, 1895, p. 3; London *Times,* April 22, 1895, p. 5; Article in the *Temps,* reported in London *Times,* April 23, 1895, p. 5; Reply of M. Hanotaux to the Socialists' attack in defence of the Government policy in the Palais Bourbon on June 10, 1895, p. 5.

cent powers," to use the words of the *Temps*.[90] In order to have " the necessary guarantees for rendering the security of Tonkin as complete as possible and for promoting our French commercial interests in those regions," [91] France had to interfere. Since the war of 1870-71, France had decided to act energetically in colonial matters in order to enhance her standing among the nations of the world. The intervention was nothing but the continuation of the policy of colonial expansion. France had " to figure in it " in order " to reap the advantage which the situation permitted." [92] Finally, France had placed " her alliances in the front rank of her considerations." " Even had the interests of France been less serious and less definite, we [the French] should have held it right not to remain uninterested as to the balance of power in the Far East. At the moment when the balance of power was about to be disturbed to the detriment of Russia, considerations of general policy commended such an attitude." [93]

Much more difficult to understand was the seeming vacillation of Germany. Writers and scholars were often puzzled to find an explanation. With the help of the documents published after the great war,

[90] Article in the *Temps,* reported in London *Times,* April 23, 1895, p. 5.

[91] Reply of M. Hanotaux to the Socialists' attack, London *Times,* June 11, 1895, p. 5.

[92] London *Times,* June 11, 1895, p. 5; April 11, 1895, p. 3.

[93] Reply of M. Hanotaux to the Socialists' attack, London *Times,* June 11, 1895, p. 5.

the basis of the German attitude has become under-
standable. The German Government thought that
the continued existence of Korea was of interest to
Russia and England, rather than to herself.[94] She
was careful not to be drawn into an action which
could only serve the interest of her rivals.[95] She,
therefore, moved with great caution in the early
stage of the war, refusing to interfere.[96] However,
Germany had been late in entering the stage of
colonial expansion. She had to act with the greatest
possible celerity in order to overtake her more wide-
awake competitors. It would not be in accord with
her colonial ambition that she should be left out of
such an important arrangement in the Far East as
the post-war readjustment. She needed a port in
Eastern Asia for her commerce and fleet.[97] Here
was a chance for Germany to put China in her debt
and to claim the right to establish coaling stations
on Chinese territory in return for her good offices.[98]
The terms of peace, it was believed, " would constitute a political preponderance of Japan over China,
and would exercise a determining influence on the
development of China's economic condition, and of
the sway of Japan in that country." [99] Japan was

[94] *Die Grosse Politik,* IX, 241, 254.

[95] Ibid., IX, 254, 256.

[96] Ibid., IX, 245-246, 248-249, 251-252, 254.

[97] Ibid., IX, 246, 248, 254, 255 und Fussn., 260.

[98] For the reasoning of the German Government in joining the
intervention, see *Die Grosse Politik,* IX, 261, 262, 266.

[99] Article in the *Cologne Gazette,* reported in the London *Times,*
April 22, 1895, p. 5. Also see ibid., April 9, p. 3; April 13, p. 3.

endeavoring to post herself as the sentry over all the important roads of China " in order, if necessary, to seclude her completely from the world." [100] The influence of this was bound to be felt by all the countries which had commercial relations with China. The European powers, therefore, had to ward off in time any steps prejudicial to their interests. The cooperation of Germany with Russian Far-Eastern aims would naturally result in an increased friendliness between the two powers in Europe also, which was sincerely to be desired in the interests of the German Empire.[101] Should France refuse to join the intervention, a breach in Franco-Russian relations would result. Should France join in the intervention, it would be difficult for England to stand aside, so the much desired common representation of the foreign interests in China would thus be secured.[102] Finally, to turn the attention of Russia to the Far East was to the advantage of Germany, for it would distract Russia's attention from her own eastern front.[103]

Facing the armed intervention of the three greatest military powers of Europe, Japan had no choice but to yield.[104] On May 10, 1895, together with the

[100] Article in the *Cologne Gazette,* reported in London *Times,* April 22, 1895, p. 5.

[101] *Die Grosse Politik,* IX, 266.

[102] Ibid., IX, 266.

[103] Ibid., IX, 266.

[104] Japan took from China 30,000,000 Kuping taels as compensation, by the Convention between Japan and China, for the retrocession by Japan to China of the Southern Portion of the Province

publication of the Treaty of Shimonoseki,[105] a Japanese Imperial Rescript was issued to the effect that the Government had accepted " the advice of the friendly powers." [106] By the treaty, the war in the Far East was ended, but the great historical drama which was to fill the next century had hardly begun its prologue. The total result of the intervention was a complete change of the relations between China and the Powers on the one side, and Japan and the Powers on the other. These relations were destined to foreshadow the Far Eastern politics of the future.

---

of Feng Tien, signed at Peking, November 8, 1895. *State Papers,* LXXXVII, 11, 1195 ff.

[105] Signed, April 17, 1895; ratifications exchanged at Chefoo, May 8, 1895. *State Papers,* LXXXVII, 799 ff.

[106] *State Papers,* LXXXVII, 805-806.

CHAPTER II

The Origin of the Alliance (Continued)

" It would be very shortsighted to believe that the treaty of Shimonoseki is the end of something, even of the first act in the great historical drama which will no doubt fill the next century. At most it is a prologue. Short of admitting the abdication of Europe in Eastern Asia, there is reason to think that we are much less on the morrow than on the eve of important events," remarked the *Débats* on the eve of the conclusion of the Sino-Japanese War.[1] This has been proved by later events to have been a prophecy. Before the war, the great Powers had worked more or less in harmony with regard to China and Japan. But, after the war, the perennial rivalry between the great Powers of Europe made itself felt in Far Eastern no less than in the Near Eastern affairs.

The success of the intervention had turned Russian attention toward the Far East, and the succeeding events had converted what was only a vague aspiration on the part of Russia into an object of immediate policy—a " forward policy " in that quarter of the world. After the war China had to raise money to pay the indemnity to Japan. With

[1] London *Times,* April 22, 1895, p. 5.

the cooperation of France, Russia at once proposed
to lend to China a thirty-six-year loan (beginning
with 1896) of 400,000,000 francs at 4 per cent. under
the guarantee of the Russian Government.[2] When,
in May, 1896, by request of the Russian Government,
Li Hung-Chang was sent as Chinese delegate to the
ceremony of the Czar's coronation, a secret treaty of
alliance was signed between China and Russia at
St. Petersburg. By this treaty the Chinese Government consented to " the construction of a railway
line across the Chinese provinces of Amour (*i. e.*,
Heilungkiang) and of Guirin (Kirin) in the direction of Vladivostok." In the event of an aggression
by Japan, the two High Contracting Parties pledged
themselves " to support each other reciprocally by
all the land and sea forces of which they can dispose
at that moment." China agreed to open all the ports
of China to Russian warships. The treaty was to
have " force and value for a period of fifteen
years." [3]

Though the text of the treaty was then unknown,[4]
the fact that a defensive alliance existed between
China and Russia was an open secret and an alleged

[2] Hosea B. Morse, *The International Relations of the Chinese Empire,* London, 1918, III, 53.

[3] John V. A. MacMurray, *Treaties and Agreements with and Concerning China,* New York, 1921, I, 81-82.

[4] The treaty was later published in the *London Daily Telegraph*
of February 15, 1910 by "An Admirer of Li Hung-Chang," who was,
according to M. Auguste Gérard, French Minister to China, 1893-97,
Li Ching-Mai, the son of Li Hung-Chang, then Chinese Minister at
the Court of St. James.

text was published even before the treaty was
signed.[5] Furthermore, a certain " Cassini Convention " was believed to exist,[6] the terms of which,
according to the text published by the *North China
Herald* of October 30, 1896,[7] gave Russia the right
to carry her Trans-Siberian railway to Kirin from
some station in Siberia and from Vladivostok, and
the right to work mines in Manchuria. The treaty
further provided for the employment of Russian
officers to drill the Manchurian levies, and granted
Russia a lease of the port of Kiaochou, and, on
emergencies, the use of Port Arthur and Talienwan,
which were not to be ceded to any other Power.
Finally, by this convention, China promised every
facility to Russian merchants, travellers, and trade.

To facilitate the transactions in connection with
the loan to China, as well as to carry out the railway clauses of the agreement, Russia chartered the
Russo-Chinese Bank late in 1895 (December 10),
which formed the important means to carry out the
policy of " conquest by railways." The capital of

[5] On March 27, 1896, the *North China Daily News* published a
treaty of defensive alliance between Russia and China.

[6] According to M. Auguste Gérard there never was, properly
speaking, any " Cassini Convention." The treaty of Alliance was
concluded at St. Petersburg in May, 1896, between Li Hung-Chang
and Prince Lobanov, and a railway contract was signed on September 8 following, also at St. Petersburg, by the Chinese Minister, Shu
Ching-Cheng, and the delegates of the Russo-Asiatic Bank; and
it was this contract for whose definite ratification at Peking on
September 30 Count Cassini waited before proceeding on his way
to Russia. M. Auguste Gérard, *Ma Mission en Chine, 1893-7,* Paris,
1918.

[7] First published on March 6, 1896, by the same paper.

the bank consisted of 11,250,000 gold roubles, in addition to 5,000,000 taels advanced on permanent deposit by the Chinese Government. The privileges granted to the bank included the receiving of tax returns, management of local finances, coining, payment of the interests of the public bonds, and construction of railways and telegraph lines in China, in so far as concessions were made by the Chinese Government to the bank.[8] To the bank was also granted a concession for railways in Manchuria,[9] for the purpose of which the bank organized the Chinese Eastern Railway Company with a capital of 5,000,000 roubles under Russian laws.[10]

In 1896, during the period of the scramble for concessions, Russia again secured her lion's share by forcing China to grant to her a lease of Port Arthur and Talienwan. The concession was made by two conventions:—the first signed at Peking on March 27,[11] and the second at St. Petersburg on May 7.[12]

While Russia was thus consolidating her position in Manchuria, she was at the same time reaching out to establish her hold on Korea.[13] Before

[8] For the Charter of Russo-Chinese Bank, see William W. Rockhill, *Treaties and Convention with or Concerning China and Korea, 1894-1904*, Washington, 1904, pp. 207-211.

[9] Ibid., pp. 212-214.

[10] Ibid., pp. 215-224.

[11] Ibid., pp. 50-52.

[12] Ibid., pp. 53-54.

[13] Morse, III, 104-105. Asakawa, *The Russo-Japanese Conflict*, pp. 259 ff. Vladimir (pseud.), *Russia on the Pacific and the Siberian Railway*, pp. 326 ff. Rosen, pp. 141 ff.

the Sino-Japanese War Mr. Waeber, the Russian
Representative at Seul, had already won for himself warm friends in the Court, particularly the
Queen and her party, and had succeeded in quietly
allying himself with certain Koreans among whom
the Chinese Resident, Yuan Shi-Kai, had created
dissatisfaction. After the war, when Japan took
the place of China and became predominant in
Korea, Mr. Waeber was still able to win over a large
body of Koreans whose good will the Japanese had,
in one way or another, alienated. The murder of the
Korean Queen, on October 8, 1895, instigated by
Viscount Lieutenant-General Gōrō-Miura, the Japanese Minister at Seul, dealt a heavy blow to Japanese
influence. On February 11, 1896, the King, with the
seal, accompanied by the Crown Prince and Princess,
fled for their lives to the Russian Legation, where
they stayed until February 20th of the following
year. The immediate result was a Russian ascendency in Korea.[14]

Among other things, the Russians secured, on
April 22, 1896, a mining concession along the Tumen
River, and, on August 28 of the same year, an immense timber concession on the northern frontier
and on Uinung Island. At the time of the coronation
of the Czar, it was rumored that a secret agreement between Russia and Korea had been concluded
by which Korea had obligated herself to employ Rus-

[14] Cf. London *Times,* April 6, 1896, p. 3. *North China Herald,*
April 2, 1896.

sian military instructors and financial councillors.
Whatever truth the report might have had, in June,
1896, it was made known that Korean troops would
henceforth be instructed by Russians, and in July,
1897, three Russian officers and ten soldiers entered
Seul. On September 6, the Korean Government undertook to employ them for three years, with the
result that the Royal guard and five battalions of the
Korean infantry, numbering about 3,000, came under Russian instruction. Having secured the right
to instruct Korean soldiers, the Russian Government proceeded next to effect a control of Korean
finance. A Russo-Korean Bank was organized, and
Mr. Kir Alexiev, a Russian subject, was appointed
financial advisor and general director of customs
of Korea.[15]

In March, 1898, the Russian Government recalled
all of her financial and military councillors at Seul,
and discontinued the Russo-Korean Bank. This,
however, did not signify an end of Russian activities
in Korea. In the north, besides the privileges of
mining as well as the right to construct a railway
from the mines to the shore granted by the Seul
Government in 1896, Russia secured three whaling
stations (March 29, 1899), on a twelve-year lease,
for the use of Count H. Keyserling, and also secured
many other property rights. Of much greater im-

[15] The latter post had been previously occupied by Mr. Brown, a
British subject. He was later restored to his office on the protest of
the British Government, and M. Alexiev had to content himself with
a subordinate position under Mr. Brown.

4

portance was the Russian activity in the south, where the Russian Government entertained the idea of securing a lease of Masampo which, apart from the fact of being a connecting point between Vladivostok and Port Arthur, is the best harbor in Korea. Since 1899 various threats and pressures had been exerted upon the Korean Government to attain this aim, and Russian diplomatic agents, naval officers and engineers had frequently visited the port and bought tracts of land of indifferent value.

Russian aggression in the Far East in these years was supported by her ally, the French Government. '' In almost all affairs of importance, she [France] marched shoulder to shoulder with Russia. She joined Russia in 1895 in the tripartite intervention for the retrocession of Liao-tung. She made practically the entire flotation of the Russo-French loan of 400,000,000 francs under the guarantee of the Russian Government for the relief of China.'' [16] During the Boxer uprising, the Governments of France and Russia worked hand in hand. They also cooperated with each other in various other enterprises within the Chinese Empire.

Apart from the support given to her ally in the north, France adopted an aggressive policy of her own.[17] She claimed as her sphere of influence the

[16] Mingchien J. Bau, *The Foreign Relations of China,* New York, 1922, p. 113. K. Asakawa, " Some of the Events Leading up to the War in the East," in the *Yale Rev.,* XIII, 145. Gérard, pp. 23-24. *Parl. P.,* China, No. 1 (1901), No. 280.

[17] Cf. M. Delcassé, as quoted in the London *Times,* November 25, 1899, p. 7.

three provinces bordering Tonking,[18] and extended
the claim to cover Szechwan. In March, 1897, she
secured from the Chinese Government a declaration
that the island of Hainan would not be ceded to any
other power;[19] and, in April, 1898, a promise that
" if a separate postal department were at some future time established with a European director at its
head, France equally with other Powers should have
the right to recommend a candidate for the post."[20]
On April 2, 1898, she occupied Kwang-Chow-Wan
and then pressed the Peking Government for a lease
of the port with its dependencies for ninety-nine
years.[21] From 1895 to 1899 various other concessions
and rights to build railways were granted by the
Yamen to France or to her subjects.[22]

The result of the war of 1894-5 was not wholly
satisfactory to Japan. The surrender of the Japanese Government to the " friendly recommendation " of the three Powers for the retrocession of
the Liao-tung Peninsula had greatly disappointed
the Japanese people. " No true Japanese can read
the Imperial Rescript [23] without ' tears of blood,' "

[18] On April 10, 1898, France secured from Yamen a non-alienation
declaration of the Chinese provinces bordering on Tonking. Rockhill, pp. 178, 179.

[19] Ibid., p. 173.

[20] Parl. P., China, No. 1 (1899), No. 17.

[21] The French flag was raised there on April 22, 1898. A convention
for the lease was submitted to the Tsungli Yamen on May 27, but
was not ratified by China until January 5, 1900. Morse, III, 112, 113.

[22] For details, see Morse, III, 90, 91, 122, 123.

[23] The Imperial Rescript was published together with the treaty
of Shimonoseki on May 10, 1895. Parl. P., Japan, No. 1 (1895),
enclosure 2.

was the feeling of the nation.[24] That the three Powers had interfered was bad enough, but that they had timed their interference so as to expose Japan to a maximum humiliation of embarrassment was infinitely worse.[25] During the war, Japan had already felt the danger of her isolated position. On the one hand, England was suspected of being an ally of China. On the other hand, the policy of the Russian Government was not so certain, and a sudden Russian attack on the exposed flank of the Japanese in the event of military operations on the continent was not beyond the region of imagination.[26] The intervention after the war definitely convinced the Japanese statesmen that, if Japan wanted to "take its place side by side with the other nations of the world,"[27] it was not enough for her to meet them on the field, but that she had to be prepared to meet them at the diplomatic table as well.

The reformation in Japan was accomplished by an enormous increase of her population, along with an immense growth of her trade and industries.[28] She thus desired East Asia, particularly Manchuria and Korea, as her market and as a supply region for raw materials and food products and a field for immigration.[29] Consequently, the Russian advance

[24] London *Times,* June 25, 1895, p. 11.

[25] Cf. Ibid., June 25, 1895, p. 11.

[26] Rosen, I, 134-135.

[27] The Memorial to the newly restored Emperor by the Lords of the four great clans of Satsuma, Choshiu, Toza, and Hizen in 1868.

[28] Asakawa, pp. 1-7.

[29] Ibid., pp. 7 ff.

in Manchuria and Korea could not be looked upon without concern by the Japanese Government whose ambition could now be realized only by an understanding with Russia for the common spoil or by an agreement with England to check the Russian advance.

Of the two, the Japanese preferred the former—that is, an understanding with Russia.[30] They believed that it was much easier to effect a Russo-Japanese understanding than an Anglo-Japanese alliance, for, in the first place, excluding the element of trade restriction from Russian policy, her expansion towards Korea and Manchuria could not be seriously objectionable to England;[31] in the second place, England was still in favor of isolation and not yet ready for an alliance, much less with Japan; and, in the third place, Japan had nothing to offer to England for an alliance, nor was she strong enough to defend British interests on the continent. Even granting that an alliance with England could be effected, the Japanese position in the Far East would still be precarious in the face of a hostile Russia.[32] Finally, such an alliance might call forth

[30] According to Hayashi (p. 87), a Russo-Japanese Alliance or a Russo-Franco-Japanese Alliance received only the support of minorities in Japan. But the opinion of a few elder statesmen, like Ito, Inouye, etc., who were in favor of an understanding with Russia, was enough to influence the Government policy.

[31] Cf. London *Times,* April 9, 1898, p. 6.

[32] Cf. Rosen, I, 165.

a war with Russia for which Japan was not then prepared.[33]

Thus, despite the fact that Russia had led the tripartite intervention, Japan approached her time and again for some understanding. Nor was the ground for such an understanding entirely lacking. To Korea, apart from the fact that large Japanese settlements existed in all the Korean ports, and most of the trade was in their hands, the Japanese people had attached an exaggerated importance, based upon historical reminiscences of former wars and conquests in the country as well as upon strategical considerations. In any case, Korea was considered in Japan as nothing short of one-half of her vitality, and a country upon which Japan's fate as a nation depended.[34] Nothing of this sort could be said of Manchuria. The Japanese people did not possess there such large vested interests.[35] Although the three Eastern Provinces seemed to promise a more important economic future than Korea, it could not be said that Russian preponderance there would be so threatening to the safety of Japan as would be her preponderance in Korea.

[33] Some Japanese thought that an Anglo-Japanese Alliance was fraught with danger to Japan who should not have been involved in England's world-wide troubles, and that England would have made a mere catspaw of her weaker ally. H. N. G. Bushby, " The Agreement between Great Britain and Japan," in *Nineteenth Century*, LI, 376-377.

[34] Vladimir (pseud.), p. 327. Asakawa, pp. 14-30, 49-52. London *Times*, November 11, 1899, p. 7.

[35] Asakawa, pp. 30-32.

From the Russian point of view, the situation was reversed. In Manchuria, Russia had enormous vested interests. " Besides its immense wealth still unexploited, Manchuria possesses the great Port Arthur, which is the only nearly ice-free naval outlet for Russia in her vast dominion in Asia." Both politically and economically, Manchuria alone was more valuable for Russia than the rest of her Asiatic territories. For Russia, Manchuria was the keynote of her Eastern policy.[36] In Korea, Russian vested interests were slight. The Peninsula was only important to her from a strategical and political point of view.[37]

The Japanese Government well understood the situation, and believed that an understanding with Russia was possible, on the basis of a Russian preponderance in Manchuria in return for a Japanese protectorate over Korea. The Japanese seized upon the coronation of the Czar in May, 1896, as a good opportunity, and sent Field Marshal Marquis Aritomo Yamagata as their representative to the ceremony, with a commission to reach an understanding with the Russian Government regarding Korea.[38] The negotiations resulted, finally, in the signing of the Yamagata-Lobanov Protocol on June 9, 1896.[39] Matters of more immediate interest to the two

---

[36] Ibid., pp. 32-46, 48-49.

[37] Ibid., pp. 46-47. London *Times,* December 25, 1895, pp. 5 and 7; November 11, 1899, p. 7.

[38] Asakawa, p. 263.

[39] Rockhill, p. 432.

Powers were settled at Seul between the Japanese
and Russian ministers by a memorandum signed in
the preceding month (May 14).[40] But the agreements, placing Russia and Japan on a par with one
another in Korea as they did, satisfied neither of the
contracting parties. Their terms were soon violated
by the Russians, who imposed the engagement of
Russian services upon the Korean Government.[41]

Failing to reach a satisfactory agreement with the
Russian Government, by the Yamagata-Lobanov
Protocol, the Japanese Government, through Mr.
Motono, then Chargé d'affaires at St. Petersburg,
tried hard in the following year to ascertain " under
what approximate conditions Russia would be willing
to come to a friendly understanding with Japan in
regard to Korea." However, they were unable to
elicit " from any one in authority anything but the
vaguest assurances of good will." [42] The lease of
Port Arthur and Talienwan to Russia by the Chinese
Government increased considerably the popular excitement in Japan against Russia. But the Japanese
Government took a more practical view of the situation. They thought that hitherto Russian activities
in Korea had been centered on the acquisition of an
ice-free port on the coast of Peninsula. Now, she had
secured such a port in Manchuria. Korea, hitherto
the only bone of contention between Russia and

[40] Rockhill, pp. 430-431.
[41] Hayashi, pp. 91-92. Rosen, I, 151-153. Asakawa, pp. 267-269.
[42] Rosen, I, 146.

Japan, needed no longer be a cause of friction between two countries whose interests were not in conflict anywhere else.[43] They therefore only " took
note " of the Russian occupation of the Liao-tung
Peninsula when they were notified of it. Meanwhile,
they approached Baron Rosen, then Russian Minister at Tokio, for " a complete and truly friendly
understanding with Russia," and suggested, as its
basis, " a reciprocal engagement to refrain from any
interference with each other's policy, Russia's in
Manchuria and Japan's in Korea." [44] " The official
proposal was in the shape of a brief *note verbale,*
in which the Japanese Government declared its willingness to consider Manchuria with its littoral as
being entirely outside the sphere of Japanese interests, provided the Russian Government was prepared to make the same declaration with regard to
Korea." The Russian Government, however, was
not willing to give up Korea altogether, and the reply only mentioned that " the Russian Government
took note with great satisfaction of the Japanese
Government's declaration that it considered Manchuria with its littoral as being entirely outside the
sphere of Japanese interests, but that it could not
make a similar declaration in regard to Korea." This

[43] Ibid., pp. 156-157. Vladimir (pseud.), pp. 327-328.
[44] In March, 1898. Rosen, I, 189. According to Hayashi (p. 93),
" In January, 1898, Russian Foreign Minister proposed, acting under
the direct instructions of the Czar, to negotiate an agreement with
Japan, in regard to Korea."

was the end of the negotiation and the matter was allowed to drop, temporarily at least.[45]

In April, 1898, to allay the growing popular excitement in Japan, a " lame and pointless " convention, known as the Rosen-Nissi Convention, was signed by the Japanese and the Russian Governments. It stated that both countries " recognize definitely the sovereignty and entire independence of Korea," and " pledge themselves mutually to abstain from all direct interference in the internal affairs of that country." Both countries agreed not to send " military instructors or financial advisers, without arriving beforehand at a mutual agreement on this subject," and, finally, the Russian Government promised not to obstruct " the development of commercial and industrial relations between Japan and Korea." [46]

Thus, the fact that Japan would not be satisfied with anything short of a protectorate over, and ultimately, an eventual conquest and annexation of Korea,[47] and that Russia refused to stay out of the Peninsula entirely,[48] made impossible a satisfactory agreement between the two countries. Nevertheless,

---

[45] Rosen, I, 157-158.

[46] Rockhill, p. 433.

[47] Cf. Rosen, I, 164. In October, 1900, the suggestion from Korea that Japan should support her neutralization somewhat after the Belgian model, met a decided refusal from Japan. London *Times*, October 30, 1900, p. 3.

[48] Cf. an article in *Das Vaterland*, the extract of which was published in London *Times*, February 25, 1896, p. 5.

even after the Anglo-Japanese Alliance was concluded, the Japanese Government did not abandon
the idea of a possible understanding with Russia.[49]
They did everything to cultivate friendly relations
with Russia. When the Grand Duke Cyril was visiting Tokio, he was received by Prince Arisugawa
with a " pointedly intimate kind of hospitality such
as had never yet been extended to any royal visitor
by any member of the Imperial family." [50] This
much could not be said of Russian proceedings in
Korea. Russia did not comply promptly with the
spirit of the Rosen-Nissi Convention, and there was
no end to the activities of Russian naval authorities
on the southern coast of Korea.[51]

Though the Japanese Government preferred an
understanding with Russia to an Anglo-Japanese
agreement, they did not fail to realize that the interest of Great Britain in the Far East was a common
one with that of Japan. A group of statesmen of
the younger generation, therefore, strongly advocated an Anglo-Japanese alliance. They argued that
Russia was not willing to give up Korea entirely,
much less to let Japan assume sole control over that
Peninsula. It was therefore useless to approach
Russia for an understanding. The right thing for
Japan to do was to make an alliance with Great
Britain to counteract the machinations of the three

[49] Rosen, I, 158-159.
[50] Ibid., pp. 160-161.
[51] Ibid., p. 161.

intervening Powers, whose friendship need never be expected in a serious crisis.[52]

The standing aloof of Great Britain from the Triple Entente had unquestionably produced a very friendly feeling among the Japanese.[53] Immediately after the intervention, the Japanese Minister at St. Petersburg in a telegram to the Japanese Government (May, 1895), suggested that Japan should draw to her side the friendship of Great Britain.[54] Since then, '' an opinion gradually spread both amongst the public and in the official world at Tokio that an alliance with Great Britain would be beneficial.'' [55] The aggressive action of Russia in China and Korea further aroused the Japanese public and convinced them that Japan had to work in concert with England, and, if need be, to '' strike a strong blow in the common cause.'' [56]

One of the leading advocates of an Anglo-Japanese alliance was Count Hayashi, who, writing in *Jiji Shimpo* in June and July, 1895, said, in substance:

[52] Hayashi, p. 113. Cf. London *Times,* June 25, 1895, p. 11.

[53] Cf. London *Times,* June 17, 1897, p. 7. Since that date public opinion in Japan had been very favorable toward England. For a brief summary of Japan's public opinion toward England before the alliance of 1902, see H. N. G. Bushby, "The Agreement between Great Britain and Japan," in the *Nineteenth Century,* LI, 375-377.

[54] *The (Japanese) Journal of International Law and Diplomacy* (in Japanese language), March, 1927, XXVII, No. 3, 62-63.

[55] Hayashi, p. 86. London *Times,* May 1, 1897, p. 6; March 18, 1898, p. 4; April 9, 1898, p. 7; June 3, 1898, p. 10.

[56] Ibid., April 9, 1898, p. 7; June 3, 1898, p. 10.

If, however, the Continental Powers are going to curb our just aspirations, to fulfill which we have poured our life and money, then we too must endeavor to ourselves make an alliance which shall counteract their machinations.

He then went on to say:

Russia certainly intends to obtain a predominating position, and in that case England's position in China might well become precarious. In this country all are agreed that the question must finally be settled by the sword, but England is not in a good strategical position for such a course, for struggle would be settled on land and not on sea.

If, however, England and Japan should make an alliance the problems of the Far East would be already settled. If the events of the late war have proved to the English statesmen that China is merely a big idol, then they may in time come to realize that Japan, though she is young and inexperienced, is earnest and energetic. China is no longer the Power of the Far East, nor is Japan yet it. Russia is trying to be it. But the real Power in the Far East is England. If she casts her lot in with Russia she can no longer be it, for Russia can coerce China by land which England cannot oppose. But if England casts in her lot with Japan, then she will more than ever be the Power of the Far East, for she is the deciding factor at present. England and Japan together can control China and ensure the maintenance of peace in the Far East.[57]

Nevertheless, apart from the fact that the elder statesmen of Japan preferred a Russo-Japanese understanding, there were other practical difficulties to be overcome before an Anglo-Japanese alliance could be concluded. On the one hand, England at the beginning did not feel the need of an alliance, much

[57] Hayashi, pp. 113-114.

less one with Japan. On the other hand, there was really little that Japan could offer for the making of such an alliance. The latter point was so obvious that even the advocates of the alliance did not overlook it. Count Mutsu, commenting on the project of the alliance, in August, 1896, said in substance:

The idea of an alliance with Great Britain is certainly great, but I am afraid that I have to say we cannot expect too much from it. It is true that England is anxious to protect her interest in the Far East; but will her interest be protected by an alliance with Japan? We ought to reflect on the strength of our army and naval forces. They are merely sufficient to protect ourselves. They are not in a position to fight on the mainland or on the sea far from our coast, to protect British interest. England certainly would not enter into an alliance with Japan if, in doing so, only Japanese interest is protected. At the time of the intervention, Prince Ito had expected British help to oppose the Powers' demand, but what the British Government did was to advise us to yield. That shows the real attitude of the British Government. The Anglo-Japanese alliance therefore, for the time being at least, can be nothing but a sweet dream.[58]

Arguments like these were very persuasive. Japan at once took steps to develop her commerce and industries, and to build up her army and navy, in order to be able to fight Russia, if necessary, and to be worthy to be an ally of Great Britain.[59] Meanwhile, she did not fail to act together with Great Britain

[58] *The (Japanese) Journal of International Law and Diplomacy*, March, 1927, XXVI, No. 3, pp. 59, 61. Cf. Hayashi, pp. 110-112. London *Times*, April 9, 1898, pp. 6, 7.

[59] London *Times*, February 6, 1896, p. 6; August 29, 1896, p. 9.

in the Far East, and nothing that could be done to
win over the friendship of England was left undone.
As Minister in Peking and then in St. Petersburg,
Count Hayashi tried continuously to cultivate the
society of the British representatives at these
places.[60] In 1897, the Emperor sent his son, Prince
Arisugawa, to represent him at the Queen's Jubilee.[61] In 1898, when England sounded the Japanese Government about England's proposed occupation of Weihaiwai, the latter replied that "Japan
would have no objection to its being held by a Power
disposed to assist in maintaining the independence of
China."[62] The attitude and the action of the Japanese Government greatly facilitated the subsequent
British occupation of the port.[63]

When, in March, 1898, Mr. Joseph Chamberlain,
then English Secretary of State for the Colonies, expressed to the Japanese Minister in London, Mr.
Kato, at a public banquet "the readiness of Great

[60] Hayashi, pp. 82-83.

[61] Rosen, I, 149.

[62] *Parl. P.*, China, No. 1 (1899), No. 35, enclosure. Also see *British Documents on the Origins of the War, 1898-1914,* ed. by Gooch
and Temperley, London, 1927, I, 21. Cf. "The Russian Government
had expressed to Japan their desire that the possession of Weihaiwei
after evacuation should be secured to China, and asked whether this
Government (Japan) would agree with them to that end, as others
would be willing to join them in it. The reply of the Japanese Government was that they could give no undertaking of this kind." *Parl.
P.,* China, No. 1 (1899), No. 30.

[63] *Parl. P.,* China, No. 1 (1898), No. 143; China, No. 1 (1899),
No. 35, 79, 82, 85, 112, 113, 118, 231. *Brit. Doc.,* I, 30-31 (No. 46);
31-32. The attitude of the Japanese Press toward the British occupation of Weihaiwei was also favorable. China, No. 1 (1899), No. 82.

Britain to enter into an agreement with Japan for the settlement of relations in the Far East,''[64] Mr. Kato immediately sent a long telegram to Count Okuma, Foreign Minister at Tokio, and urged on him the advisability of such an agreement.[65] Though no serious steps toward such an alliance were taken either by Japan or England at this time, the friendly relations between these two countries were already such as to produce the impression abroad that England and Japan were in close alliance.[66]

For more than half a century England had occupied a leading position in the councils of the Western Powers in China. There she had maintained a high prestige and had developed great commercial interests. The Sino-Japanese War and the diplomatic campaigns which accompanied and followed it turned the tables against Great Britain. Since then, China had leaned more on the intervening Powers— Russia, France, and Germany [67]—who were working more or less in harmony in the Far East.[68]

Standing alone, and unable to check the advance of the Continental Powers, particularly Russia,

[64] Hayashi, p. 83.

[65] Ibid., p. 83.

[66] Supplement to the Joint Memorial of Chang Chih-Tung and Sheng Hsuan-Huai, *Parl. P.,* China, No. 1 (1899), No. 108, enclosure. Cf. London *Times,* February 1, 1898, p. 3.

[67] Morse, III, 101, 102. Interviews of Li Hung-Chang, London *Times,* May 25, 1896, p. 6; August 4, 1896, p. 8.

[68] Cf. London *Times,* June 23, 1897, p. 20. *Par. Deb.,* February 8, 1898, 4th Series, LIII, 127-128. *Parl. P.,* China, No. 1 (1898), No. 132.

Great Britain resorted to the "policy of compensation." To balance the Franco-Russian loan of
July, 1895, she made, in 1896 and 1898, two loans to
the Chinese Government through the Hongkong and
Shanghai Banking Corporation, in cooperation with
the Deutsch-Asiatische Bank.[69] To keep the balance
of power in the Far East from being disturbed by
the German occupation of Kiao-Chou and the Russian occupation of the Liao-Tung Peninsula, she secured from China a lease of Weihaiwei " for so long
a period as Port Arthur shall remain in the occupation of Russia." [70] As compensation for the cession
of Kwangchowwan to France, China was compelled
to agree that the limits of British territory at Hongkong should be enlarged.[71] Also, Great Britain obtained from China a declaration as to the non-
alienation of the Yangtse basin, the declaration as to
the Inspectorship of the Customs, the opening of the
" Inland Waters " of China to steam navigation,
the opening of Nanning and Siangtan (subsequently
changed to Yochow) as treaty ports, and many railway concessions which, up to the end of November,
1898, were the longest in mileage granted to a single
Power.[72]

[69] Morse, III, 53-54.
[70] State Papers, 1897-98, XC, 16-17. Parl. P., China, No. 1 (1898),
Nos. 129, 130. Morse, III, 117, 118.
[71] State Papers, 1897-98, XC, 17-18. Morse, III, 119-120.
[72] 2800 miles; compared to Russia, 1,530 miles; Germany, 720
miles; Belgium, 650 miles; France, 420 miles; America, 300 miles.
Parl. P., China, No. 1 (1898), No. 459. Morse, III, 124.

But England was not interested in a policy of spheres of influences and the ultimate dismemberment of China.[73] British interests in the Far East were principally commercial.[74] She wanted an " open door " and, as a corollary, the maintenance of the independence and the integrity of China.[75] It was only after unsuccessful attempts to oppose the Powers' demands to China that the British Government resorted to a policy of counter-demand. Every compensation granted was therefore an indication of failure, rather than of the success of the British policy. As a result, not only were her commercial

[73] Balfour, *Par. Deb.*, April 29, 1898, 4th Series, LVI, 1582, 1583. Morse, III, 113.

[74] Balfour at Manchester, London *Times,* January 11, 1898, p. 8. Curzon at Bolton, ibid., January 26, 1898, p. 6. *Parl. P.,* China, No. 1 (1898), p. 133. To give some idea of the British trade in the Far East, the following quotations are taken: " The British shares of China's total foreign trade was considerably above 70 per cent, or more than £32,000,000 per annum; . . . . The Far East trade was actually 20,000,000 more per annum than our annual trade exports and imports to India, and represented about 1/6 of our world-trade. And that on a virgin field for the greater part unopened and capable of indefinite expansion." Mr. A. Colquhoun at the Royal United Service Institution, London *Times,* March 10, 1898, p. 12. " Great Britain and her colonies do within a fraction of two-thirds of the entire import and export trade of China, ... Turning to the carrying trade we find that . . . . the commanding position of British shipping, amounting to almost three-fourth of the foreign trade and considerably more than half of the coastwise trade, is now manifest, ..." Official returns and annual report for 1898 of the Chinese Imperial Maritime Customs, London *Times,* August 21, 1899, p. 5.

[75] Curzon, the Under-Secretary for Foreign Affairs, *Par. Deb.*, 4th Series, March 1, 1898, LIV, 332, 338-339. Balfour at Manchester, London *Times,* January 11, 1898, p. 8. Cf. ibid., October 25, 1895, p. 9.

interests seriously threatened,[76] but her prestige was greatly injured. To most British writers and statesmen, this situation seemed to be very humiliating, especially to a Power which had opened China single-handed and had since then occupied a leading position there in the councils of the Powers.

The voice of alarmists was everywhere heard.[77] By these it was believed that a combined assault upon Great Britain's commercial supremacy had been deliberately staged by the Continental Powers, whose pledges were not to be trusted.[78] If Russia, France, and Germany took possession of portions of China, or divided the whole of China, an exclusive system would be imposed, and imposed mainly against the commerce of Great Britain.[79] They reasoned that, by the occupation of Manchuria, Russia would gain a portentous increase of military strength by being supplied with an irregular cavalry and a hardy population, and thus would attain a position which England might find difficult to challenge when Russia's time for closing the door arrived. The incorporation of Manchuria might

[76] *Parl. P.,* China, No. 1 (1898), Nos. 13, 14, 38, 51, 57, 59, 65, 75, 78, 79; China, No. 1 (1899), No. 469; China, No. 2 (1899), Nos. 2, 8, 13, 16, 17, 23.

[77] London *Times,* November 11, 1895, p. 9; December 20, 1897, p. 9; March 28, 1898, p. 11. *Par. Deb.,* 4th Series, March 1, 1898, LIV, 303-304, 321; March 24, 1898, LV, 804; LVI, 1673-74; August 10, 1898, LXIV, 782. *Parl. P.,* China, No. 1 (1899), Nos. 25, 319.

[78] *Par. Deb.,* February 8, 1898, 4th Series, LIII, 127-128; March 1, 1898, LIV, 303, 304. *Parl. P.,* China, No. 1 (1899), No. 319.

[79] *Par. Deb.,* March 1, 1898, LIV, 306, 317, 321; April 5, LVI, 274; April 29, LVI, 1631, 1632. *Parl. P.,* China, No. 1 (1899), No. 25.

occupy Russia a considerable time, but, when this was accomplished, she would be in a position to descend upon Pechili. Since no natural barriers existed between Pechili and Yangtze, it was only a question of time before Russia would gain control of the whole country.[80] Furthermore, according to these alarmists, the English position in the Far East did not merely concern England alone. It was an Imperial question, and it concerned some of her colonies. Unless the independence and integrity of China were secured, England would not only lose the Chinese market, but would endanger the safety of her colonies, of Hongkong, the Straits Settlements, and also her possessions in Burma and the Malay Peninsula, and Russian attack on India would be no longer impossible.[81] Consequently, they urged the Government to adopt a strong and definite policy.[82] This opinion was voiced by the *Times* in a leading article on July 30, 1898:

But unfortunately the country is still waiting for some substantial evidence, for some material facts, to show that Her Majesty's Government have ceased to rely upon mere

[80] *Parl. P.*, China, No. 1 (1899), No. 25, *Par. Deb.*, 4th Series, LVI, 1673-1674; August 10, 1898, LXIV, 781; February 8, 1899, LXVI, 197.

[81] *Par. Deb.*, 4th Series, April 5, 1898, LVI, 279; August 10, LXIV, 782; March 28, 1901, XCII, 165.

[82] London *Times*, March 10, 1898, p. 12; April 12, p. 7; April 25, p. 9; April 26, p. 11; April 30, p. 11; August 2, p. 7; August 9, p. 7; August 11, p. 9; August 16, p. 7; September 6, p. 7; September 24, p. 9; February 27, 1899, p. 9; March 2, p. 9, *Par. Deb.*, March 1, 1898, 4th Series, LIV, 307-8; February 8, 1899, LXVI, 231; LXVIII, 1393 ff.; March

paper " assurances " for the protection of British interests in face of the practical activity of other Powers. While we are lulled to sleep for months by Parliamentary statements of a more or less disingenuous character, other nations are acting with indefatigable energy. While we go on talking about a policy of open doors, other nations are consolidating and extending their spheres of exclusive influence at such a rate that there will soon be no door to open. It does not need that the Yangtze Valley should be either mortgaged, leased, or ceded to another Power in order to deal irreparable injury to British trade and British enterprise. That result will follow upon the adroit manipulation of railway and industrial concessions obtained by other nations through the political action of their Governments and the free use of State resources. . . . . In a word, we have secured no " open door," we have no " equality of opportunity," and even in what we fondly hoped was a sphere formally and fully secured to British interests other nations are constructing their railways and consolidating their interests, while nowhere, neither in North nor South nor Middle, does it seem possible for British capitalists to gain a footing.

Are we to go on forever, trying to keep out the ocean with a mop or are we going to take the world as we find it, and to secure at least some area of Chinese territory where British enterprise may have a chance ? [83]

The British Government, however, was not so easily disturbed. At the Guildhall Banquet on November 9, 1895, the Marquis of Salisbury, then British Prime Minister, advised the British public

---

30, 1900, LXXXI, 849; August 2, 1900, LXXXVII, 468. On March 1, 1898, a resolution was passed in the House to the effect: " That it is of vital importance for British commerce and influence that the Independence of Chinese territory should be maintained."

[83] London *Times,* July 30, 1898, p. 11.

not to view what had taken place in the Far East with unnecessary disturbance or alarm, and said: " Depend upon it, whatever may happen in that region, be it in the way of war or in the way of commerce, we are equal to any competition which may be proposed to us. We may look on with absolute equanimity at the action of any persons, if such there be, who think that they can exclude us from any part of that fertile and commercial region, or who imagine that if we are admitted, they can beat us in the markets of the world." [84] In 1898, after the German occupation of Kiauchow and the Russian occupation of the Liaotung Peninsula, the First Lord of the Treasury, Mr. A. J. Balfour, was still of the conviction that " so far as the open door—in the only true legitimate sense—is concerned, it has never been shut," [85] and that " now, after all the months of active diplomacy, we find ourselves commercially and strategically in a far stronger position than we did before, and can look into the future with feelings of far greater confidence and assurance." [86] At Albert Hall the Prime Minister went even further: " We shall maintain against all comers that which we possess, and we know, in spite of the jargon about isolation, that we are amply competent to do so." [87]

[84] London *Times*, November 11, p. 6.
[85] *Par. Deb.*, August 10, 1898, 4th Series, LXIV, 829.
[86] Ibid., April 29, 1898, LVI, 1597.
[87] Cf. Ibid., February 8, 1898, LIII, 38, 94, 95; April 5, LVI, 237; August 10, LXIV, 829. London *Times*, January 18, 1898, p. 9.

Even as late as September, 1899, Sir Claude Mc-
Donald, then British Minister at Peking, had this to
report: " I do not think that the pessimistic tone
adopted by many critics of our policy is altogether
justified by facts or results. I think we have, on the
whole, more than held our own." [88]

Nevertheless, the British statesmen were not un-
aware of all the possible dangers that might arise
as a result of inaction on the part of the British
Government.[89] They were fully determined that the
door of China should not be shut and that the predominance of any Power at Peking should not be
tolerated.[90] But, in this early period, they did not
want to become involved in European quarrels,[91]
and they did not believe that the situation in the Far
East was as threatening as had been declared, or
that England was as helpless as some imagined.[92]

[88] London *Times*, September 29, 1899, p. 4.

[89] *Par. Deb.*, March 1, 1898, 4th Series, LIV, 312; June 10, LVIII,
1432-1436; LXVI, March 13, 1899, pp. 590-591. London *Times*, May
14, 1898, p. 12.

[90] *Par. Deb.*, February 8, 1898, 4th Series, LIII, 30; Salisbury,
February 8, LIII, 38-39; Curzon, the Under-Secretary for Foreign
Affairs, March 1, LIV, 331-332. Brodrick, the Under-Secretary for
Foreign Affairs, LXXVI, 83. Balfour at Manchester, London *Times*,
January 11, 1898, p. 8; Sir M. H. Beach, the Chancellor of the Ex-
chequer at Swansea, ibid., January 18, p. 7.

[91] As late as 1897 (the Queen's Jubilee year) the principle of isolation was even put into verses saying that England needed no allies,
that *le cas échèant* it could fight the whole world alone, with the
refrain: " We've got the ships, we've got the men, we've the money
too ! " Isaac don Levine, *Letters from the Kaiser to the Czar*, New
York, 1920, p. 48.

[92] *Par. Deb.*, Salisbury, February 8, 1898, 4th Series, LIII, 38-41;
Balfour, LIII, 94, 95; Curzon, March 1, LIV, 337; April 5, 1898,

They therefore adopted a policy of patience and
watchfulness, in order to avoid precipitate action
that might needlessly disturb the peace of the Far
East.[93] Not until 1898, did a group of British statesmen begin to feel the danger of their isolated position
not only in the Far East but in all parts of the
world as well,[94] which since the Triple Entente of
1895 had been a favorite subject of ridicule on the
part of the foreign press.[95] Certain influential members of the British Cabinet began to desire a policy
of alliances as a substitute for the traditional principle of " splendid isolation." [96]

In the Far East, Great Britain could ally herself
with Japan, or with Germany, with the adherence of

LVI, 327; LVIII, 1386, 1387, August 10, LXIV, 74; February 8,
1899, LXVI, 224; LXXVI, 84; February 15, 1901, LXXXIX, 284;
March 28, XCII, 184. London *Times,* November 11, 1897, p. 8. Mr.
Jamieson, British Consul at Shanghai, at a meeting of the London
Chamber of Commerce. Even the *Times* which had advocated a
strong policy in the Far East throughout these years, in an editorial
on December 23, 1897, made the following remarks: " With a strong
Minister on the spot and the Government and the country determined to safeguard their immense Chinese trade, we should manage
to hold our own, even without the sympathy of other European
Powers." London *Times,* December 23, 1897, p. 7.

[93] Brodrick, the Under-Secretary for Foreign Affairs, in the Commons, *Par. Deb.,* LXXII, 814; LXXVI, 85, London *Times,* November 11, 1899, p. 11.

[94] *Par. Deb.,* February 8, 1898, 4th Series, LIII, 132-134; March 1,
LIV, 303-304.

[95] London *Times,* April 24, 1895, p. 5; April 25, p. 5; May 2, p. 5;
May 3, p. 9; May 6, p. 5; February 1, 1896, p. 8; December 23,
1897, p. 3; December 25, p. 3; March 30, 1898, p. 11. *Parl. P.,* China,
No. 1 (1899). No. 14, enclosures 1 and 2.

[96] Chamberlain at Birmingham, London *Times,* January 31, 1898,
p. 8; May 14, p. 12. Chamberlain in the Commons, *Par. Deb.,* June 10,
1898, LVIII, 1432-1436. Cf. *Brit. Doc.,* I, vii.

Japan and, perhaps, the United States, or come to an understanding with Russia. In 1895, at the time of the Tripartite intervention, Great Britain had held aloof and had refused to give to Japan the much desired help to oppose the demand of the Continental Powers, for British statesmen well knew that " at that time, Japan had occupied Port Arthur," and that " the enemy [of Great Britain] was Japan." [97] The intervention had thwarted Japanese ambitions on the Continent, and, since then, in order to oppose the Russian advance, Japan had adopted the policy of the open door and the maintenance of the integrity and independence of China, and had cooperated heartily with England. This policy did not fail to secure a response, for Japan was soon considered as a friend by the British public and statesmen. They began to advocate an alliance with Japan, and argued that Japan was a " natural ally " of Great Britain in the Far East.[98] The most eloquent advocate of such an alliance was, perhaps, Sir Ellis Ashmead-Bartlett, who, preaching this gospel to the Commons, observed:

I consider the rise of the Japanese power in the East has been very providential for this country. I do not know what

[97] Sir W. Harcourt defending the Government policy in 1895 in the Commons, *Par. Deb.*, March 1, 1898, 4th Series, LIV, 323-324.

[98] *Par. Deb.*, February 8, 1898, 4th Series, LIII, 129-131, 302-306; March 1, LIV, 307-309; April 5, LVI, 286; April 29, LVI, 1672-1674; February 8, 1899, LXVI, 198; August 7, LXXVI, 70; March 30, 1900, LXXXI, 853. London *Times*, December 23, 1897, p. 7; December 31, p. 3; February 1, 1898, p. 3; March 26, pp. 7, 11; April 4, p. 11; April 9, p. 7; April 27, p. 11.

our position would have been now if we had to face a combination of Russia and France, and possibly of Germany as well, in the Far East. There is a very great and strong Power growing up in Japan, and by the help of Japan alone can we retain our position in the Northern Pacific. By their help alone can we keep Russia out of China. . . . . By using the power of Japan, they (the British Government) can, if they choose, control the whole Chinese question and the Northern Pacific.[99]

On another occasion, preaching the same gospel, he said:

Let us hope Her Majesty's Government at last realise that co-operation with Japan is our main lever and hope in the East. With Japan we can do exactly as we please in the Northern Pacific, whereas without Japan our task will be arduous, and even difficult. For five years I have been urging this Anglo-Japanese entente as the best and almost the only means of saving China and of upholding British interests in those regions. I trust that at last Her Majesty's Government have, even with slow and halting feet, realised this vital principle of politics, and that Japan will have all our support in her useful and beneficent efforts.[100]

Nevertheless, there were certain practical difficulties in the way to an Anglo-Japanese Alliance. The foreign policies of the country could not be segregated into water-tight compartments. It was therefore impossible for England to be the enemy of Russia in Asia, and, at the same time, the friend of Russia in Europe and elsewhere. An alliance with Japan would mean that England had to be prepared

---

[99] *Par. Deb.,* March 1, 1898, 4th Series, LIV, 305-306.
[100] Ibid., August 7, 1899, LXXVI, 70.

to wage war all over the world against Russia and her allies. Japan, though a rising Power, did not possess world-wide interests. Would it be wise, therefore, for England to ally herself with Japan in the Far East, and thus incur the enmity of Russia, and, perhaps, to fight her alone, in all parts of the world? Furthermore, British interests in the Far East were principally commercial, and therefore demanded peace. An alliance with Japan might provoke an unnecessary war, and thus disturb the peace that was so valuable to British trade. Finally, in British high quarters, there was a prejudice against a non-Christian Yellow race.[101]

There were, then, the other alternatives: an alliance with Germany, adhered to by Japan and, perhaps, the United States; or a friendly understanding with Russia. For generations British relations with Germany had been friendly, but, since 1894, the sky of the Anglo-German relations had been darkened by successive events.[102] Open conflicts of interests had existed between the two Powers, not only in the Near East and in Africa, but also in Asia. The growing German industry and sea power further aroused the jealousy and hostility of Great Britain.

Under these circumstances, the British Government turned first to Russia, early in 1898, for a friendly understanding.[103] It reasoned that Russia

[101] Ibid., February 8, 1899, LXVI, 198.
[102] Gooch, pp. 208-231. Cf. London *Times,* December 25, 1897, p. 3.
[103] Many British statesmen preferred an understanding with Russia to an alliance with Germany. " German proceedings in China,"

and Great Britain, especially in the Far East, had
to meet, but they need not meet in anger.[104] China
was large enough for both. Banish the elements of
territorial designs and of trade restrictions from her
policy, and Russia's undertakings in Manchuria and
her project of coming down to an ice-free port on the
Pacific would not be injurious to British interests
and, therefore, could not be seriously objectionable
to England.[105]

On January 17, 1898, the English Ambassador at
St. Petersburg was instructed to ask M. de Witte
whether it was not possible for England and Russia
to work together in China.[106] The English Ambas-

---

argued Mr. Asquith, "were much more difficult to reconcile with the
professed objects of the policy of Her Majesty's Government," and
"Germany had nothing to offer in an alliance." *Par. Deb.,* June 10,
1898, 4th Series, LVIII, 1346-50. Cf. ibid., February 8, 1898, LXVI,
238. Edward Grey. London *Times,* October 11, 1898, p. 7; Lord
Kimberly, ibid., January 26, 1899, p. 5. Some were even willing to
abandon Manchuria to Russia. *Par. Deb.,* 4th Series, LXVI, 243;
LXXXI, 871.

[104] Edward Grey, *Par. Deb.,* 4th Series, LVI, 1661; Salisbury, ibid.,
LVIII, 1370. Cf. Count Mouraviev, China, No. 2 (1899), No. 23.

[105] Mr. Balfour was the first British statesman to declare in a
speech at Bristol, on February 5, 1896, that there was no objection
to Russia obtaining an outlet to the Pacific. Cf. *Parl. P.,* China,
No. 1 (1898), Nos. 76, 103, 108, 123, 128, 133. *Par. Deb.,* Curzon, the
Under-Secretary for Foreign Affairs, March 1, 1898, LIV, 337;
LVIII, 1370; Marquess Lansdowne, August 6, 1901, XCVIII, 1364.
London *Times,* Balfour, January 11, 1898, p. 8; March 7, p. 11; May 2,
1899, p. 9. In the Commons, Mr. Balfour argued: "That railways
by whomsoever constructed and under whatsoever conditions they
may be constructed, cannot but be on the whole a benefit to British
and to general trade." *Par. Deb.,* April 5, 1898, 4th Series, LVI, 231.
Cf. Ibid., April 29, 1898, LVI, 1593.

[106] *Brit. Doc.,* I, 5.

sador also suggested that any understanding, in order to be really effective and lasting, had to extend to the general area of their respective interests, and not to be confined to the important questions affecting the Far East.[107] The overtures were at first favorably received by the Russian Government. They suggested, however, that, in the first instance, they should proceed to treat the Chinese affairs which were very pressing.[108] To this the British Government agreed, and proposed a " partition of preponderance "—that the valley of Huang-Ho and the territory to the north of it should be regarded as subject to Russian influence, and the Yangtze valley as subject to British influence.[109] The Russian Government seemed disposed to agree,[110] but, at this juncture, England secured from China certain political and commercial advantages,[111] and a loan by the Anglo-German Syndicate was also signed. This gave excellent excuse for the Czar to refuse to pursue the discussion of the broader questions, and the negotiations were dropped.[112]

[107] Ibid., I, 6.
[108] Ibid., I, 9.
[109] Ibid., I, 8, 12-13; Cf. I, 2.
[110] Ibid., I, 10, 13.
[111] These included the declaration for the non-alienation of the Yangtze basin, the declaration for the Inspectorship of the Customs, the opening of the " inland waters " of China to steam navigation, and the opening of Nanning and Siangtan as treaty ports. According to Mr. J. A. C. Tilley, " These concessions having been secured, the understanding with Russia became a matter of comparative indifference at that time to Her Majesty's Government." The negotiations were therefore dropped. *Brit. Doc.,* I, 2.
[112] *Brit. Doc.,* I, 16.

As soon as the proceedings for an Anglo-Russian rapprochement seemed to have reached an *impasse,* Mr. Chamberlain, the powerful Colonial Secretary of the British Cabinet, opened negotiations (end of February, 1898) with the German Minister at London for an Anglo-German alliance.[113] The Kaiser suggested that this alliance should be with the Triple Alliance, with the addition of Japan and America. The negotiations lasted with intervals throughout the year 1898, and because of the lack of sincerity on the part of the Kaiser and his advisers, finally led to no result. Among other reasons, and not one of the least, was the attitude of the Kaiser and Count von Bülow, who did not wish to endanger the good will of Russia, nor to fight for the English interests in the Far East.[114]

[113] Hermann Freiherr von Eckardstein, *Lebenserinnerungen,* X, *und politische Denkwürdigkeiten,* Leipzig, 1921, pp. 292-296. Levine, *Letters from the Kaiser to the Czar,* New York, 1920, pp. 47-49, 53. Gooch, pp. 298-312. Many British statesmen were then advocating an alliance with the Central Powers, particularly Germany. *Par. Deb.,* February 8, 1898, 4th Series, LIII, 132-134; March 1, LIV, 303-304, April 5, LVI, 286; August 2, LXIII, 1012. Lord Kimberly, London *Times,* January 26, 1899, p. 5; February 27, p. 9; Chamberlain at Leicester, ibid., December 1, p. 7.

[114] The German Minister told the Prussian Parliament in plain words: "Germany was not going to enter into alliances for the good will, pleasure, and advantages of other countries, but only exactly as far as they suited German interests." *Par. Deb.,* 4th Series, XCII, 187. Nor was a partial agreement regarding the Far East alone possible, for, although in Asia German interests might have been the same as those of Great Britain, she had a much greater interest in not joining an alliance for special operations in the East, for her interest in Europe was a thousand times as great as any that she had in Asia. Besides, she did not wish to risk any conflict with

Having been unable to reach a general and lasting understanding with either Russia or Germany, Great Britain turned to a policy of partial and temporary agreements in the Far East.[115] " Animated by a sincere desire to avoid in China all cause of conflict on questions where their interests meet," Great Britain and Russia agreed on a " partition of spheres for concessions for the construction and working of railways in China," *i. e.*, Russia to the north of the Great Wall, and Great Britain in the

Russia in the Far East which would expose her to attack on two frontiers in Europe—Russia on her Eastern and France on her western frontier. Nor did she want to bear the brunt of explosion in Russia; she desired to release her own eastern frontier in Europe by encouraging Russia in the Far East. Mr. Brodrick, the Under-Secretary for Foreign Affairs, June 9, 1899, *Par. Deb.*, 4th Series, LXXII, 804. Prince von Bülow, Imperial Germany, tr. by Marie A. Lewenz, London, 1916, pp. 49, 50. *Letters from the Kaiser to the Czar*, pp. 9, 10, 12, 13, 16, 17, 25, 38-39, 41-43, 45, 52. Cf. *Par. Deb.*, August 7, 1899, 4th Series, LXXVI, 83. The Berlin *Neueste Nachrichten*, London *Times*, October 28, 1895, p. 5. The *Hamburger Nachrichten* (Prince Bismarck's organ), London *Times*, May 16, 1898, p. 7; the *Cologne Gazette*, reproduced by the *Norddeutsche Zeitung*, April 6, 1898.

[115] On January 15, 1896, Great Britain and France signed an agreement in which the two governments agreed to extend and to render common to both Powers all commercial and other privileges conceded in the two Chinese provinces of Yunnan and Szechuen to Great Britain or France. *State Papers*, 1895-96, LXXXVIII, 13-16. On March 30, 1900, Mr. Brodrick, the Under-Secretary for Foreign Affairs, made the following remarks in the Commons: "It is the policy of the Government, without creating further responsibilities necessitating the employment of a large number of troops, to keep open the waterways of China for our trade, and to secure to British subjects a full share of opportunities to open out China while securing from all countries the recognition of the principle of the open door." *Par. Deb.*, 4th Series, LXXXI, 888.

basin of the Yangtze. Each promised not to obstruct, directly or indirectly, the other's application for railway concessions in the latter's assigned region.[116]

The following year witnessed the Boxer uprising in China. Taking advantage of the situation, Russia proceeded to occupy Manchuria, and by the 10th of October, Russian troops had practically established control over the whole of Southern Manchuria.[117] In addition, she seized the railway from Tientsin to Peking (subsequently surrendered to joint use and occupation of the Powers), and the railway from Tientsin to Shanhaikwai and thence north (not given up till February, 1901), and she also occupied Yingkow, the port of Newchwang.[118] Not only were British potential interests in the Far East thus threatened, but property rights of British subjects

[116] *State Papers,* 1898-99, XCI, 92. First suggested by Mr. Lessar, Russian Chargé d'Affaires at London, to Mr. Balfour. China, No. 2 (1899), No. 13.

[117] Ever since then Russia refused a definite restitution of the region to China, and promised only to restore the Three Eastern Provinces "after a normal state of things has been re-established in the Chinese Empire, and when a central and independent Government has been established in the capital, sufficiently strong to guarantee Russia against the renewal of the disorders" caused by the Boxer uprising. The *Messenger Officiel* (St. Petersburg), quoted in *Par. Deb.,* May 21, 1901, 4th Series, XCIV, 738. Also *Parl. P.,* China, No. 1 (1902), Nos. 14, 31; No. 2 (1904), Morse, III, 321-325. Count Lamsdorv told the Japanese Government that Russia would be perfectly right even if she chose to make occupation (of Manchuria) permanent.

[118] She also seized the coal mine at Tongshan and claimed a concession at Tientsin. *Parl. P.,* China, No. 5 (1901), No. 89; China, No. 7 (1901), Morse, III, 321-325.

in North China were actually disregarded by Russian military authorities.[119] Russia's bold steps in those months were not difficult to understand. Since October 9th, 1899, England had been at war with the Boers, the early successes of whom had greatly prejudiced British prestige all over the world.

" The position of Great Britain," wrote a contemporary historian, " at the opening of the conflict [the Boer war] was one of ' splendid ' if not risky isolation. France and Russia seemed incurably hostile; Germany was less unfriendly, but scarcely a friend; the United States, though our [British] outspoken sympathy in the Spanish war had softened the angry memories of Venezuela, stood aloof from the controversies of Europe; Japan had not yet made her choice between London and Petrograd; Austria and Italy took no active part in Weltpolitik. This loneliness was intensified both by the setting and the incidents of the war." [120] If Great Britain ever needed an ally, it was at this time. Notwithstanding this situation, to retard the attainment of Russian aims in the Far East, Great Britain did not turn to Japan. Once again she approached Germany and reached an agreement with her on October 16, 1900. The agreement, recorded in an exchange of notes, was made in four articles.[121] Article I upheld the

[119] *Parl. P.*, China, No. 7 (1901), Nos. 1, 7, 21, 39, 45, 76, 77, 81, 84, 86, 95, 103, 149, 153, 154, 174, 187, 189.

[120] Gooch, p. 308.

[121] *State Papers*, 1900-01, XCIV, 897 ff. Later on, the German Chargé d'Affaires at St. Petersburg gave assurances that no hostility

principle of the open door in China. Article II disclaimed any territorial designs upon China on the part of the Contracting Powers, who pledged themselves to the maintenance of Chinese integrity. Article III provided that if another Power made use of the complications in China in order to obtain territorial advantages, the signatories were to discuss common actions. The last article provided that " other Powers interested " should be invited to " accept the principles recorded in it [the agreement]." [122]

The agreement, though praised by British statesmen as a " diplomatic success " and a " substantial advance on what had gone before," [123] soon proved to be without value to England. When Russia was pressing Peking in the following spring for the ratification of a secret treaty with Alexeiv, the Russian commander-in-chief in the Far East, and the Tartar General of Mukden had made of Manchuria

---

to Russia was implied, and that Germany had been driven to come to terms with England by Russia's having declined, at the commencement of the complications, to entertain proposals made by Germany for assuring her position in the Yangtsze.—*British Doc.*, I, 331-332.

[122] The principles recorded in the Anglo-German agreement of October 16, 1900, were later accepted by Russia. *Parl. P.*, China, No. 5 (1900), and enclosure, Austria (ibid., No. 5, (1900), No. 6), Japan (ibid., No. 5 (1900), No. 7, enclosure 2), France (ibid., No. 5 (1900), No. 81), Italy (ibid., No. 5 (1900), No. 9, enclosure), and the United States (ibid., No. 5 (1900), No. 10, enclosure 3). Both Russia and France accepted the principles with reservation while Japan adhered to the agreement as a signatory Power. Also see ibid., China, No. 5 (1900), No. 4.

[123] Viscount Cranborne, *Par. Deb.*, December 16, 1900, 4th Series, LXXXVIII, 152-153. Cf. Lord Salisbury at Guildhall, London *Times*, November 10, 1900, p. 12.

a virtual Russian protectorate,[124] and, when Lord
Lansdowne asked the German Government to cooperate with England and Japan to oppose the Russian
demand, the reply from the Berlin Cabinet was that
the Anglo-German agreement of October 16, 1900,
did not include Manchuria.[125] On March 15, the Chancellor declared in the Reichstag: " It is clear from
the text that it does not include Manchuria, and we
made it clear in the negotiations. Nothing can be
more indifferent to us than what happens in Manchuria. There are no real German interests there.
We only watch over German interests in China, and
we leave it to England to look after her own." [126]

---

[124] The secret agreement was believed to be signed on the 22d of
November, 1900. Several alterations were proposed later. *Parl. P.,*
China, No. 2 (1904), Nos. 5, 42. Count Lamsdorv, the Russian
Minister for Foreign Affairs, refused to communicate the text of the
agreement, and declined to discuss the versions received by England.
Ibid., China, No. 6 (1901), Nos. 163, 169, 171, 211. *Brit. Doc.,* II,
38-39; 47; 49; *Parl. P.,* China, No. 6 (1901), Nos. 9, 11, 14, 31, 35,
75, 85, 97, 130, 136, 139, 140, 154, 158; China, No. 2 (1904), Nos. 2,
3, 4, 6, 14, 35.

[125] Both Lord Lansdowne, the British Foreign Minister, and Viscount Cranborne, the Under-Secretary for Foreign Affairs, admitted
that Manchuria was not included in the agreement so far as the principle of open door was concerned, but held that, as regards the integrity of China, Manchuria was not excepted. " There is no limit," said
Viscount Cranborne, "to the territorial clause. It applies to the
whole of the Chinese Empire; but the open-door clause is obviously
limited—limited, in the first place, to the ports, the littoral, and
rivers of China, and, in the second place, limited to those ports in
which the contracting Powers have influence." *Par. Deb.,* July 29,
1901, 4th Series, XCVIII, 267. Cf. ibid., March 19, XCI, 405; March
22, XCI, 853; March 28, XCII, 183; July 29, XCVIII, 300; August 6,
XCVIII, 1360. *Brit. Doc.,* II, 27-31.

[126] *Parl. P.,* China, No. 6 (1901), No. 187. London *Times,* August
6, 1901, p. 7. Gooch, p. 326.

But, early in 1901, Chamberlain returned to the project of a general alliance with Germany.[127] England was ready, the Colonial Secretary told Baron von Eckardstein, then First Secretary of the German Embassy, to solve outstanding questions with the German Empire, especially with regard to Morocco and the Far East. Thus despite the difference between the German and British interpretations of the Anglo-German agreement regarding Manchuria, Lord Lansdowne suggested to Eckardstein on March 18, that a " defensive agreement " between Great Britain and Germany would be desirable. The latter replied by suggesting an Anglo-German-Japanese pact, which, he knew, would be agreeable to Mr. Hayashi, the Japanese Ambassador at London, to maintain the open door and the independence and integrity of China. On March 20, Holstein went even further and made the suggestion that the proposed alliance should be with the Entente of 1895 with the adherence of Japan. By March 25, the chief points were fixed. A defensive alliance was to be agreed upon and a separate alliance entered into with Japan with reference to the Far East. This scheme, however, again failed, as it had in 1898 and 1899, on account of insincerity on the part of the Berlin Government, and, in July, a final opportunity for a rapprochement presented by the Moroccan Mission to London was also allowed to pass. By the

[127] Otto Hammann, *Zur Vorgeschichte des Weltkrieges,* Berlin, 1919, ch. v. Gooch, pp. 324 ff. *Brit. Doc.,* II, ch. x.

end of October, an oratorical duel between the Chancellor and the Colonial Secretary took place over the conduct of the German troops in the war of 1870, which greatly agitated the temper of the Governments and the peoples of both countries. The British Government finally realized that an Anglo-German alliance was impossible.[128]

Standing alone, with prestige greatly prejudiced by the events in Asia as well as in Africa, and with her troops occupied in the Boer war, Great Britain was practically helpless against Russian encroachment in Manchuria.[129] At the time of the Boxer uprising, she had to invoke the help of Japan to defend her own interests in China.[130] In the North China campaign, Japan had proved that her military strength was equal to that of the countries of Europe,[131] and throughout the time of trouble, she

[128] Gooch, pp. 326-330. London *Times,* September 20, 1901, p. 7; January 7, 1902, p. 7.

[129] In these days " in Russia, Germany and Austria, in Italy, Spain and France, in Belgium, Holland, and even in Switzerland, there seemed to be a considerable body of popular opinion vehemently hostile to England." *The Review of Reviews,* VI, No. 3, p. 26.

[130] *Parl. P.,* China, No. 1 (1901), Nos. 14, 32, 122.

[131] *Parl. P.,* China, No. 1 (1901), No. 242; No. 5 (1901), Nos. 32, 79. London *Times,* September 10, 1901, p. 7. The growing power in Japan was evident even before the North China campaign. On November 11, 1899, the *Times* observed: " She (Japan) has bided her time and consolidated her strength. She has created a formidable navy far surpassing that which overthrew China on the seas. The enormous strides she has made in the development of her material resources are strikingly illustrated by the growth of her foreign trade. With a population of only 40 millions, the imports and exports of Japan, ... have already outstripped those of China

had cooperated heartily with the British Government.[132] United, England and Japan would be the masters in the Far East; separated, neither England nor Japan would be able to check the advance of the northern colossus. Thus, when on March 9, 1901, the Japanese Ambassador asked the British Government " How far may Japan rely upon the support of Great Britain in case Japan finds it necessary to approach Russia? " [133] the question received serious consideration. In a Memorandum drawn up for the British Foreign Office, Mr. Bertie summed up the situation as follows:

What Japan feels, or, rather, what is felt in that country, is that the Russian danger is advancing rapidly, and that it will not be long before Russia attempts to bring Korea within her sphere. Therefore, if Japan must fight for Korea, she had better do so over the Manchurian Agreement, before the Russian railway is completed.

---

with her 400 million inhabitants. The Japanese finances are in a very creditable state, ... The country has borne with ease the extraordinary charges for the increase of armaments, amounting to 22 millions sterling for the navy and 10 millions for the army, while the regular departmental estimates for the two departments, which were $1\frac{3}{4}$ millions before the war, are now $5\frac{1}{4}$ millions. . . . . Japan is in a strong and a solvent position. It is true the programme of naval construction and military reorganization which she started after the war has not yet been completed, but by far the greater part of the work, about $\frac{2}{3}$ of the whole, will be finished, by the end of the current financial year." London *Times*, November 11, 1899, p. 11.

[132] *Parl. P.*, China, No. 3 (1900), Nos. 121, 129, 134, 146, 170, 181, 188, 190, 191, 193, 235, 252, 260, 265, 266, 267, 276; China, No. 1 (1901), Nos. 22, 23, 32, 122, 123, 124, 149, 173.

[133] *Brit. Doc.*, II, 41.

If France were allowed to side with Russia, and they crushed Japan, the result might be a renewal of the triple understanding—viz., Russia, France, and Germany. Those three Powers would become supreme in China, and we should go to the wall.

If Russia alone, or in combination with France, defeated Japan, and we came to the rescue to prevent the obliteration of Japan, we should incur the lasting enmity of Russia and France, and a defeated, and probably ungrateful, Japan would not be of much use to us as against Russian encroachments.

It has been suggested that if Japan defeated Russia there would be grave danger to European interests in the Far East.

A great military and naval Power, with unbounded natural resources and an immense population such as Russia, is not likely to accept defeat permanently. She would reorganize for a further trial of strength, but such trial might be a long way off, and it would be greatly retarded by Japan being allowed to take as the spoils of war the Liaotung Peninsula. Its possession by Japan would be a guarantee that there would be no reconciliation between Russia and Japan. This would be an advantage to England and Europe. The yellow danger would be kept in check by Russia and the Russian danger by Japan.

If we do nothing to encourage Japan to look to us as a friend and a possible ally against Russia and France, we may drive her to a policy of despair, in which she may come to some sort of terms with Russia. I do not say that it is probable, but it is possible, and our interests would greatly suffer if she did.[134]

With such an understanding of the situation, when the project of an Anglo-German or an Anglo-Ger-

[134] *Brit. Doc.*, II, 43. King Edward also considered it most essential that England should give Japan her hearty support on all occasions when it was possible to do so. Ibid., II, 92.

man-Japanese alliance failed, the British Government was ready for an alliance with Japan alone.[135]

Ever since the Sino-Japanese war, Russian activities in Korea had been a nightmare for the Japanese statesmen. Time and again they had approached the Russian Government for a solution, but nothing had resulted except two pointless conventions which had not satisfied the Japanese people. After several years of attempts for a peaceful settlement had failed, most Japanese writers and statesmen were definitely convinced that a Russo-Japanese agreement upon the basis suggested by Japan was, under the circumstances, impossible. At the same time, the growing strength in Japan and her part in the North China campaign had inspired them with greater confidence in their country's ability to protect her own interests.[136] Therefore, by 1901, the nation was almost unanimously against an understanding with Russia, which in its opinion would be, at best, only a temporizing expedient, and as a result Japan would lose prestige at home and abroad.[137] The Russian encroachments upon Manchuria in 1900 and 1901 did not directly concern Japan and were not so considered, but the Japanese statesmen feared that

[135] On Feb. 13, 1902, Marquess Lansdowne made the following remarks on the floor: "No other Power has interests in Far East at all comparable to those of Great Britain and Japan; and therefore it is that this agreement is made between Great Britain and Japan alone." *Par. Deb.*, 4th Series, CII, 1175.

[136] Cf. London *Times*, November 8, 1901, p. 6.

[137] Ibid., November 8, 1901, p. 6. Cf. the summary of two articles in Yomiuri Shinbun, London *Times*, November 2, 1896, p. 13.

Manchuria, under the military and political control of Russia, might become the Russian stepping-stone to Korea.[138] They fully realized that a failure to reach an agreement with Russia regarding Korea would mean a war between the two countries. They were therefore willing to fight Russia over the question of the Manchuria agreement before the Siberian railway was completed,[139] and they believed they could beat Russia on the field in a single-handed combat. But Russia did not stand alone: she was in alliance with France in Europe. In case a war broke out between Japan and Russia, France would surely come to the assistance of her ally in the north.[140] In a combat against the great Franco-Russian combination, Japan could not expect to win. Ever since the Tripartite intervention, Japan had welcomed the friendship of Great Britain. An Anglo-Japanese alliance to hold the ring for Japan in a possible war with Russia was sure to elicit a hearty welcome from the whole Japanese nation.[141]

[138] Ibid., March 26, 1901, p. 5. *Brit. Doc.*, II, 92, 97, 105.

[139] *Brit. Doc.*, II, 41, 43.

[140] The *Figaro* of the 8th of May, 1901, definitely declared that M. Delcassé had arranged with the Russian Minister to support Russia in her actions in regard to Manchuria and Korea. H. N. G. Bushby, "The Agreement between Great Britain and Japan," in the *Nineteenth Century*, LI, 375.

[141] Japan was ready to go to war with Russia in the early part of 1901 and was anxious that England and Germany would not allow France to help Russia. *Brit. Doc.*, II, 41, (43); II, 92. In the early part of 1901, even Ito was in favor of an Anglo-Japanese alliance. Hayashi, p. 165, footnote. *The (Japanese) Journal of International Law and Diplomacy*, March, 1927, XXVI, No. 3.

The negotiations for an Anglo-Japanese alliance started—strangely enough—from a suggestion of the First Secretary of the German Embassy Baron von Eckardstein in March when the German and British Governments were discussing a general alliance between the two countries.[142] In replying to Lord Lansdowne's offer of a " defensive agreement " between Great Britain and Germany, Eckardstein made the suggestion of an Anglo-German-Japanese pact. Being informed of this possibility, Mr. Hayashi,[143] the Japanese Ambassador, immediately advised the Tokio Government of the desirability of such a combination. On April 16 he

[142] Hammann, ch. v. Pooley, p. 12. Hayashi, pp. 119 ff. Baron von Eckardstein, *Lebenserinnerungen,* 2d ed., 1920, II, 280-281. *Brit. Doc.,* II, 60, 89, 96-100. Baron Eckardstein, however, in his report on March 19, gave the initiative of an alliance to Lord Lansdowne. *Die Grosse Politik,* XVII, 41-42. But in another place he declared that on the 16th of March he had told Lord Lansdowne: " If there were a defensive alliance covering all eventualities, Germany would of course be in a position to localize a war between Russia and Japan by influencing France." Eckardstein, II, 280-281. The German Government was not sincere in this transaction. The question of having Germany join the Anglo-Japanese Alliance was left by the Japanese Government to the discretion of the British Cabinet, which found out later that Germany, as shown by her action in China, was by no means really friendly to Great Britain, and thus dropped her. See *Brit. Doc.,* I, 332, 333. II, 26-27, 97, 103, 104, 110, 120-121. "A timely outburst of Anglophobia (in Germany), which even the most indulgent British statesmen could hardly overlook, made it impossible to admit Germany into the alliance, ..." A, B, C, Etc., " British Foreign Policy—Reconsidered," in the *National Review,* XL, 347. Cf. ibid., pp. 350 ff. A, B, C, Etc., " British Foreign Policy," in the *National Review,* XLIII, 732-733.

[143] He took his office as the Japanese Ambassador at the Court of St. James in May, 1900.

received the authorization to sound Downing Street
on his own responsibility, and this he did on the following day.[144] On account of Lord Salisbury's absence from London and Cabinet changes in Tokio,
the discussions were not resumed until July 31, when
both Lord Lansdowne and Hayashi agreed to look
forward to negotiations for a definite agreement.[145]
But it was not until October 8, after the Japanese
Government had carefully considered the question
and formed a definite policy supporting an Anglo-
Japanese alliance, that Hayashi was formally given
the power to negotiate an alliance with Great
Britain.[146] On November 6, Lord Lansdowne handed
to the Japanese Ambassador the first draft of the
proposed treaty the terms of which were in accordance with the understanding they had previously
reached in several meetings.[147] While progress was
thus being made in the negotiations for an Anglo-
Japanese alliance, Prince Ito was visiting St. Petersburg, and, on his way back to Berlin, despite his
early approval of an alliance between London and
Tokio, he put up a strong opposition to the proposed
project.[148] The opposition from the first statesman

[144] *Brit. Doc.*, II. 89

[145] Ibid., pp. 90-91. The last opportunity for a rapprochement
between the German and British Governments was let slip in
the same month, just a few days before this meeting of Lansdowne
and Hayashi.

[146] Hayashi, p. 128.

[147] *Brit. Doc.*, II, 99-100. The oratorical duel between the Chancellor of Germany and the Colonial Secretary of the British Government started at the end of October.

[148] Hayashi, pp. 149 ff.

of Japan, supported by Count Inouye and other
friends, was indeed very strong and could be
thwarted by nothing less than an Imperial command which was given in a Council of Elder Statesmen on December 7.[149] Consciously or unconsciously,
Prince Ito's visit to Russia had served as a spur
upon England to hasten the negotiations.[150] The
final draft of the treaty was signed in London by
Lord Lansdowne and Mr. Hayashi on January 30,
1902,[151] and was published eleven days later in London and twelve days later in Tokio.[152]

[149] Hayashi, p. 165.

[150] See *Brit. Doc.*, II, 57-58. Hayashi, pp. 123 ff. About the same
time Mr. Kurino was packed off to Paris to talk about a Triple Alliance between Russia, France, and Japan. Pooley, p. 12.

[151] For the several drafts (and amendments) of the treaty of alliance of January 1902, see *Brit. Doc.*, II, 114 ff.

[152] The Japanese Government insisted on early publication of the
treaty. *Brit. Doc.*, II, 100, 102, 120, 121. The British Government
also felt " that it could not be kept secret for long, and that as we
should certainly have it dragged out of us in Parliament it was much
better to make a clean breast of it at once." *Brit. Doc.*, II, 137. The
Treaty was published one day later in Tokio on account of the fact
that February 10 was a holiday in Japan. Before its publication the
substance of the agreement had been communicated to the United
States and German Governments. *Brit. Doc.*, II, 121-123. *Par. Deb.*,
CII, 1246, 1247.

CHAPTER III

The Alliance, 1902-05

The treaty, signed on January 30, 1902, declared that the Governments of Great Britain and Japan desired to maintain " the *status quo* and general peace in the Extreme East," to uphold " the independence and territorial integrity of the Empire of China and the Empire of Korea," and to secure " equal opportunities in those countries for the commerce and industry of all nations." The two Powers denied any " aggressive tendencies " as to either China or Korea. But " having in view, however, their special interests, of which those of Great Britain relate principally to China, while Japan, in addition to the interests which she possesses in China, is interested in a peculiar degree politically as well as commercially and industrially in Korea, the High Contracting Parties recognized that it will be admissible for either of them to take such measures as may be indispensable in order to safeguard those interests if threatened either by the aggressive action of any other Power, or by disturbances arising in China or Korea, and necessitating the intervention of either of the High Contracting Parties for the protection of the lives and property of its subjects." If, as a result, war should ensue between one of the allies and a third Power, the other ally agreed to maintain a strict neutrality and prevent other Powers from joining in hostilities against its ally. If, however, a second hostile Power should engage in the war, the two allies would wage war together and make peace in common. Neither ally would enter into separate arrangements with another Power to the prejudice of the interests described in the instrument, without consulting the other. They promised to communicate with each other fully and frankly whenever these interests might be in jeopardy. The Agreement was to come into effect immediately after the date of its signature, and was to remain in force for five years from that date. In case neither ally notified the other, a year before 1907, its intention of terminating the treaty, it was to remain in force until a year after such a notice of expiration was given. But, if the date of expiration should come at a time when one of the allies was at war, the alliance was to continue, *ipso facto,* until peace should be concluded.[1]

In England, the Agreement was well received, though the approval cannot be said to have been universal.[2] It was praised by its supporters as an

[1] For text of the treaty, see MacMurray, I, 324 ff. Sir T. H. Sanderson in a letter to Sir E. Satow, said: "There is nothing beyond the agreement itself except an interchange of notes promising one another docking facilities and expressing the intentions of later [the two] Governments to keep up their naval forces in the Far East." *Brit. Doc.,* II, 137.

[2] The *Spectator* and a few other pro-Russian papers objected to the alliance, because they thought the Anglo-Japanese combination was detrimental to a friendly understanding between England and

instrument that would do much for " the preservation of peace in the Far East and all over the
world."[3] But others raised objections, and the criticisms ran from Mr. Michie's mild disparagement
that " much as we may admire the skilled workman-
ship of the Anglo-Japanese Treaty, the best can be
said for it is, that it is after all only a wooden leg,
a brittle substitute for the sinewy member which it
replaces,"[4] to Mr. Zeta's severe condemnation that
" the provisions of Lord Lansdowne's alliance, as it
stands, can only be regarded as in the highest degree untimely, unnecessary, unequal, and injurious."[5] In Japan, the publication of the alliance was
welcomed by the whole nation with the utmost en-
thusiasm. The Japanese celebrated its signing as a
great victory. Not a dissentient word was heard,
even from those who had earlier been in favor of
a friendly arrangement with Russia.[6]

Russia. For English opinion of the alliance see *Par. Deb.,* CII, 1273,
1276, 1280; CX, 753; etc. Also see " England and the Powers," in
the *Monthly Review,* London, VI, No. 3, p. 11. Charles Bill, " The
Imperial Outlook," in the *Monthly Review,* XI, No. 3, p. 29. A. Maurice Low, " The Anglo-Japanese Alliance," in the *Forum,* New York,
XXXIII, 196. " The Treaty with Japan," in the *Living Age,* Boston,
CCXXXII, 697.

[3] London *Times,* February 12, 1902. Cf. *Par. Deb.,* CII, 1311-12.
Review of Reviews, New York, XXV, 460.

[4] A. Michie, " Anglo-Japanese Alliance," in *Blackwood's Edinburgh Magazine,* Edinburgh, CLXXI, 444.

[5] Zeta, " The Anglo-Japanese Alliance, and After," in the *Fortnightly Review,* London, LXXVII, 365 ff. For other criticisms and
comments see *Par. Deb.,* CII, 1175, 1179, 1290, 1294, *Arena,* XXVII,
453.

[6] See the *Japan Daily Herald,* February 13, 1902, Also see " The
Changing East," in the *Quarterly Review,* London, CXCVI, 219

In the United States, though she was not a party
to the alliance, and although her Government did not
express any official opinion on it, the treaty was
hailed by the Press and the people as a measure
that would secure the open door in China without
involving the United States in political complications with European Powers.[7] In Germany, the alliance was regarded as directed against Russia and
as a sure instrument to prevent an Anglo-Russian
understanding. Thus, the Kaiser informed Lascelles,
the British Ambassador at Berlin, that he had heard
of it " with interest and satisfaction," and he was
surprised " that the agreement had not been concluded earlier."[8]

Only one Power was displeased; that was Russia.[9]
The Russian Government was greatly discomforted
by the alliance and acknowledged it as a diplomatic
check, if not a defeat, though the Russian Government pretended to affect calm, and even indifference.[10] To serve as a warning to Japan, who, Russia
believed, was intoxicated by her alliance with a great

A. Maurice Low, " The Anglo-Japanese Alliance," in the *Forum*,
XXXIII, 197. " The Anglo-Japanese Alliance," in the *Nation*, New
York, LXXIV, 144.

[7] See " The Anglo-Japanese Alliance," in the *Nation*, New York,
LXXIV, 144. Seiji C. Hishida, *The International Position of Japan
as a Great Power*, New York, 1905, p. 226. Also see *Par. Deb.*, CII,
1246-47.

[8] *Brit. Doc.*, II, 122, 123.

[9] Both Italy and Austria-Hungary looked upon the alliance with
favor. *Brit. Doc.*, II, 123, 129, 142.

[10] *Brit. Doc.*, II, 130-131. For Russian and French Governments'
attitude toward the alliance, also see ibid., II, 123-124, 124-125, 125-
126, 128, 130, 131, 135-136.

Power like England,[11] and to maintain her prestige
in the eyes of the Chinese, Russia, in conjunction with
France, on March 16, declared:

The allied Governments of Russia and France have received a copy of the Anglo-Japanese Agreement of the 30th
January 1902, concluded with the object of maintaining the
status quo and the general peace in the Far East, and preserving the independence of China and Korea, which are to
remain open to the commerce and industry of all nations, and
have been fully satisfied to find therein affirmed the fundamental principles which they have themselves, on several
occasions, declared to form the basis of their policy, and
which still remain so.

The two Governments consider that the observance of these
principles is at the same time a guarantee of their special
interests in the Far East. Nevertheless, being obliged themselves also to take into consideration the case in which either
the aggressive action of third Power, or the recurrence of
disturbances in China, jeopardizing the integrity and free
development of that Power, might become a menace to their
own interests, the two allied Governments reserve to themselves the right to consult in that contingency as to the means
to be adopted for securing those interests.[12]

This declaration was soon followed by a *com-
muniqué officiel,* dated March 20, stating that:

The Imperial Government, appreciating the friendly communications made in this regard to Russia by the Japanese
and English Governments, has received the conclusion of
that convention with the utmost calm. The principles that

---

[11] *Brit. Doc.,* II, 137.

[12] MacMurray, I, 325-326. *Brit. Doc.,* II, 135-136. *Parl. P.,* China,
No. 2 (1904), No. 50.

7

have guided Russian policy have remained and still remain invariable; Russia insists on the independence and integrity of China—a friendly neighboring country—as well as on that of Korea; Russia desires the maintenance of the *status quo* and the general pacification of the Far East. By the construction of the great Siberian Railway, with a branch running through Manchuria to a port always free of ice, Russia is favoring the extension, in those regions, of the commerce and industry of the whole world. Would it be in her interests actually to set up obstacles to that?

The intention, expressed by England and Japan, to contribute to the attainment of the same aims which are invariably pursued by the Russian Government, can only appeal to the sympathy of Russia, in spite of comments emanating from certain political spheres and from various organs of the foreign press, which have made an effort to present under a quite different aspect the impassive attitude of the Imperial Government in regard to a diplomatic act which, in its view, does not at all change the general situation of the political horizon.[13]

Much was said as to the one-sidedness of the terms of the first alliance. Some believed that England alone benefited by the arrangement, for England's chance of confronting a European coalition was much greater than that of Japan.[14] Others thought that the alliance was one-sided, because the Far East formed the whole foreign policy of Japan, while to

[13] MacMurray, I, 326.

[14] M. Alcide Ebary, whose opinion on such matters, according to the *Saturday Review*, was worthy of sincere respect, endeavored to demonstrate England alone benefited by the arrangement. "The Anglo-Japanese Treaty," in the *Saturday Review*, London, XCIII, 196.

England it was only a part of her Imperial policy.[15]
A close examination of the instrument and a careful
inquiry into its origin shows, however, that neither
was the case. In fact, a treaty of this kind could not
be one-sided. The truth was that Great Britain and
Japan had common interests to defend in the Far
East.[16] Japan wanted to prevent Russia from domi-
nating Korea; and Great Britain, considering the
importance of the geographical position of that
peninsula, was not willing to see Korea pass into the
hands of Russia.[17] Great Britain wanted to maintain
the *status quo* and the open door in China. To this
Japan had no objection so long as the open door and
the integrity and independence of China were
threatened to her disadvantage.[18] Japan was anxious
to have Great Britain keep the ring for her in a
war against Russia; Great Britain was afraid lest
Japan would join Russia in regard to China and
Korea.[19] The power of England was essential to
Japan, and the power of Japan was essential to
England. Neither could look on with indifference

[15] Mr. Henry Norman, criticising the alliance in the House of
Commons, said: "By this treaty British policy would in future be
tied hard and fast to the wheels of Japanese policy." *Par. Deb.*, CII,
1276. Cf. ibid., CII, 1292-3. The *Spectator*, February, 1902.

[16] Mr. Balfour declared on July 7, 1902, in the Commons, that the
Agreement with Japan was entered into for a "common object."
Par. Deb., CX, 943. Cf. ibid., CII, 1285, 1295. *St. Papers*, XCV, 85.
Stafford Ransome, "Japan's Imperial Policy," in the *Fortnightly
Review*, LXXVII, 567.

[17] *Brit. Doc.*, II, 91, 92, 97. Hayashi, pp. 125, 129.

[18] *Brit. Doc.*, II, 91, 97. Hayashi, pp. 120, 125, 129.

[19] *Brit. Doc.*, II, 98. *Par. Deb.*, CII, 1296.

while the power of the other in the Far East was being crushed by a hostile combination.[20]

For these reasons they united. It was true that, though India was not included in the Agreement,[21] Japan's special interests, politically as well as commercially and industrially, were recognized by England, but, after all, if Korea had to fall into the hands of one of her two neighboring Powers, Japan was naturally preferred by Great Britain as the protector of that country. Although India was not included, by virtue of the alliance, in case a war broke out between Great Britain and a hostile combination, the former could at least be freed from any danger in the Extreme East, for any attack from the hostile Powers on China or Korea would automatically bring in the forces of Japan.

The gain on the side of England from the alliance was best summed up in the following words:

What it [the treaty of alliance] does for this country is to liberate us from all anxiety with regard to our interests in that vast sphere of the earth vaguely known as the " Far East." We have acquired the usufruct of one of the most powerful fleets existing, and of the ports and coaling stations of Japan. This alone renders almost laughable any suggestion that French or German intervention in conjunction with Russia would be a serious menace. It would also render a

[20] *Par. Deb.*, CII, 1287. Cf. ibid., CII, 178, 1295. Zeta, " The Anglo-Japanese Alliance, and After," in the *Fortnightly Review*, LXXII, 375.

[21] England had suggested to include India in the Agreement, but Japan rejected, and the project was dropped. *Brit. Doc.*, II, 102, 104.

hundred times more dangerous an attempt to disturb the *status quo* in the Persian Gulf. . . . . With regard to ourselves another possibility arises which we may set down as pure gain. If this country were to become engaged in war with any European Power from causes not Asiatic, the interests of England in the Far East would be henceforth either safe from attack or an attempt to injure them would almost certainly be followed by the appearance of our ally in the field. . . . . In such a contingency the appearance of Japan on the scene would infallibly mean the disappearance of our enemies, whoever they might be, from those regions.[22]

To Japan, the gain was that " it seemed that the agreement safeguarded Japan's position in Korea, it greatly relieved her from working under the nightmare of a European coalition against her, it strengthened her voice with that of England at the court of Peking, and it added to the weight of whatever Japan might undertake to do in foreign relations." [23]

In order to understand the real significance of the terms described by the treaty, we have to go deeper than the wording of the instrument seems to indicate. The treaty was aimed at Russia.[24] In its preamble

[22] " The Anglo-Japanese Treaty," in the *Saturday Review*, XCIII, 196. Cf. Charles Bill, " The Imperial Outlook," in the *Monthly Review*, XI, No. 3, p. 29. " The Changing East," in the *Quarterly Review*, CXCVI, 219-220. *Par. Deb.*, CIX, 1266.

[23] T. Iyenaga, " The Anglo-Japanese Alliance from the Japanese Point of View," in the *Review of Reviews*, XXV, 461. Cf. *Arena*, Boston, XXVII, 453.

[24] The whole Continental Press agreed on this point. Russia's joy over the conclusion of the treaty was not sincere. Edwin Maxey, " The Anglo-Japanese Treaty," in the *Arena*, XXVII, 452-454. Cf. *Brit. Doc.*, II, 89, 91-92, 97. Hayashi, p. 125.

it declared the desire to maintain "the *status quo*
and general peace in the Extreme East." The sincerity on the part of the allies to maintain peace in
the Extreme East could not be doubted,[25] only that
the peace they wished for was one on their terms.
To Great Britain, these consisted of a recognition
of British special interests in China or at least in
the Yangtze Valley, "the territorial *status quo* in
China and its adjoining regions, and equal opportunities for the development of the commerce and
industry of all nations within those regions, as well
as with the limits of the Chinese Empire."[26] To
Japan the terms meant a free hand for her in Korea,
and a recognition of her special interests—though
these had then to be created—in China.[27] But Great
Britain and Japan were not the arbiters of those regions, and their interests were not the same as those
of the other Powers. Russia, for one, also had interests there. If she, too, maintained a policy like
that of Great Britain and Japan, that is, to maintain
peace only on her own terms, then, to avoid conflicts
in the Extreme East, was an impossibility. Thus it
lay with Russia to decide whether the Anglo-Japanese Agreement was to secure general peace in Asia.

[25] Hayashi, pp. 166, 168-169. *Brit. Doc.*, II, 103, 109, 112.

[26] The Anglo-Japanese Agreement, January 30, 1902, Article I.
MacMurray, I, 324. The Marquess Lansdowne to Sir C. MacDonald,
forwarding Agreement between Great Britain and Japan of January
30, 1902. *State Papers*, XCV, 84-85. See also *Brit. Doc.*, II, ch.
xi. Hayashi, ch. iv.

[27] The Anglo-Japanese Agreement, January 30, 1902, Article I.
MacMurray, I, 324. *Brit. Doc.*, II, ch. xi. Hayashi, ch. iv.

As to the *status quo* mentioned in the preamble, the question arises: What was meant by the *status quo?* [28] At the time of the signature of the Anglo-Japanese Alliance, the Russian troops were still in occupation of Manchuria. When asked in the Parliament whether the *status quo* recognized by the Anglo-Japanese Treaty also recognized the Russo-Chinese Convention of November 12, 1900, signed by the local Russian authorities and the Tartar General, Lord Cranborne said: " The Russian Minister for Foreign Affairs informed Her Majesty's Ambassador at St. Petersburg that it [the Russo-Chinese Convention of November 1900] was in the nature of a *modus vivendi*.[29] A temporary Agreement of that kind does not bring in question the international status of Manchuria under public treaties." [30]

[28] In international law the phrase *status quo* is used " to denote actual possession by rights of conquest, occupation or otherwise, at some particular moment, which has to be defined with as much exactness as possible in the proposals for a treaty of peace, or in the treaty itself." " When on the conclusion of a treaty of peace the belligerents agree mutually to restore all their conquests, they are said to revert to the *status quo ante bellum.*" Sir Earnest Satow, *A Guide to Diplomatic Practice,* London, 1917, I, 155-158. Cf. Lassa F. L. Oppenheim, *International Law,* London, 1906, II, 287. William E. Hall, *International Law,* Oxford, 7th ed., 1917, p. 599. Albert Sorel, *L'Europe et la revolution française,* Paris, 1904, p. 159.

[29] Count Lamsdorff, the Russian Foreign Minister, explained the local and temporary character of the Agreement of November, 1900, as " a *modus vivendi* for the duration of the simultaneous presence of Russian and Chinese authorities in Southern Manchuria." *Parl. P.,* China, No. 2 (1901).

[30] *Par. Deb.,* CIV, 1270. Both Lord Lansdowne and Lord Cranborne had declared in unmistakable terms that Manchuria was a

" The Japanese held that all regularly arranged conventions between China and the Powers were included in the phrase *status quo,* and were therefore recognized under the treaty. These included the leases of Kiaochow, Port Arthur, Talienwan, and Wei-Hai-Wei, besides the convention with the Russo-Chinese Bank relative to the Manchurian Railway. Equally with this, the Anglo-German Agreement of October 16, 1900, the Anglo-Russian Agreement of May, 1899, and the assurances of the Chinese Government as to the non-alienation of the Yang-tse-kiang region were all recognized by the new treaty." [31] An investigation of the British documents leaves no doubt that to this interpretation of the *status quo* the British statesmen also agreed.[32]

In the preamble the allies declared themselves to be " specially interested in maintaining the independence and territorial integrity of the Empire of China and the Empire of Korea, and in securing equal opportunities in those countries for the commerce and industry of all nations." Having these

---

part of the Chinese Empire and was included in the treaty of January 30, 1902, between Great Britain and Japan. *Par. Deb.,* CII, 1180, 1247.

[31] Hayashi, p. 118. Cf. Alfred Stead, " The Anglo-Japanese Agreement," in the *Contemporary Review,* LXXXI, 442.

[32] *Par. Deb.,* 4th Series, CII, 1247; CIII, 584. *Brit. Doc.,* 109. It should be noted that the interpretation of the *status quo* in the treaty of January 30, 1902, by the British and the Japanese Governments was different from the universally accepted meaning of that phrase. Cf. above, p. 93, footnote 28. Cf. Alfred Stead, " The Anglo-Japanese Agreement," in the *Contemporary Review,* LXXXIII, 442.

ends in view, they mutually recognized, by Article I,
" the independence of China and Korea," and declared themselves to be " entirely uninfluenced by
any aggressive tendencies in either country." But,
in the same article, we find the following words:
" Having in view, however, their special interests
of which those of Great Britain relate principally to
China, while Japan, in addition to the interests which
she possesses in China, is interested in a peculiar degree politically as well as commercially and industrially in Korea, the High Contracting Parties recognize that it will be admissible for either of them
to take such measures as may be indispensable in
order to safeguard those interests if threatened
either by the aggressive action of any other Power,
or by disturbances arising in China or Korea, and
necessitating the intervention of either of the High
Contracting Parties for the protection of the lives
and property of its subjects."

Such a provision, when carried to its logical conclusion, was nothing less than a mutual recognition
that both contracting parties would have a free hand
in taking whatever measures they might please,
without regard to the wishes of the Chinese or
Korean Governments, to foil the aggressions of
other Powers or put down local disturbances, and
therefore a right to intervention in the domestic
affairs of those countries. This would nullify the
very independence, and, in many cases, impair the
very integrity, the maintenance of which the allies

professed to be specially interested in, and pledged
mutually to recognize. Nor could the "special interests" recognized by the treaty be regarded as
consistent with the principle of open door.

The real fact was that the allies wanted to safeguard their special interests in China and Korea.
The words which declared their respect for the open
door, and the independence and integrity of China
and Korea, were merely fine phrases used for the
purpose of disguising the real purport of the alliance and of silencing the objections of the other
Powers. They may be likened to the courteous
formula which conceals a social rebuff. Furthermore, they could be made use of by the allies in protesting against the proceedings of other Powers
which might endanger their interests in those
regions.[33]

The alliance was offensive as well as defensive.[34]
An instrument which ordered a third Power, Russia,
to get out of Manchuria, a place which was occupied
by her troops, and out of Korea, where she had as
good a claim as that of any other Power, while at
the same time asserting the allies' special interests

[33] On February 13, 1902, Lord Cranborne, the Under-Secretary
for Foreign Affairs, made the following remarks in the House: "We
are not international knights-errant who are going to make binding Agreements because of the good looks of any Power." *Par. Deb.*,
CII, 1285. Cf. ibid., CII, 1178, 1311. *Brit. Doc.*, II, 99.

[34] Cf. *Par. Deb.*, CII, 1273, 1276. A, B, C, etc., "The Alliance with
Japan," in the *National Review*, London, XXXIX, 154. A, B, C,
etc., "British Foreign Policy—Reconsidered," in the *National Review*,
XL, 346. Also see *Saturday Review*, XCIII, 196.

in China—in the case of Japan, these special interests hardly existed—and giving Japan, a party to
the alliance, a free hand in Korea, could not be said
to be purely defensive.[35] The fact that Russia was
aggressive in Manchuria and Korea, did not prove
that the allies were defensive. At the time of the
conclusion of the Anglo-Japanese Alliance of January 30, 1902, both China and Korea were independent countries. Neither Russia, nor Great Britain,
nor Japan had any rights in those countries; they
had only interests there. Under the Agreement,
either of the high contracting parties might independently take action, if, in the judgment of that
Party alone, its interests were threatened in the
manner described by the treaty.[36] It was true that
this was conditioned by Article V which provided
that " whenever, in opinion of either Great Britain
or Japan, the above mentioned interests were in
jeopardy, the two Governments would communicate
with one another fully and frankly." This was in
order to obviate, in advance, differences of opinion as

---

[35] In fact, " if Russia requires a permanent argument for remaining [in Manchuria] she would simply have to make an easy adapta-
tion of the words in which the High Contracting Parties to the Anglo-
Japanese Treaty contemplate intervention for the protection of their
special interests against foreign aggression or internal disorder. An
excuse for the latter plea was never likely to be wanting, and Russia,
again by the truly ' celestial ironies,' might choose, if she liked, to
regard Anglo-Japanese policy as the unreasonable aggression upon
her special interests which would justify her in maintaining the
occupation of Manchuria upon Anglo-Japanese principles." Zeta,
in the *Fortnightly Review* (1902), LXXVII, 378.

[36] *Par. Deb.*, CV, 40.

to the actual existence of the circumstances whereby alone the obligations contemplated by Article III, that is, to conduct war in common and to make peace in mutual agreement, could be deemed to have arisen. But in case either Great Britain or Japan should take up a quarrel with another Power, the cause of which, in the opinion of the other ally, was not in the defense of their respective interests, but was distinctly aggressive, and should be in the danger of being crushed by a hostile combination, the other ally could still by the force of the treaty come to her assistance, for it was provided by the treaty that either of the high contracting parties was to be allowed " to take such measures as might be indispensable," in order to safeguard its interests. Now, it was a well-known fact that it was to the Japanese interest that British power in the Far East should not be curtailed, and *vice versa*. It would have been strange, therefore, if the allies should not have exploited the utility of that provision to its full extent when occasion arose.

The strength of the alliance was soon seen in several connections. Only two months after its publication (on April 8, 1902) Russia came to an agreement with China in regard to Manchuria,[37] based on Prince Ching's counter-proposals, which were wholly approved by Japan and, in the main, by

---

[37] The abrupt condescension on the part of Russia was principally effected by the new alliance. See, Asakawa, p. 214. *Yale Review,* XIII, 143. *Brit. Doc.,* II, 126.

Great Britain.[38] Russia promised thereby, provided
that no disturbances should have arisen, and that
the action of other Powers should not have prevented it, to withdraw gradually all its forces from
the three Eastern Provinces as follows:—from the
regions west of the Liao River, by October 8, 1902;
from the rest of the province of Mukden and the
entire province of Kirin, by April 8, 1903; and
finally, from the province of Heilung-Kiang, by October 8, 1903. Pending the evacuation, the numbers and the dispositions of the Chinese forces in
Manchuria were to be determined by consultation
between Russian and Chinese officers, but, after the
evacuation was completed, the Chinese Government
was to have the right to increase or diminish its
troops in the Manchuria provinces only with the
condition that, in doing so, the Russian Government
was to be notified.[39]

In still another connection, the strength of the
alliance was felt. This was during the time of the
diplomatic negotiations preceding the evacuation of
Shanghai in the latter part of 1902,[40] when Japan
gave the " most cordial and complete support "
to the objections which her ally raised against the
German condition that " the Peking Government
and the Yangtse Viceroys should have engaged not

[38] The United States 57th Cong., 2d Sess. *H. Doc.* No. I, pp. 277-
279.

[39] MacMurray, I, 326 ff.

[40] The evacuation of Shanghai took place on November 1, 1902.

to grant to any Power special advantages of a political, military, maritime or economical nature, nor to allow the occupation of any other points commanding the river either above or below Shanghai." [41]

In Korea, the alliance had for a time the effect of strengthening Japan's position at Seul. Shortly after its conclusion the Russian Minister notified the Tokio Cabinet that, so far as his Government was concerned, Japan was at liberty to have a free hand in Korean affairs. [42]

The real test of the strength of the alliance, however, did not come until the time of the diplomatic negotiations which Japan had taken up directly with Russia in regard to Manchuria and Korea, and during the war that followed. By the Russo-Chinese Convention of April 8, 1902, Russia promised to evacuate Manchuria at three different periods within the ensuing eighteen months. By the date set for the first evacuation, October 8, 1902, it had been completed, [43] and, on October 28, Prince Ching was able to inform the British Minister at Peking that " Their Excellencies the Minister Superintendent of Northern Ports and the Military Governor of Mukden have now severally reported by telegram that all the railways outside the Great Wall have been handed back, and that the Southwest portion of the

[41] Brit. Doc., I, 335; II, 144-5. Par. Deb., CXVIII, 212. Parl. P., China. No. 3 (1902), Nos. 25, 30.

[42] "The Cloud in the Far East," in Macmillan's Magazine, London, LXXXVIII, 358.

[43] Parl. P., China. No. 2 (1904), No. 65, enclosure 2.

Mukden province as far as the Liao River has been completely evacuated by Russian troops.'' [44]

The second part of the evacuation, covering the strategically most important section of Manchuria, was to occur, according to the Russo-Chinese Convention, on April 8, 1903. When this date drew near, no withdrawal of the Russian troops had taken place.[45] Instead, new demands in seven articles were handed to the Chinese Foreign Office. These demands included, among other things, the non-alienation, by lease or sale, of any portion of Manchuria to another Power, the perpetuation of the system of government then existing in Mongolia, and the closing of the Manchuria provinces against foreign trade, by forbidding China to open new ports or towns therein.[46] Later, upon the repeated refusal of these demands by the Chinese Government, even heavier demands were made.[47]

Simultaneously with the suspension of the evacuation of Manchuria and her pressure upon the Peking Government for the new demands, Russia, after suddenly notifying the Korean Government, on April 13, 1903, began to work the timber concessions which she had secured in 1896, and, early in May, occupied

[44] Ibid., China. No. 2 (1904), No. 66, enclosure.

[45] Ibid., China. No. 2 (1904); Nos. 67, 106, 116, 122, 128, 130, 137, 156.

[46] For the version of these demands, see, ibid., China. No. 2 (1904). No. 94. Also see ibid., Nos. 77, 78, 81, 82, 86, 127.

[47] Ibid., China. No. 2 (1904), Nos. 95, 98, 109, 110, 114, 117, 119, 121, 123, 125, 126, 134, 141, 143. Cf. ibid., China, No. 2 (1904). Nos. 133, 136, 139, 142, 147, 154, 156, 157, 159, 160.

Yong-am-po, a point near the mouth of the Yalu River.[48]

Now, the Manchurian Agreement of April 8, 1902, signed by China and Russia, was not entirely satisfactory to either Great Britain or Japan.[49] Failure on the part of Russia to carry out her promised evacuation of the three Eastern provinces and her recent aggressive actions in both China and Korea, gave Japan an opportunity to negotiate directly with Russia alone,[50] in order to reach a binding agreement which would secure once for all "an amicable adjustment of the questions between Japan and Russia, concerning their respective special interests in Korea and Manchuria."[51]

The basis for such an adjustment, proposed by Japan, was contained in the six articles delivered on August 12 to Count Lamsdorff by Mr. Kurino.

[48] Asakawa, pp. 289 ff. The sudden change of attitude on the part of Russia toward active aggression was due to the ascendency of a military party in that country. "Russia and Japan," in the *Quarterly Review* CXCIX, 603-4. *Brit. Doc.*, II, 131-132, 202-203, 223, 237-238, 239.

[49] *Parl. P.*, China. No. 2 (1904), Nos. 52, 55.

[50] The Manchurian Question engaged the serious attention of the British Government in 1903, and both the United States and Great Britain were anxious for some settlement in Manchuria with Russia. *Par. Deb.*, CXXI, 639, 789, 917; CXXVI, 190. The Japanese Government, however, insisted on negotiating directly with Russia alone, and was not willing to have either Great Britain or the United States join her in the negotiations. *Brit. Doc.*, II, 208-209, 210-211.

[51] Ibid., II, 215. According to MacDonald, it was the "sincere and earnest wish of the Japanese Government and people that peace should have been maintained." *Brit. Doc.*, II, 215-217. Cf. ibid., II, 224-225.

These articles, though professing to respect the independence and territorial integrity of China and Korea, and to maintain the open door in those countries, proposed a reciprocal recognition of Japan's preponderating interests in Korea and Russia's special interests in railway enterprises in Manchuria, and a recognition of the right of Japan to take in Korea, and of Russia to take in Manchuria, necessary measures, even to the extent of sending troops, for the protection of their respective interests, or for suppressing insurrection or disorder liable to create international complications. Finally, Russia was to recognize the exclusive right of Japan to give Korea advice and assistance, including even military support.[52]

These provisions,[53] if agreed to by Russia, would have recognized Russia's special economic interest in Manchuria, and have established Japan's protectorate over Korea, which was clearly contradictory to the professed spirit of the alliance between England and Japan, concluded only eighteen months previously.[54] Throughout the negotiations between

[52] Asakawa, pp. 303-304.

[53] The essential features of these articles were never altered in the later notes from Japan throughout the negotiations between Japan and Russia. For the details of the Russo-Japanese negotiations preceding the war, see Asakawa, chs. xviii, xix.

[54] In October, 1903, Baron Koruma informed MacDonald, that " he thought the Russians would continue to consolidate their position in Manchuria. This the Japanese could not prevent, but the negotiations, if brought to a successful conclusion, would permit the Japanese to consolidate their position in Korea, which they would strain every nerve to do." *Brit. Doc.*, II, 220. Cf. Calchas, " First Principles in the Far East," in the *Fortnightly Review*, LXXXI, 203 ff.

8

Russia and Japan, the British Government had been
" fully and accurately informed " as to the progress
of events,[55] yet no objection was raised by it to the
basis of the understanding which Japan proposed to
Russia.[56] Instead, the British Government gave
Japan its complete support and approval.[57] This
gave further confirmation of the observation above
made that the alliance of 1902 was concluded to safeguard the allies' special interests in China and
Korea, and showed that the allies' declared intention to maintain the open door and the independence
and integrity of China and Korea was not sincere.

[55] *Brit. Doc.,* II, 244. Cf. Ibid., II, 206-207, 208-209, 213-214, 217,
220, 220-221, 224-225, 233-234, 237-238, 242-243, 243-244, 245.

[56] Lansdowne to Durand, British Minister at Washington: "Our
feeling is that considering the nature of demands upon which Japan is
insisting we should not be justified in putting even moral pressure
upon her to abate them. We might, moreover, incur lasting resentment of Japan if we were to stand in her way and deprive her of an
opportunity which she is apparently determined to turn to account.
If she were to miss her chance now she might suffer for it hereafter."
Brit. Doc., II, 243. Cf. Ibid., II, 246-247, 250, 251.

[57] Marquess Lansdowne to Sir Claude MacDonald: "His Majesty's
Government have, however, never concealed from themselves that the
interests of Japan in Korea are of a special kind. . . . . His Majesty's Government would welcome a recognition by Russia of the
special interests of Japan in Korea. They have themselves, in the
Anglo-Japanese Agreement, already admitted that Japan has such
interests, and they consider that it would be to their advantage that
the position of Japan in that country should be strengthened." *Brit.
Doc.,* II, 209. Cf. ibid., II, 209-210, 218, 219, 225, 227-228, 232-233,
237, 240, 240-241, 243. The British Government had protested against
Russian actions in Peking and made representations favorable to
Japan at St. Petersburg. *Parl. P.,* China No. 2 (1904), pp. 55, 58.
Par. Deb., CXXII, 298; CXXIX, 345. They had also urged the Chi-
nese Government to refuse the Russian demands. China, No. 2 (1904),
Nos. 79, 80, 81, 82.

This was made even more obvious by the highhanded measures which Japan took in Korea during the period of war.[58]

When the war broke out, Great Britain immediately declared her " strict neutrality." [59] Throughout the war, as anticipated, Japan had been the victor and more than able to hold her own.[60] Great Britain was therefore naturally satisfied with keeping her neutrality,[61] despite the fact that both France

[58] On February 23, 1904, fifteen days after the outbreak of war, Japan forced Korea to sign a treaty which practically gave Japan a protectorate over Korea. In two subsequent treaties Japan was given the right to recommend a financial adviser and a diplomatic adviser to the Korean Government whose consent had to be obtained before the Korean Government could deal with any matter concerning finance and foreign relations of the country (concluded on August 22, 1904), and the right to control and administer the post, telegraph and telephone service in Korea (concluded on April 1, 1905). Henry Chung, *Korean Treaties,* New York, 1919, pp. 213-214, 214-215, 215-218. Cf. F. A. McKenzie, *The Tragedy of Korea,* London, 1908, pp. 108 ff.

[59] State Papers, XCVII, 476 ff. The outbreak of hostilities occurred on February 8, and British neutrality was formally declared on February 11.

[60] It was based upon this anticipation that the alliance of 1902 was drafted in such a way that it only went into effect if one of the contracting parties was attacked by a combination of Powers. In defending Articles II and III of the treaty of alliance, Lansdowne said: " Japan has a strong navy and a strong army, and might very fairly expect to hold her own in a single-handed encounter with any other Power; but if she were to be threatened with an attack by more than one Power she would undoubtedly be in imminent peril; and it is in that imminent peril that we desire to come to her succour." *Par. Deb.,* CII, 1178.

[61] At this time, Great Britain did not want a great European war which was dreaded, in fact, more than anything else. Moreover, she had reasons not to irritate Russia, for she had entertained the hope, though still vague by this time, of reaching an understanding with

and Germany had been guilty of helping Russia in violation of their neutrality.[62] Nor was this disliked by Japan,[63] who was in fact anxious that Great Britain should not enter the war, for her entry was sure to draw in France, and perhaps also Germany, to fight on the side of Russia. At a European conference at the end of the conflict, no matter which side

---

Russia, in order to complete her policy of seeking the Empire's security in alliances. Cf. Count Okuma, " Diplomacy and the War," in the *Independent,* New York, LIX, 432. Calchas, " First Principles in the Far East," in the *Fortnightly Review,* LXXXI, 194 ff. There was no doubt, however, that Great Britain would go to the assistance of Japan, had the latter been defeated by Russia and in danger of being obliterated. In defending the treaty of 1902 in the House, Mr. Balfour said: " If Japan is in difficulties with a single Power, Great Britain still can go to the assistance of Japan if she wants to go." *Par. Deb.,* CII, 1295. Cf. *Brit. Doc.,* II, 224, 228-229; John B. Walker " The Conquest of Asia by Russia," in the *Cosmopolitan,* New York, XXXVI, 386.

[62] The Russian Baltic fleet on her route to the Far East had coaled and made use of French ports and bases which were clotted along the routes to the Far East. H. W. Wilson, " Japan's Trafalgar," in the *National Review,* July, 1905. As to Germany, the Kaiser had promised the Czar, even before the outbreak of hostilities, neutrality of the most benevolent kind, and during the period of war, he had disregarded utterly any semblance of neutrality in the direction of limiting the sale of ships or *materiel de guerre* to Russia. The *Nation,* New York LXXVII, 519. Alfred Stead, " The War: Korea and Russia," in the *Fortnightly Review,* LXXXII, 101-102. Cassell's *History of the Russo-Japanese War,* London, III, ch. lxii. Also see Letters from the Kaiser to the Czar. Contrast these to the British declaration that His Majesty's Government had resolved " to prevent, as far as possible, the use of His Majesty's harbours, ports, and coasts, and the waters within His Majesty's territorial jurisdiction, in aid of the warlike purposes of either belligerent." British Circular to Public Offices for the Observance of Neutrality in the War between Russia and Japan, February 10, 1904. *State Papers,* XCVII, 482-484.

[63] *Brit. Doc.,* II, 244, 245, 251. Cf. ibid., II, 97.

won the war, Japan could not expect to dictate her own terms as she later did at Portsmouth.

For about a year and a half after the outbreak of hostilities, Japan won an unbroken series of victories on both land and sea. At the request of President Roosevelt, both belligerents sent their delegates to the United States, and the peace conference opened officially on the 9th of August, 1905, at Portsmouth, New Hampshire. On September 5, the treaty of peace was signed.

The Portsmouth Treaty provided among other things: (1), That Japan's " paramount political, military, and economic interests " in Korea be recognised; (2), That the rights of Russia by lease and concessions in the Liaotung Peninsula be transferred to Japan; (3), That the southern section of the Manchurian railway and the southern portion of the island of Saghalin be ceded to Japan; (4), That the troops of both countries be withdrawn from Manchuria (not including the Liaotung Peninsula), and that the number of railway guards maintained there be kept as small as possible; and (5), That their respective railways in Manchuria, except in the Liaotung Peninsula, be exploited exclusively for commercial and industrial, but in no wise for strategical, purposes.

By Article III of the treaty the Russian Government declared that it had " not in Manchuria any territorial advantages or preferential or exclusive concessions in the inpairment of Chinese sovereignty

or inconsistent with the principle of equal opportunity.'' By Article IV Japan and Russia reciprocally engaged '' not to obstruct any general measures
common to all countries which China may take for
the development of the commerce or industry of
Manchuria.'' [64]

About three months and a half after the Portsmouth treaty, Japan and China reached an agreement in which the Chinese Government consented to
all the transfers and assignments made by Russia
to Japan in their treaty of peace in so far as they
concerned herself.[65] In a supplementary agreement,
Japan was given the right to retain for fifteen years
the military railway line constructed between Antung
and Mukden, and China and Japan agreed to or-
ganise a joint stock company of forestry for the
exploitation of the forests in the regions on the right
bank of the Yalu River.[66]

On November 7, 1905, two months after the Portsmouth treaty, Japan forced Korea to sign a treaty
which gave Japan the right to take full charge of the
foreign relations of Korea, and directly led to the
complete annexation of that country five years later
by Japan.[67]

---

[64] MacMurray, I, 522 ff. *State Papers*, XCVIII, 735 ff.

[65] The agreement also provided that in regard to the leased territory and the matter of railway construction and exploitation, in case
any question arose, the Japanese Government was to decide it in
consultation with the Chinese Government. MacMurray, I, 549 ff.
State Papers, XCVIII, 740 ff.

[66] MacMurray, I, 551 ff. *State Papers*, XCVIII, 742 ff.

[67] Japan forced Korea to sign on July 24, 1907, another treaty by
which Japan was given the right to take over the internal adminis-

Were the alliance not in existence in 1904, Japan, being not sure of the attitude of the German and British Governments, and fearing that a war with Russia meant in effect a conflict with the military and naval forces of the great Dual Alliance, would not have dared to plunge into such a dangerous adventure. The treaty of 1902, by giving reassurance to Japan, had therefore, as a matter of fact, hastened the war in the Far East.[68] But, if the Anglo-Japanese agreement had failed to maintain peace in the Far East, it had at least the effect of restricting the area of hostilities and localising the war.[69] It was true that France had nothing to gain and everything to lose in a war in the Far East, and therefore could not be really zealous in joining Russia in a combat against Japan;[70] nevertheless, she would have surely

tration of Korea, and, finally, on August 29, 1910, the treaty of annexation. Henry Chung, *Korean Treaties*, pp. 223-224, 225 ff., respectively.

[68] During the time of the negotiations preceding the war, it was Great Britain who at the intimation of her ally had frustrated Delcassé's contemplation of an offer of mediation, and rejected Lamsdorv's request that the British Government should offer assistance in bringing about a pacific resolution. *Brit. Doc.*, II, 229-230, 236, 240, 240-241, 244. Cf. *Par. Deb.*, CXXIX, 41; CXLI, 28.

[69] Before the outbreak of hostilities, Marquess Lansdowne in a despatch to MacDonald made to Japan the following promise: " His Majesty's Government . . . . will on their side fulfill, both in letter and spirit, their obligations under the agreement, which imposes upon them the duty of using their efforts in order to prevent other Powers from joining in hostilities against their ally." *Brit. Doc.*, II, 244. There was no doubt that the British Government later did keep her promise.

[70] Cf. Edwin Maxey, " The War in the East and the Possible Complications," in the *Arena*, XXXI, 353 ff. J. C. O'Laughlin, " The War and the Powers," in the *Outlook*, New York, LXXVI, 735 ff.

been dragged in, had the alliance not been in existence. Then, to save Japan from being crushed by a coalition, Great Britain was sure to enter the war to maintain the balance in favor of Japan.[71] Regardless of whether Germany and the United States would throw in their weight, a world war would be already in existence.

By the war and the treaties that followed,[72] Japan had gained the long-hoped-for complete and exclusive control over Korea, acquired a strong foothold on the Continent, and planted her " special interests " in Manchuria. As for England, henceforth she needed not to fear the Russian advance toward the east, and China, particularly the Yangtse Valley, was made secure for her factories and merchandise, whilst France, having put all her funds in Russia, had to curtail her colonial aspirations with regard to which there had been considerable jealousy in England before the Russo-Japanese war.[73] Furthermore, Great Britain had taken advantage of the

[71] On February 13, 1902, Marquess Lansdowne declared in the House: "The Obliteration of which (Japan), by a coalition of Powers, we could not in any circumstances tolerate." *Par. Deb.*, CII, 1178. Cf. ibid., CII, 1177, 1295.

[72] The Treaty of Peace at Portsmouth between Russia and Japan, September 5, 1905. The treaty between China and Japan, confirming all the transfers and assignments made by Russia to Japan by the treaty of Portsmouth in so far as they concerned China, and the additional agreement to the treaty, December 22, 1905. The treaty between Japan and Korea, by which Japan assumed charge of the foreign relations of Korea.

[73] Andrew M. Pooley, *Japan's Foreign Policies*, London, 1920, pp. 12-13.

war in the Far East to send a military expedition
into Tibet, in order to consolidate her position there,
and had forced the latter country to sign the treaty
of Lhasa on September 7, 1904.[74]

The treaty of 1902 between Great Britain and
Japan, therefore, did not contribute to the maintenance of the *status quo* and general peace in the extreme East. Nor did it contribute to the maintenance
of the independence and integrity of the Chinese and
Korean Empires. It did, however, directly or indirectly, restrict the area of hostilities, seal the fate
of the Korean nation, create Japan's special interests in Manchuria side by side with those of Russia,
greatly strengthen the position of both Japan and
Great Britain in China, and immensely enhance their
prestige at the Court of Peking. In fact, the advantages of the first alliance to the allies were so obvious that, when the second treaty was announced,
there was hardly any objection to it in either Great
Britain or Japan.

[74] MacMurray, I, 578-580. This treaty was later ratified by China
in a convention with Great Britain on April 27, 1906. MacMurray,
I, 576-577.

CHAPTER IV

THE ALLIANCE, 1905-11

The treaty of 1902 was to last for five years and could not be terminated by either party without twelve months' notice to the other.[1] It was made for the preservation of peace, and, should peace unfortunately be broken, it was expected to restrict the area of hostilities.[2] After the war between Russia and Japan, the efficacy of the old alliance no longer existed, and the new situation in the Far East as a result of the war, needed new provisions.

Meanwhile, a diplomatic revolution was rapidly taking place in Europe. The British statesmen, after four years' intermittent negotiation with the Berlin Government, finally found that a general agreement between Great Britain and Germany was impossible.[3] They immediately turned to the Dual Alliance. In the Spring of 1903 King Edward made a visit to Paris for the first time for more than three

---

[1] Article VI of the Alliance of 1902.

[2] Despatch to His Majesty's Minister at Tokio, forwarding Agreement between Great Britain and Japan of January 30, 1902. *State Papers,* XCV, 84-86. *Par. Deb.,* CII, 1178.

[3] The Japanese Alliance itself—from which Germany was excluded—was an indication that Great Britain was beginning to emancipate herself from German influence, which had hitherto weighed so heavily on her foreign policy. Cf. A, B, C, Etc., "British Foreign Policy," in the *National Review,* XLIII, 735.

years.[4] Three months later the King's visit was returned by President Loubet. Not long after a treaty was signed between England and France, under which differences of a judicial order were to be submitted to the Permanent Court of Arbitration in accordance with Article 16 of the Hague Convention.[5] This treaty was soon followed by the memorable Agreement of April 8, 1904, which settled the differences between the two countries in all parts of the world where their interests came into conflict.[6]

Having secured the friendship of France, Great Britain naturally desired a reconciliation with Russia, the other party to the Dual Alliance. Ever since Russia had turned to the East, the bone of contention between that country and Great Britain had been the Far East. By the treaty of 1902 with Japan, the British statesmen had hoped that, once the British policy in the Far East had been definitely defined and supported by a force that could not be challenged, Russia would come to terms with Great Britain in that part of the world, and that it would then be possible for the two countries to reach a general understanding.[7] During the Russo-Japanese

[4] For the revolution of Anglo-French relations, see Gooch, pp. 330-331, ch. x. Graham H. Stuart, *French Foreign Policy,* 1898-1914, New York, 1921, André Tardieu, *La France et les Alliances,* 3d. ed., Paris, 1910.

[5] Signed at London, October 14, 1903. State Papers, XCVI, 35.

[6] *State Papers,* XCVII, 31 ff.

[7] *Par. Deb.,* 1296-7, *Brit. Doc.,* II, 130. Cf. A, B, C, Etc., "British Foreign Policy—Reconsidered" in the *National Review,* XL, 345 ff., and "British Foreign Policy," in the *National Review,* XLIII, 729 ff.

war and the negotiations which preceded it, the British Government, though supporting her ally, had taken great care not to encourage the latter to proceed to extremities,[8] lest Great Britain should incur the permanent resentment of Russia and thus make impossible an Anglo-Russian understanding in the future. The same consideration had later prevented a very imminent war between these two countries after the famous Dogger Bank incident during which unarmed British fishermen were fired upon by the Russian fleet.[9]

The war in the Far East had revealed the undreamed-of weakness of Russia, from whom Great Britain, for a considerable time at least, had little to fear. Consequently, much of her old jealousy of the Slavic Power died out.[10] Russia had long been one of the mainstays of the world's peace. Her eclipse removed her corrective weight in the European balance and the world's most effective barrier to Ger-

[8] *Brit. Doc.*, II, 241.

[9] For the Dogger Bank Incident, see Cassell, III, ch. lxviii; *Brit. Doc.*, IV, 5-40.

[10] The war in Asia added a new burden of $1,200,000,000 to Russia's former loan of $3,400,000,000 of foreign indebtedness. Her navy was practically destroyed. She sank from the rank of third largest naval power to that of seventh; from 447,315 the tonnage of her fleet went down to 227,343. In her army she sustained a loss of over three hundred thousand officers and men. In addition to these was her internal movement for radical reforms which claimed, for the time being at least, practically all her brains and initiative. See Wolf von Schierbrand, "Japan as a Commercial Rival," in the *World To-day*, Chicago, IX, 1168. Coloniensis, "Can We Trust Russia?", in the *Fortnightly Review*, LXXXI, 754 ff. Calchas, "The Limits of Japanese Capacity," in the *Fortnightly Review*, LXXXII, 786.

man aggression. The result was an immediate German preponderance in Europe.[11] England now, for the first time since the Napoleonic war, realized that Russia was necessary to the European balance and to the world's peace.[12] Therefore, she earnestly desired Russia's friendship. There was, moreover, a danger that Russia would come to terms with Germany, the signs of which were becoming daily clearer on the political horizon of Eastern Europe since Russia had met her defeat in her Asiatic conflict.[13]

To win Russia over and to be careful not to drive her to a policy of despair, in which she might ally her-

[11] Russia's defeat was Germany's opportunity which the Berlin Government was not slow to make use of. The result was the first Moroccan Crisis. For the effects of the Russo-Japanese War on the European situation, see Frederic Austin Ogg, "European Alliances and the War," in the Review of Reviews, XXXII, 295 ff. An Italian Statesman, "The Influence of the Far Eastern War on the European Situation," in the National Review, XLVI, 402 ff. E. J. Dillon, "Russia and Germany," in the Contemporary Review, LXXXVIII, 609 ff.

[12] Sir Charles W. Dilke, "Present English Foreign Policy," in the Independent, LIX, 1513.

[13] Germany was most active during this period to win over Russia. "Her conduct during this recent war—that was, the more than benevolent neutrality observed; the furnishing Russia with abundance of small arms, ammunition, cannon; the sale to Russia of transports, converted cruisers of fleet type, etc.; the taking up in Berlin of Russia's most difficult war loan (after failure even in Paris) and material assistance in several previous loans; most of all, though, the proofs of sympathy given by the Kaiser, such as the telegram of farewell to the Viborg Guard Regiment, the sending military deputations, and, lastly, the interview with the Czar at Björko—all these things and more of them went to show what the Kaiser's object was." Wolf von Schierbrand, "Japan as a Commercial Rival," in the World To-day, IX, 1169. Cf. Alfred Stead, "Japan and Russia; Germany and Great Britain," in the Fortnightly Review, pp. 488 ff.

self with Germany, England had to be sincerely conciliatory toward St. Petersburg. But Japan was the
ally of England, and English Far-Eastern policy
rested on the alliance with the island Empire in the
East. So long as Japan and Russia remained enemies, an effective obstacle to the Anglo-Russian understanding existed, and Russia and England could
not become real friends. The British statesmen well
understood this, and were shrewd enough to see that
only moderate demands on the part of Japan for
conclusion of peace, could provide a starting point
for increasing friendly relations between Japan and
Russia. To attain this aim, Japan had to be relieved
of all apprehension of vindictive action on the part
of Russia in the future. This could be best done by
promptly concluding a new alliance with Japan.[14]

The treaty of 1902 between England and Japan
had not covered India. After the Russo-Japanese
war there was a growing fear in England that the
defeat of Russia in the East might divert her energy
toward Central Asia and the northwestern frontier

[14] On September 5th Sir H. Mortimer Durand, the British Ambassador at Washington, wrote to President Roosevelt: "(Lansdowne)
also asked me to let you know privately that the agreement between
England and Japan, the substance of which I communicated to you
when I was at Oyster Bay, was signed not long afterwards. His Majesty's Government felt that by promptly concluding this agreement,
and thereby relieving Japan of all apprehension of vindictive action
on the part of Russia in the future, they would make it easier for
Japan to moderate her demands, and they believe that their action
had the result they anticipated." The private papers of Colonel
Roosevelt, quoted by Tyler Dennett in his book *Roosevelt and the
Russo-Japanese War*, New York, 1925, p. 258, footnote.

of the Indian Empire.[15] Russia, though having sustained a great loss in the recent war, still appeared to be a serious danger to the Indian frontier. This danger seemed to be a hundred times more real, if one considered the close relations between Russia and Germany at this time, for the Kaiser certainly would have no hesitation in giving the necessary encouragement and support to the Czar, since his aim was to divert Russia's attention from Europe and to win her over by working together with Russia in Asia. In view of these considerations, it was, therefore, not a surprise that British statesmen should have been willing to sign a new treaty with Japan.

Japan, too, needed a new alliance. By the summer of 1905, Japan, though having won an unbroken series of victories, was rapidly becoming exhausted. She had put forth her maximum strength, the trial of which might result in a serious disaster to the nation.[16] The Mikado's ministers preferred, therefore, to have an early peace, rather than to run a most dangerous risk. It was this inside-view of the nation's real strength,[17] together with the resolute

[15] "China Station," "A Russo-Japanese War," in the *Contemporary Review*, LXXXI, 424 ff. R. E. C. Lond, "Russia, England and the War," in the *World To-day*, VIII, 45. William Weber, "The Anglo-Japanese Treaty Again," in the *Nation*, New York, LXXXI, 443. *Brit. Doc.*, IV, 124.

[16] See B. L. Putnam Weale (pseud.), *The Truce in the East and Its Aftermath*, New York, 1907, ch. vii.

[17] According to Mr. Putnam Weale, "the real position at the front was well understood privately in Downing Street." *The Truce in the East and Its Aftermath*, p. 171.

attitude assumed by the Czar's Plenipotentiaries immediately after their appointment, that caused the Tokio Cabinet to realize that their position at the peace conference could not be too strong and that there could be no peace, should Japan have refused to agree to moderate and reasonable terms. To fortify Japan's position at the peace conference and to provide for any contingency of Russia coming back in the near future, nothing could have been better for Japan than a new treaty with her old ally England.[18]

The second Alliance was signed at London on August 12th, three days after the opening of the peace conference at Portsmouth.[19] As its aim was different from that of the Alliance of 1902, so were its terms. It could hardly be said to be a renewal of the old; it was virtually a new instrument.

[18] For the reasons of both Japan and England to renew the alliance in 1905, see Herbert Paul, "The New Alliance," in the *Nineteenth Century,* LVIII, 513 ff.; "The Fear of Russia and the Defence of India," in *Blackwood's Magazine,* CLXXVII, 589 ff. Putnam Weale, *The Truce in the East and Its Aftermath,* pp. 170-171. See also *Brit. Doc.,* IV, 121-123, 127, 138-140.

[19] The negotiations for the renewal of the Anglo-Japanese Alliance were commenced in London in the early part of 1905. *Brit. Doc.,* IV, 120 ff. As the peace conference was still in progress, the British Government deemed it unwise to publish the new treaty, and the announcement of its conclusion was thus held back till September 6, one day after the Portsmouth conference was signed. The news of the formation of the alliance, however, was reported in the papers on August 25th, and even before that President Roosevelt of the United States was made aware through Sir Durand of the negotiations that were in progress and the nature of the terms. Dennett, p. 257.

The objects of the new alliance,[20] as declared in its preamble, were: (1) The consolidation and maintenance of the general peace in the regions of Eastern Asia and of India; (2) The preservation of the common interests of all Powers in China by insuring her independence and integrity and the principle of the " open door "; (3) The maintenance of the territorial rights of the High Contracting Parties in Eastern Asia and India, and the defence of their special interests in those regions.

The treaty provided: That, if, in the opinion of either of the High Contracting Parties, any of these rights and interests were in jeopardy, the British and Japanese Governments would communicate with each other fully and frankly, and would take common measures to safeguard them; That, if either ally should be involved in war in defence of its territorial rights or special interests in Eastern Asia and India, by reason of unprovoked attack or aggressive action on the part of a hostile Power or Powers, the other ally would at once conduct the war in common, and make peace in mutual agreement with it; That Great Britain recognised that Japan possessed paramount political, military, and economic interests in Korea, and, therefore, the right to take necessary measures of guidance, control, and protection to safeguard and advance those interests, provided always that such measures would not close the door of Korea to the commerce of the

[20] For the text of the Alliance of 1905, see MacMurray, I, 900 ff.

9

world; That Japan recognised that Great Britain had special interests in all that concerned the security of the Indian frontier, and, therefore, the right to take necessary measures in the proximity of that frontier for safeguarding her Indian possessions; That neither of the high contracting parties would enter into an agreement with a third Power to the prejudice of the objects of the treaty, without consulting the other; That, as regards the Russo-Japanese war, Great Britain would continue to maintain strict neutrality, unless some other Power or Powers should join in hostilities against Japan; That the conditions under which armed assistance should be afforded, and the means by which such assistance was to be made available, would be arranged by naval and military authorities of the two countries, who would co-operate fully and freely with one another. The last article was but a repetition of Article VI of the old alliance, with the exception that it provided that the new agreement should remain in force for ten, and not five, years from the date of its signature.

In England, as one writer observed: "This treaty was approved by all sections of the people, and the Liberal party, by the mouths of Mr. Asquith and Sir Edward Grey, had given their blessing to the diplomacy of Lord Lansdowne in the matter of the Japanese Alliance.[21] Parliament was not even

---

[21] Lord Lansdowne belonged to the Conservative Party, which was then in power.

consulted on the subject. Vast and far-reaching obligations had been silently placed upon the shoulders
of these islands without any discussion in the House
of Commons and very little in the Press. It was
taken for granted that . . . . alliance with the
brown conquerors of the Russians is in the language of the omnibus or the Stock Exchange, ' good
business ' for England.'' [22]

In Japan, the Press united in its praise.[23] They
not only received the new instrument with '' open
arms and enthusiastic acclaim,'' but also compared
it favorably with the old alliance, for the new treaty

[22] '' Coloniensis,'' '' The Seamy Side of the Alliance,'' in the *Monthly
Review*, XXI, No. 2, pp. 1-2. Cf. An Observer, '' Possible Effects on
England of Japan's Triumph,'' in the *Nation*, New York, LXXXI,
315. Mr. '' Coloniensis,'' in criticising the new alliance, said: '' The
Japanese Treaty, while barring the way to an understanding with
regenerated Russia, not only prevents the federation of the British
Empire, but hastens the establishment of the Australian Republic
under the suzerainty of the United States, which is the idea of many
Australian working men. For these reasons I hold that the Japanese
Treaty of Alliance is an instrument showing not wisdom but cunning;
not strength but decadence; and that the appearance of Japanese
troops in the Hooghly is more likely to break than consolidate the
British Empire.'' For other adverse criticisms, see William Weber,
'' The Anglo-Japanese Treaty Again,'' in the *Nation*, New York,
LXXXI, 443.

[23] The *Japan Daily Herald*, September 28, 29, 30, 1905. Japan's
welcome to the new alliance was, however, not without exception.
Viscount Tani, who had opposed the alliance between England
and Japan since its very beginning, when interviewed by Nippon's
representative, said that '' he thought the alliance would throw Germany into the arms of Russia, and when the two Powers were united
there was no telling what might not happen. It was simply an illusion, or rather delusion, to think peace had been secured by the
new compact. Rather it tended to disturb it.'' The *Japan Daily
Herald*, October 2, 1905.

recognised Japan's exclusive control over Korea, and guaranteed Japan against any insane design of Russian *revanche*.[24]

In comparing the terms of the second alliance with those of the first, several important changes must be noted.[25] It was for the control of Korea that Japan went to war with Russia, of which she now came out as a victor. At the time the second alliance was concluded, Japan was still in military occupation of Korea. British statesmen knew that no one could now stop Japan's imperialistic designs in that country without incurring her lasting resentment, and they were, therefore, least willing to do that themselves. Consequently, the new alliance declared, in its preamble, the desire of the high contracting parties to insure the independence and integrity of the Chinese Empire and the principle of the " open door " within the territory of that country, but made

[24] In the United States, the new alliance was received with favor. In France it was welcomed as exercising a salutary restraint upon Japanese ambition and therefore as a strong influence for peace. The *Saturday Review*, C, p. 392. In Berlin it was largely received with indifference, although a part of the German Press interpreted the new treaty as a menace to Germany, Russia and France. *Japan Daily Herald*, September 9, 30, 1905. In Russia the press heaped violent abuse on the Treaty, remarking that it destroyed the political equilibrium of Europe, and regarded the convention as an attempt to enslave more than half of Asia. *Japan Daily Herald*, September 7, 1905.

[25] Cf. " The Treaty with Japan," in the *Saturday Review*, C, pp. 424-425." The Anglo-Japanese Treaty: A Great Human Document," in the *Outlook*, LXXXI, 292 ff. Archibald Hurd, " The Anglo-Japanese Fleets in Alliance," in the *Fortnightly Review*, LXXXIV, 829 ff. Alfread Stead, " Peace in the Far East," in the *Fortnightly Review*, LXXXIV, 599 ff.

no reference to the maintenance of the independence
and territorial integrity of Korea. Instead, Article III of the treaty provided:

Japan possessing paramount political, military, and economical interest in Korea, Great Britain recognises the right
of Japan to take such measures of guidance, control, and protection in Korea as she may deem proper and necessary to
safeguard and advance those interests, provided always such
measures are not contrary to the principle of equal opportunities for the commerce and industry of all nations.

In a despatch to the British Ambassadors at St.
Petersburg and Paris on September 6, Lord Lansdowne justified this change by saying: '' The new
treaty no doubt differs at this point conspicuously
from that of 1902. It has, however, become evident that Korea, owing to its close proximity to
the Japanese Empire, and its inability to stand
alone, must fall under the control and tutelage of
Japan.'' [26]

As a compensation to Great Britain, Article IV of
the instrument provided:

Great Britain having a special interest in all that concerns
the security of the Indian frontier, Japan recognises her right
to take such measures in the proximity of that frontier as she
may find necessary for safeguarding her Indian possessions.

It was in view of these provisions that the allies
made it clear in the preamble that the new alliance
was to cover India as well as Eastern Asia, and that

[26] MacMurray, I, 518-519. Cf. *Brit. Doc.*, IV, 132.

it had for its object the maintenance of their territorial rights and the defence of their special interests in those regions.

The main purpose of the first alliance was to hold
the ring for Japan in her war against Russia, whilst
that of the second alliance was to deprive Russia of
any hope of success in any future aggressive policy
toward India and Eastern Asia, and, by so doing,
to turn her attention once again toward Europe, and
thus to bring her ultimately to the side of the allies.
Therefore, while the first alliance provided that
either ally would come to the assistance of the other
contracting party, only if the latter should have
become involved in war against a combination of
Powers, the second alliance provided that war with
one hostile Power should be a sufficient cause for
common action.

Finally, the new alliance differed from its predecessor in that it was to last for ten, and not five
years, though still with the same self-extending provision. This was an evidence of the growing friendship between the two allied nations, and of their
confidence in each other.[27]

The direct results of the new alliance were that
" the ' white peril ' passed forever from Japan. The
Europeans of Europe could no more confront her

[27] A longer period for the second alliance was first suggested by
Japan. *Brit. Doc.,* IV, 122, 129. It is significant to note that the desire to maintain the *status quo* in the extreme East was not regis-
tered in the second alliance, nor was there any further denial of
aggressive tendencies on the part of the allies in China and Korea.

from neighbouring ice-free coasts, nor spreaded
. . . . across the huge helpless continent of China
to the south. The fleets of Europe could no more
challenge her predominant power in her home seas.
. . . .To Britain it afforded a compensation of in-
estimable value, for Britain was no longer wholly
invulnerable against attack . . . . her vital problems of offence and defence were no longer confined
to British coasts and to the continent of Europe
. . . . her great imperial frontiers were in oceans,
thus sea power rendered her still secure, except
along two great land frontiers in America and Asia.
Of these, the Canadian frontier was not adjacent to
that of a great military power, nor was it a factor
of danger or weakness in practical politics at that
time. The Indian frontier, on the other hand, was
both a danger and a weakness. For against the military might of a Russian advance, (with the support, perhaps, of Germany,) upon India, the right
arm of Britain and her chief source of strength—
seapower—was of little avail, and, at the same time,
she failed in military strength. Consequently at the
one point where she lay open to attack in a vital part,
Britain was weakest in the power of defence. It was
in respect of this fatal weakness, however, that the
Japanese Alliance lent invaluable strength.'' [28]

[28] E. John Solano, " The World Influence of Britain and Japan,"
in the *Monthly Review*, XXI, No. 2, pp. 11-12. Cf. Archibald Hurd,
" The Anglo-Japanese Fleets in Alliance," in the *Fortnightly Review*,
LXXXIV, 830 ff.

The second treaty declared its object to be " the consolidation and maintenance of the general peace in the regions of Eastern Asia and of India," but neither of the contracting parties was willing to concede any of its imperialistic claims in these regions: therefore, " general peace " could only be maintained by putting a high price upon war. Should Russia, or some other Power, have decided to maintain an unyielding attitude in Asia, the value of this declaration would have been *nil*. The second object of the treaty, as declared in its preamble, was " the preservation of the common interests of all Powers in China," and the maintenance of " the independence and integrity of the Chinese Empire," and of the " open door " therein. These clauses were, as one writer remarked, " but diplomatic humbug designed to deprive the treaty of its sting so that the other Powers could raise nothing to object," for they were heftily bludgeoned into oblivion by the next and concluding clause of the preamble which declared that the third—the real—object of the alliance was " the maintenance of the territorial rights of the high contracting parties in the regions of Eastern Asia and of India, and the defence of their special interests in the said regions."

As was its predecessor, the alliance was a defensive and offensive instrument, although it provided that the other contracting party would come to the assistance of its ally only " if by reason of unprovoked attack or aggressive action " on the part of a

third Power, " either contracting party should have
been involved in war in defence of its territorial
rights or special interests.'' At the time of the conclusion of the second alliance, Great Britain possessed territorial rights in India, Burma, and Hongkong, and had—or at least claimed to have—special
interests in the Yangtse Valley. But Japan at this
time had, or claimed to have, special interests: she
had no " territorial rights '' whatever in the regions
of India and Eastern Asia. " In India, she had none;
in Eastern Asia, she had not yet acquired any. . . . .
It is true that Port Arthur and the Kwangtung
peninsula were occupied by the Japanese forces
at the time; it is also true that Japan had also occupied the Sakahalin Island. In these regions, however, Japan could have no other territorial rights
than those involved in military occupation. The
Russo-Japanese War was not yet brought to the
end, when, on August 12, 1905, the new alliance
treaty was signed at London. The peace conference at Portsmouth had been in session only three
days, and it was not known what form the peace
treaty would take. Even the international law principle of *uti possidetis*—the principle which legalises
the state of territorial possession at the moment of
the conclusion of peace, unless stipulations to the
contrary are contained in the treaty—could not,
therefore, be held to be operative. In Korea, Japan
had not yet acquired any territorial rights. In spite
of the fact that the country was overrun by Japa-

nese forces and placed under Japanese military occupation, Korea was still an independent nation.
At the time of the conclusion of the second Anglo-
Japanese Alliance, therefore, Japan did not possess
a foot of territory, either by acquisition, by lease, or
by conquest, on the continent of Asia.'' [29]

Furthermore, the treaty recognised the right of
freedom of action of Japan in Korea, and of Great
Britain in the proximity of the Indian frontier. An
instrument in which both of the signatory Powers
pledged themselves to defend with all their forces
something which one of the contracting parties did
not possess,[30] and mutually recognised their right of
freedom of action in some independent countries, or
in the territories of some independent countries, had
certainly leaped over the bound within which an
agreement can be called purely defensive. Finally,
whether the treaty was merely defensive depended
upon the exact meaning which the contracting parties attributed to the terms '' territorial rights ''
and '' special interests,'' the interpretation of which
by the allies, as seen in the light of later events,
again defeated the assertion that this alliance was
formed exclusively for defensive purposes.

Owing to the financial and physical drain of the
Japanese war and the grave domestic problems

[29] G. Zay Wood, *China, the United States and the Anglo-Japanese
Alliance,* New York, 1921, pp. 60-61.

[30] The "territorial rights" of Japan, which the British and Japanese Governments had in mind, referred, of course, to her future
lease of the Liaotung Peninsula and annexation of Korea, and possibly her acquisition of the southern half of the Sakhalin Island.

which that war had made manifest, Russia could
not hope alone to confront the great Anglo-Japanese
combination in the Far East. To pursue her ambition in China in face of that hostile combination,
she had to ally herself with another Power who was
strong enough and willing to throw its weight together with Russia, into the scales against Great
Britain and Japan. France was her ally in Europe,
and, before the war, had given her most useful support in Asia. But, since 1904, France had come to
terms with England, and she had finally realised
the folly of diverting the attention of the Dual Alliance from Europe by supporting Russia's aggression in distant Asia. There was only one Power
whose interests in Asia were coincident with those of
Russia. This Power was Germany who, in her hun-
ger for colonial expansion, was anxious to acquire
territory on the continent of Asia. The victory of
Japan and the new Anglo-Japanese Alliance were
equally a death-blow to the hopes and ambition of
Germany, as well as of Russia. Furthermore, the
German Kaiser had always wished to encourage
Russia's aggressive programme in the Far East, so
as to divert her attention from Europe.

Had Asia been the only consideration of the Russian statesmen, they might have allied themselves
with the Berlin Government in order to pursue their
ambition in the Far East. There were, however,
other considerations which were more important
than this. The imperialistic policy of Germany in-

cluded the principle of race-federation, which
brought her, with regard to the future of Austria-
Hungary, into the sharpest possible conflict of interest with Russia in Europe. " The great Pan-
German Empire was to cut Europe in twain from
north to south, and to bar Russia from all the Western world. Eastward it would fence in the Russian
frontier with German bayonets for over a thousand
miles. Westward it would give the keys of both the
European sea-gates of Russia—in the Baltic to the
north and in the Mediterranean to the south—into
the keeping of German naval power." [31] Then there
was the old score between France and Germany. So
long as Alsace-Lorraine remained in the hands of
her enemy, France would never come to an amicable
agreement with the victor of the Franco-Prussian
war. Now, Russia was in alliance with France. A
defensive and offensive agreement between Russia
and Germany would mean a dissolution of the Dual
Alliance which the Russian statesmen were loath to
abandon.

The Russo-German relations, in fact, had never
been more intimate since the disintegration of the
Dreikaiserbund than during the trying days of the
Russo-Japanese war. Before the outbreak of hos-
tilities, the Kaiser had encouraged the Czar to fight
Japan, and had assured him that he need not fear a

---

[31] E. John Solano, "The World Influence of Britain and Japan,"
in the *Monthly Review*, November, 1905, XXI, No. 62, p. 21.

German attack on the western front of Russia.[32] During the time of war, Germany had rendered valuable services to the Russian forces by selling to them ships and *materiel de guerre,* and by coaling the Baltic fleet of the Czar.[33] On July 28, 1904, Russia paid for these favours by concluding a one-sided commercial treaty with Berlin. As the war with Japan went on, it became daily clearer that there was little chance of victory for Russia. The Kaiser grasped the significance of this, and took advantage of this opportunity to force the Czar into a Russo-German alliance.

On October 27, the Kaiser telegraphed to the Czar: " For some time, the English Press has been threatening Germany that she must on no account allow coals to be sent to the Baltic fleet on its way out. It is not impossible that the Japanese and British Governments may launch joint protests against our coaling your ships, coupled with a summons to stop. The result of such a threat of war would be the inability of your fleet to proceed for want of fuel. This new danger would have to be faced by Russia and Germany together, who would both have to remind your ally France of her obligations. . . . . In this way a powerful combination of the three Conti-

---

[32] *Letters from the Kaiser to the Czar.* Austria also assured Russia that she needed not to fear an attack on her southern front, in exchange for a Russian promise of neutrality in the event of an attack by Italy. Szilassy, *Der Untergang der Donau-Monarchie,* Berlin, 1921, p. 180.

[33] Above, ch. iii, footnote 62.

nental Powers would be formed, and the Anglo-Saxon group would think twice before attacking it." [34] Two days later the Czar replied: " Of course, you know the first details of the North Sea incident from our Admiral's telegram. Naturally it completely alters the situation. I have no words to express my indignation with England's conduct. I agree fully with your complaints about her behaviour concerning the coaling of our ships by German steamers, whereas she understands the rules of keeping neutrality in her own fashion. It is certainly high time to put a stop to this. The only way, as you say, would be that Germany, Russia and France should at once unite upon arrangements to abolish English and Japanese arrogance and insolence." [35]

The results of these correspondences were a preliminary agreement signed on December 11 by which Russia promised to " stand by " Germany, and Germany to supply coal to the Russian fleet, and a final treaty of alliance signed at Björko on July 24 of the next year in which it was provided: I. If any European State shall attack either Power the other will aid with all its forces. II. Neither will conclude a separate peace. III. The Treaty shall come into force on the conclusion of peace with Japan, and may be cancelled at a year's notice. IV. Russia will make its terms known to France and invite her to sign it as an ally. When, however, the Russian Am-

[34] Quoted in Gooch, p. 379.
[35] Ibid., pp. 379-380.

bassador at Paris sounded the French Government, the reply only strengthened the belief of Lamsdorv and Witte that the Björko treaty was incompatible with the Dual Alliance, and that France could never join a German league and recognise the settlement of 1871. After Witte became Prime Minister, on October 20, the treaty was officially denounced by Russia.[36]

After the treaty of Björko was denounced, Russia soon showed signs that she had emancipated herself from German leadership, and that she had begun to lean towards England.[37] The growing friendship between Russia and Great Britain finally crystallised into the Anglo-Russian Convention of August 31, 1907, which removed all the causes of antagonism between the two traditional rivals.[38] Russia, having failed to form a combination against the Anglo-Japanese Alliance, and having finally decided to bury the hatchet with England, naturally desired also to reach an understanding with England's ally in the Far East.

Before the war of 1904-5, Japan had wished to reach a peaceful settlement with Russia by delimiting their spheres of influence in Eastern Asia— Japan in Korea and Russia in Manchuria. The war

[36] For the details about the Björko Treaty, see The Kaiser's Letters to the Czar, *The Willy-Nicky Correspondence,* ed. by N. F. Grant, London, 1920. Alexander Iswolsky, *Memoirs,* London, 1920. Count S. I. Witte, *Memoirs,* New York, 1921. Gooch, pp. 378 ff. Emile J. Dillon, *The Eclipse of Russia,* New York, 1918.

[37] Gooch, pp. 388 ff.

[38] MacMurray, I, 674 ff.

had showed to Japanese statesmen its tremendous risk, and they were anxious to avoid the re-occurrence of such a war. During the period of war, Japan had incurred a very heavy national debt; the peace had brought to her no indemnity from Russia. In order to increase her wealth and to pay the debt, Japan had to devote her energy to trade and industries for the development of which peace had to be maintained, and a reconciliation with Russia was necessary. And, above all, the real objective of Japanese policy was China, and not Russia.[39] Japan and Russia, remaining hostile, could thwart the projects of each other in the regions of the Chinese Empire; but if they cooperated, much could be gained by both at the expense of that country.

On July 30, 1907, the Governments of Japan and Russia, " desiring to consolidate the relations of peace and good neighbourhood " between the two countries, and " wishing to remove for the future every case of misunderstanding," concluded an agreement by which " each of the High Contracting Parties engages to respect the actual territorial integrity of the other, and all the rights accruing to one and the other parties from the treaties, conventions and contracts in force between them and

[39] During the negotiations preceding the Russo-Japanese Convention of 1910, the Japanese Ambassador at St. Petersburg confessed to Iswolsky, the Russian Minister for Foreign Affairs, " that the real objective of Japanese politics was not Russia, but China." Iswolsky to the Russian Ambassador in London, January 13, 1910, in B. de Seibert, *Entente Diplomacy and the World*, New York, 1921, p. 13.

China," and in which they pledged themselves to
" recognise the independence and territorial integrity of the Empire of China " and the principle of
open-door therein, and to " sustain and defend the
maintenance of the *status quo.*" [40] A month and
a half before this convention France and Japan, animated by the same desire of removing " all cause of
misunderstanding for the future " between the two
countries, agreed to respect the independence and
integrity, as well as the principle of the open-door
of China. The two Powers, " having a special interest in having order and a pacific state of things guaranteed especially in the regions of the Chinese Empire adjacent to territories where they have the
rights of sovereignty, protection or occupation,"
pledged " to support each other for the peace and
security in those regions, with a view to maintaining the respective situation and the territorial rights
of the two Contracting Parties in the Continent of
Asia." [41]

Until the outbreak of hostilities between Russia
and Japan in February, 1904, it is probable that
Japan had formed no deliberate plan to obtain for

[40] MacMurray, I, 657-658. According to Dr. E. J. Dillon, " Russia
and Japan have been wending steadily in the direction of partner-
ship ever since the treaty of Portsmouth. To my knowledge one of
them was ripe and ready for a defensive and offensive alliance at
the close of the year 1905, and also to my knowledge the matter was
actually mooted and couched in a twofold proposition at that time.
But nothing came of the proposal, which the other side considered
premature." E. J. Dillon, "A Dual Alliance for the Far East," in the
Contemporary Review, XCVIII, 107.

[41] Ibid., p. 640.

10

herself a special and permanent position in South Manchuria,[42] and to disregard the independence and integrity of China and the principle of open-door which she had several times before pledged herself to respect. Her formal declaration of war admitted of no other interpretation than that one of her war aims was to drive the Russians out of Manchuria, and to restore the same to China. " So soon, however, as she found that victory was within her grasp she began with characteristic energy to pave the way for the absorption of the whole of Southern Manchuria." [43] After the conclusion of peace, Japan immediately proceeded to consolidate her position in South Manchuria, and to exact from China various concessions concerning mines, forests, and the construction and administration of railways which went much further than the privileges and rights accorded to her by the treaty of Portsmouth. This was not all; she also used these undertakings, obtained, as they were, often by threat from China, and interpreted them in such a way as to extend her control, political and economical, over South Manchuria, not infrequently in violation of China's integrity, and to exclude other Powers therefrom.[44]

[42] As late as during the Russo-Japanese negotiations immediately preceding the war, Japan still expressed her willingness to recognise Manchuria as outside her sphere of interest, if the Russians would reciprocate by recognizing Korea as outside theirs.

[43] Lancelot Lawton, " The Powers and the Far East," in the *Fortnightly Review*, XCV, 819.

[44] Ibid., pp. 817-838. W. W. Willoughby, *Foreign Rights and Interests in China*, 1927, I, 169 ff. Stanley K. Hornbeck, *Contemporary*

In the matter of commerce, state aid and various devious methods were used to enable her merchants to compete with and to undersell the citizens of other countries.[45]

With both Russia and England willing to hold their hands, Japan had at this time practically a free hand in dealing with China.[46] In 1909, however, the United States launched out a program of energetic intervention. A group of American banking interests joined with certain British firms to obtain from China the right to construct a railway from Chinchou to Aigunon, the northern border of Manchuria. Simultaneously, the American Secretary of State proposed a " neutralization " of all the railways of Manchuria. According to this plan the ownership of all the lines in Manchuria were to be vested in China, but their administration was to be entrusted temporarily to an international commission representing the interested Powers who were at the same time to supply China with funds in order to buy up existing lines and build new ones.[47]

Politics in the Far East, New York, 1916, ch. xv. Archibald R. Colquhoun, "Agree with Thine Adversary," in the *Fortnightly Review,* XCVIII, 496 ff.

[45] Lancelot Lawton, " The Powers and the Far East," in the *Fortnightly Review,* XCV, 817-838.

[46] Commenting on the relations between China and Japan, Mr. Saint Nihal Singh said: " In her (Japan's) recent dealings with China, the methods of Japan have invariably been those of a pugilistic bully." Saint Nihal Singh, "Asia for the Japanese," in the *Contemporary Review,* XCVIII, 346-347.

[47] Willoughby, pp. 175-178. Hornbeck, pp. 260-261.

Knowing that England's real interest in China was for the open-door and integrity of that country, and that the most she could expect from her ally was that the latter should stand aloof and place no obstacle in her way towards conquering Manchuria, Japan, in order to check the American designs, turned to Russia.[48] The Russo-Japanese convention of 1907 bore " an exclusively negative character." As a set-off against the United States, Japan now desired a new treaty which would contain " positive provisions " for the cooperation between the two countries to exploit China.[49] On December 24, 1909, referring to Secretary Knox's neutralization plan, Count Komura, the Japanese Minister for Foreign Affairs, told the Russian Ambassador at Tokio that " he considered it to be the right moment for Russia and Japan, who had undertaken the first step towards an understanding in 1907, now to decide on the second step. The joint interests in Manchuria

[48] The Russian Ambassador at Tokio to Iswolsky, December 2-15, 1909, in Siebert, pp. 9-10. The same to the same, December 11-24, 1909, in ibid., p. 10. The same to the same, December 31, 1909–January 13, 1910, in ibid., pp. 11-12. According to the *Fortnightly Review*, " the Russo-Japanese agreement was rendered almost inevitable by the European situations in those years, especially the Balkan Crisis. But there is no doubt that it was hastened and ensured by the action of Washington." Cf. " Mr. Knox and Count Aehrenthal " in the *Fortnightly Review* (1910), XCIV, 198 ff. Cf. T. F. Millard, " Our Blundering Diplomacy in the Far East," in the *American Magazine*, New York, LXX, 424. " Secretary Knox's Diplomatic Game," in *Current Literature*, New York, XLVIII, 366. W. B. H., "A Chance for Statesmanship," in the *World's Work*, New York, XXI, 13805.

[49] The Russian Ambassador at Tokio to Iswolsky, December 31, 1909–January 13, 1910, in Siebert, pp. 11-12.

should serve as a basis for the future development of political relations.'' [50] The Russian foreign minister fully realized that the standpoint of her country was '' analogous to that of Japan.'' [51] He was therefore willing to cooperate with Tokio, and agreed that the basis for the proposed political understanding should consist of '' the maintenance of the *status quo* in Manchuria, the definite demarcation of the special Russian and Japanese interests and their protection against aggression on the part of a third Power.'' [52]

The consummation of these negotiations was the signing of a Russo-Japanese convention on July 4, 1910, which consisted of a public and a secret document. The first, in the words of the Russian Minister for Foreign Affairs,[53] '' promoted closer joint action between Russia and Japan in the questions of the Manchurian railways and confirmed anew the firm resolution of both Governments to maintain the

[50] The Russian Ambassador at Tokio to Iswolsky, December 11-24, 1909, in Siebert, p. 10. It shall be remembered in this connection that the meeting between Prince Ito and M. Kokovsoff, the Russian Minister of Finance, by which Japan hoped to reach an understanding with Russia concerning affairs in Manchuria, was scheduled to take place at Harbin on October 26, 1909. T. F. Millard, "Our Blundering Diplomacy in the Far East," in the *American Magazine,* LXX, 423.

[51] Iswolsky to the Russian Ambassador at London, December 31, 1909, in Siebert, p. 14.

[52] The Russian Ambassador at Tokio to Iswolsky, February 23–March 8, 1910, in Siebert, p. 15.

[53] Iswolsky to the Russian Ambassador in London, June 11-24, 1910, in Siebert, pp. 16-18.

status quo in these districts.'' [54] The second '' defined more precisely the two spheres of interest (in Manchuria) as well as the limitations to which they subjected themselves in order to reinforce their mutual relations and to preserve the position proper to them in Manchuria from all interference on the part of the other Powers.'' [55] It was not long after this that Korea was formally annexed.[56]

The attitude of the English Government during this period—from August 12, 1905, the date of the signing of the second treaty of alliance, to its renewal on July 13, 1911—was that of neutrality. She gave no active support to Japan, or to Russia. Neither did she come forth to defend the open-door principle and China's integrity for the maintenance of which she had concluded several solemn treaties and made many pompous declarations. She remained perfectly silent and passive not only when China's interests were threatened, but even when the interests of British citizens were jeopardised.[57] The various artificial methods which Japan used to divert Manchurian trade from its normal channel were carried out, without doubt, at the expense of the trade interests of other countries, including Great

[54] MacMurray, I, 803-804.

[55] A draft of this secret treaty between Russia and Japan may be found in Siebert, pp. 17-18.

[56] August 29, 1910. Henry Chung, *Korean Treaties,* pp. 225-226.

[57] A sidelight is shown by the Kotoku trial which involved British citizens. The London Government refused to indicate the public opinion of the country to Japan. *Par. Deb.,* 5th Series, XXI, 858-860.

Britain.[58] The latter, however, made no protest. In 1907, certain British firms obtained from China the right to construct a railway from Hsinmintun to Fakumen. The Japanese Government objected to this line on the ground that a secret agreement had been arrived at in 1905 between China and Japan by which China had undertaken " not to construct any railway lines parallel to and competing with the South Manchurian Railway." [59] It was clear that " the obtaining of this undertaking as well as the action taken under it was in clear violation of the provisions of the Portsmouth Treaty," [60] and was " contrary to principles set forth in the Anglo-Japanese Agreement of 1905." [61] Not only this, " the nearest point on the proposed line was thirty-five miles distant from the South Manchurian Railway and separated from it by the Liao River," and it was also shown that " virtually no part of the trade of this fertile thickly populated district found its way to the South Manchurian Railway." [62] Nevertheless, the British Government supported the view of Tokio, and the scheme fell through.[63]

[58] B. L. Putnam Weale, *The Coming Struggle in Eastern Asia*, London, 1908, pp. 636 ff.

[59] A clause in the secret protocols to the Sino-Japanese Treaty of December 22, 1905.

[60] Willoughby, I, 172.

[61] Hornbeck, p. 259.

[62] Earl Stanhope, " Great Britain and Japan in the Far East," in the *Nineteenth Century and After*, LXVII, 540. Cf. *Par. Deb.*, 5th Series, Commons, II, 1045.

[63] When questioned in the Commons, Sir Edward Grey defended the attitude of the Government by arguing that " Japan was not

A scheme was then proposed to construct a railway from Chinchou, on the Gulf of Pechili, *via* Toananfu and Tsitsihar, to Aigun, on the Amur River. At first it was agreed that both the construction and the financing of the line should be entrusted entirely to British firms. As, however, both Russia and Japan were opposed to this undertaking, and the British Government refrained from exerting any influence in its favour, China, while retaining the British contractors, invited a group of American financiers to take up this project. The financing of this railway—a matter of somewhere about eight millions sterling—thus passed, to a large extent, out of British hands, and the British share in the orders for material was diminished by a sum computed at no less than £500,000. "Although this railway as far as Tsitsihar would, with the exception of a few miles at either end, run entirely through Mongolia and at a distance never less than 150 miles from the South Manchurian Railway, and would thus be altogether outside the Manchurian spheres of influence claimed by Japan and Russia," Sir Edward Grey supported the view of Tokio and St.

contesting the right in principle of China to extend her railway system." *Par. Deb.*, CLXXXV, 527. He also admitted that His Majesty's Government was in possession of the text of the clause of the protocol by which Japan claimed "the right of vetoing the construction of the Hsinmintun-Fakumen Railway." *Par. Deb.*, CLXXXVI, 1191. The secret protocol was communicated to the British Government in April, 1906. Cf. *Par. Deb.*, 5th Series, Commons, II, 1046, 1444-45.

Petersburg acquiesced in the scheme,[64] and instructed the British Minister at Peking and the Consul-General at Mukden to give no support to the Chinchou-Aigun scheme.[65] On June 15, 1910, Sir Edward Grey justified his action in the Commons by saying that it was " perfectly reasonable," after all that had passed, for Japan to ask for participation in a railway which might to some extent compete with her own line that was already in existence, and that " in face of the Anglo-Russian Agreement of 1899, the only reasonable course for us (the British Government) to adopt was to maintain a neutral attitude." [66]

In a memorandum dated November 9, 1909, Secretary Knox, using the suggested Chinchou-Aigun scheme as a basis, proposed a neutralization of all the railways in Manchuria, and submitted it to the British Foreign Office for its consideration. " The

[64] The Russian Government objected to this line and warned Downing Street that any support from the British Government would be considered as a violation of the agreement of 1899 between the two countries. Japan, while claiming that this line would injuriously affect the South Manchurian Railway, and demanding compensation, secretly pressed Peking not to issue an edict authorising the construction of this railway.

[65] For a brief history of the Aigun scheme see Earl Stanhope, " Great Britain and Japan in the Far East," in the *Nineteenth Century and After*, LXVII, 540-541. Lawton, in the *Fortnightly Review*, XCV, 831-882. Cf. *Par. Deb.*, Fifth Series, Commons, XVII, 1375-80. The American request that the British Government should give its support to the Aigun Railway scheme was turned down by the British Government. *Par. Deb.*, 5th Series, Commons, XV, 1038.

[66] *Par. Deb.*, 5th Series, Commons, XVII, 1389-90. Cf. ibid., 5th Series, Commons, XIV, 1126, 1451; XV, 1038; XVI, 5; XVII, 1389-90.

general principle," replied Sir Edward Grey, " entirely commends itself to His Majesty's Government so far as the preservation of the Open Door policy and equal commercial opportunity are concerned, and would in their opinion be well adapted to securing to China full control in Manchuria." [67] But soon the Russian and Japanese opposition was made known and the British Government shifted its position.[68] Both the Chinchou-Aigun scheme and the neutralization plan of the Manchurian railways were finally dropped because of lack of support.[69] When Korea was formally annexed, not even a murmur was heard from Downing Street.[70]

For an explanation of this timid and passive attitude of the British Government in the Far East, we have to look again to the general situation of Europe. It was during the life-time of the Anglo-Japanese Alliance of 1905 that a new German policy had produced periodical crises threatening the peace of Europe.[71] The first Moroccan crisis began on March 31, 1905, even before the conclusion of the

[67] *U. S. Foreign Relations,* 1909.

[68] W. B. H., " A Chance for Statesmanship," in the *World's Work,* XXI, 13804. For a brief history of the American neutralization plan of all the Manchurian railways see Willoughby, I, 17 ff.

[69] France considered the American proposal to be impracticable and supported the view of her ally. Germany merely declared her agreement in principle, as did England. Iswolsky to the Russian Ambassador at London, December 31, 1909–January 13, 1910, in Siebert, p. 15.

[70] *Par. Deb.,* 5th Series, Commons, XXVII, 153 ff.

[71] To be exact, it was from 1905 to 1914.

second treaty of alliance. This was followed, in 1908,
by the second Moroccan Crisis: the affair of Casa-
blanca. In the same year the first serious crisis in
the Near East occurred, when Austria, taking advantage of an internal revolution in Turkey, formally annexed Bosnia-Herzegovina. England realized that, in order to check the Central Powers, she
needed the Japanese alliance in the Far East and
the Triple Entente in Europe. The encroachment
of Russia and Japan in the Far East imperilled
only commercial and economic interests of Great
Britain, but the growth of German power in Europe
was a menace to the existence of the British Empire
itself. It may be contended that the London Government should have supported American policy in
China, the realisation of which would have been distinctly advantageous to the British Far Eastern
trade. This, however, England could not do, for thus
she would have lost the friendship of both Russia
and Japan, without a possibility of concluding an
alliance of a world-wide character with the United
States, as Washington was by no means willing to
give up her traditional policy of aloofness. In fine,
the injury sustained by British commerce and industry in the Far East, as a result of the violation
by Russia and Japan of China's integrity and the
principle of equal commercial opportunity for all
nations therein, was the price paid by England for
the friendship of Russia and Japan in order to carry
out successfully her policy of seeking the Empire's

security in alliances. British economical interests in the Far East were sacrificed on the altar of British political designs.[72]

Knowing that the phrase " insuring the independence and integrity of the Chinese Empire and the principle of equal opportunities for the commerce and industry of all nations in China," was merely a diplomatic gesture, we may undertake the task of estimating the results of the second alliance. It guaranteed to Japan the fruits of her victory over Russia. By forcing Russia to recognise the settlements at Portsmouth, it made possible the cooperation between Russia and Japan in exploiting China and in blocking the United States policy in Manchuria; and, finally, it facilitated the formal incorporation by Japan of Korea the fate of which was foreshadowed—even predetermined—in the first

---

[72] Cf. Lancelot Lawton, " The Powers and the Far East," in the *Fortnightly Review,* XCV, 837-8. When questioned in the Commons in connection with the Chinchou-Aigun scheme, Sir Edward Grey said: " I think that it [a neutral attitude] is the only reasonable course we could take, either on grounds of general policy or in accordance with a general sense of the construction of our treaty engagements [the agreement of 1899 with Russia]." *Par. Deb.,* 5th Series, Commons, XVII, 1390. But in a reply to St. Petersburg, he said that although Russia was formally in the right, " the point in question did not deal with the concession for a railway line but with the financing of a Chinese undertaking, and that the Russian Government itself took up a similar attitude in its endeavours to obtain the co-operation of the Russo-Chinese Bank in the building of the Hankow-Szechuan Railway." Iswolsky to the Russian Ambassador at London, December 31, 1909–January 13, 1910, in Siebert, p. 15. The stern fact is that it really was on the ground of " general policy " that Sir Edward Grey had supported the view of St. Petersburg (and of Tokio) in regard to the Chinchou Aigun scheme.

Anglo-Japanese alliance. For England, the alliance of 1905 secured the peace in the Far East, and thus enabled her " considerably to reduce her naval forces in the Far East and to strengthen her fleet in like measure in European waters . . . . where it might eventually be needed." [73] It was chiefly for this reason that the alliance of 1905 was renewed in 1911, notwithstanding the prejudice against Japan and the Japanese, entertained by British subjects in England, in the Dominions, as well as in the Far East.

[73] Sir Arthur Nicolson, the British Under-Secretary for Foreign Affairs, was reported to have said on the occasion of the renewal of the Anglo-Japanese alliance in 1911: " Since the coming into force of the Anglo-Japanese Treaty, England has been able considerably to reduce her naval forces in the Far East and to strengthen her fleet in like measure in European waters. Through this England possessed an important guarantee for the maintenance of peace in the Far East, and has been enabled to strengthen her naval forces there where they might eventually be needed." The Russian Ambassador in London to Neratov, July 4-17, 1911, in Siebert, p. 33.

CHAPTER V

The Alliance, 1911-21

The attitude of the British Government was that of the statesmen who had British interests to look after, not only in China, but in all parts of the world. It was based upon inner and accurate knowledge of the naval and military resources of the Empire, and the world-wide political situation during the years 1905 to 1911. But those who did not have such an inner and accurate knowledge of British position in *Weltpolitik*, but rather had their minds focussed upon Eastern Asia, could not be expected to be so tolerant toward Japanese aggression on the Continent.

The rising Japanese commerce and industry, and the methods used by the Japanese to undersell their commercial rivals had made the Japanese merchants the deadliest competitors of the British adventurers in the Far East, who were, therefore, bitterly opposed to the country which was their political ally.[1] In England, both inside and outside of the Parliament, there prevailed a growing impression that British interests in China were injuriously affected by the actions concerning China taken by Japan.[2]

[1] See Weale, *The Coming Struggle in Eastern Asia,* ch. vi.
[2] *Par. Deb.,* 4th Series, CLXXXV, 1195-6; *Par. Deb.,* 5th Series, Commons, II, 1045; XIV, 559, 1125, 1450-1; XV, 649, 1037-8; XVI, 1211, 1859, 2286; XVII, 1376, 1377; XXV, 1968.

One writer had this to say by way of warning to the British Public: " To-day even the man in the street is aware that the growth of Japanese power has shaken our prestige in India, in Egypt, and all over the Pacific. Our alliance with Japan and our friendship with Russia must not blind us to the fact that they are pursuing a joint policy of territorial expansion in Asia, and at the same time embarking on an unprecedented naval expenditure which cannot fail to affect us." [3]

In the Dominions, the ill feeling against Japan and against the Japanese was even more pronounced. There it was not only a question of competition for markets far from home, but a question as to their very existence. The problem of Japanese immigration in New Zealand, in Canada, and especially in Australia had done much to damage their good relations with Japan.[4] Furthermore, they were haunted by the fear that some day the Anglo-Japanese Alliance might entangle them in a contest with the United States with whom they were anxious to maintain friendly relations.[5] It was therefore

[3] A. R. Colquhoun, "Agree with Thine Adversary," in the *Fortnightly Review*, XCVIII, 503.

[4] For a detailed account of the treatment of Japanese by the Dominions see Raymond L. Buell, Japanese Immigration (*World Peace Foundation Pamphlets*), Boston, 1924, pp. 332 ff.

[5] Cf. Archibald Hurd, " The Racial War in the Pacific: An Imperial Peril," in the *Fortnightly Review,* XCIX, 1031-1046. As early as 1906, Mr. Bellairs had already raised this question in the Commons: " Whether there is any provision in the Anglo-Japanese treaty safeguarding His Majesty's dominions from being involved

only natural that large sections of opinion in the Dominions looked askance at the Oriental Alliance.[6]

The fact that, despite the existence of such ill feeling against Japan among British nationals, the Alliance was modified and not discontinued in 1911, is evidence of its importance from a political point of view. From 1905 to 1911 the course of events in Europe had shown that, sooner or later, the growing rivalry between England and Germany would lead to a war. In anticipation of such a contingency, the British Government thought it wise to renew her alliance with Japan in order to insure against trouble in the Far East. This insurance policy gave to England a further advantage in the form of being able to concentrate her naval forces in European waters. Finally, the treaty was to be a " guarantee against Japan's ill-will caused by the bad treatment of the Japanese, especially in Australia ";[7] it was

---

in war with the United States of America on behalf of Japan." *Par. Deb.*, 4th Series, CLXIII, 864. "Anglo-Japanese Treaty," in the *Independent*, LXXI, 120-121. *Minutes of the Proceedings of the Imperial Conference,* 1911 (*Parl. P.,* Dominions No. 7), p. 51.

[6] London *Times,* July 14, 1911.

[7] In conversation with the Russian Ambassador in London, Sir A. Nicolson, Under-Secretary for Foreign Affairs of Great Britain, was reported to have said: "The point in question was in reality a most delicate one, with special reference to the colonies, *i. e.,* Australia. In view of the fact that the laws in the British colonies show but little consideration for the yellow race, a lapse of the Anglo-Japanese Alliance might have led to serious friction, which would have meant continuous disquietude for England, even if it did not embody a direct danger of war." The Russian Ambassador in London to Neratov, July 4-17, 1911. Siebert, p. 32.

also to be a precaution against possible further com-
binations injurious to the British interests. Since
the signing of the July convention with Russia in
1910, Japan had been in close relation with that
country. The agreement in regard to Persia and the
Bagdad Railway, reached at Potsdam between the
Kaiser and the Czar in the same year, renewed,
temporarily at least, the friendship between Germany and Russia. In view of these international
relations, a lapse of the Japanese alliance might
have given initiative and power to a German-Russo-
Japanese combination.[8]

Japan, on her side, also had reasons for the renewal of the Alliance. For seventeen years she had
worked incessantly to avoid being diplomatically
isolated; she had not forgotten the lesson she received after the Sino-Japanese War. In order to
achieve her post-war policy of peaceful penetration
in China, she wanted an alliance to secure peace for
herself in the Far East. It was true that she could
ally herself with Germany and Russia, but a German alliance would be of doubtful value. An alliance with Russia might give Japan all that she
could desire; but Russia was Japan's enemy during the war of 1904-5, and Russia could not be expected to forget completely those unfortunate years.
A lapse of the British alliance might give an oppor-

[8] Cf. Conversation with Sir A. Nicolson as reported by the Rus-
sian Ambassador in London to Neratov, July 4-17, Siebert, pp. 32-33.
Alfred L. P. Dennis, *The Anglo-Japanese Alliance*, 1923, pp. 32-33.
Par. Deb., Commons, XXII, 2595.

11

tunity to Russia to secure her revenge. The renewal
of the Anglo-Japanese Alliance, though excluding
the United States of America from the scope of its
operation,[9] was, therefore, still beneficial to Japan,
for it gave the impression throughout the Far East
that Great Britain acquiesced in Japan's aggressive
policy in China, and it prevented Russia from think-
ing of coming back upon her former rival. It thus
forced Russia to remain a friend of Japan.[10]

The denunciation by Japan, on July 16, 1910, of
her existing treaty of 1894 with England, was to
take effect on July 16, 1911. This denunciation was
followed by the promulgation of a new Japanese tariff to take effect on July 17, 1911. In the early
spring of 1911 Japan and England found themselves
negotiating for a new treaty of commerce and navigation which was signed on the 3d of April.[11] Since
May the Imperial Conference had been in session in
London. For the first time the British Government
took the Dominion representatives into its confidence in matters concerning foreign policy.[12] This

[9] In fact, Japan " could not, and did not expect half of the English-
speaking world to range itself on her side against the other half.
This was what she never counted upon." " Japan, America, and the
British Alliance," in the *Fortnightly Review*, XCIV, 204. Cf. a
leading article in the " Jiji," a very influential paper in Japan, July 16,
1911. Also see *Review of Reviews*, XLIV, 603.

[10] Cf. " Japan and the Powers," in the *Nation*, New York, XCV, 95.

[11] *Parl. P.*, Japan, No. 1 (1911), p. iv. For a text of the treaty see
ibid., pp. 1 ff.

[12] On June 2, 1911, a resolution was carried unanimously in the
Imperial Conference to the effect: "(a) that the Dominion shall be
afforded an opportunity of consultation when framing the instruc-

occasion was utilised by the British Government to
explain to the Prime Ministers of the self-govern-
ing Dominions the reasons for the necessity of a
renewal of the Anglo-Japanese Alliance, and their
unanimous approval of the renewal was secured.[13]
Finally, an arbitration treaty between the United
States and England was pending for ratification.[14]
The time was therefore opportune for the negotiation of a renewal of the Anglo-Japanese Alliance.[15]

The third version of the Alliance was signed on
July 13, 1911.[16] The reason for the revision of the
earlier treaty was given in the preamble which

---

tions to be given to British delegates at future meetings of the Hague
Conference, and that Conventions affecting the Dominions provi-
sionally assented to at that Conference shall be circulated among
the Dominion Governments for their consideration before any such
Convention is signed; and (b) that a similar procedure, where time
and opportunity and the subject matter permit, shall as far as possible be used when preparing instructions for the negotiation of other
International Agreements affecting the Dominions." *Minutes of Proceedings of the Imperial Conference*, 1911, pp. 130-132.

[13] This fact does not appear in the *Minutes of the Proceedings of
the Imperial Conference*, 1911. The British Colonial Secretary, however, told the House six days after the signing of the third edition
of the Anglo-Japanese Alliance: "The Prime Ministers of the self-
governing Dominions were consulted before the Alliance was renewed,
and unanimously approved of the renewal." *Par. Deb.*, 5th Series,
Commons, XXVIII, 1018. Cf. ibid., XXVIII, 1257.

[14] This proposed arbitration treaty later fell through, for it was not
ratified by the United States Senate.

[15] The European international situation at this time was also grave.
The famous "Mansion House Speech" by Lloyd George, which gave
warning to Germany that England was prepared to stand by France,
was given only a week later, and the Agadir crisis was rapidly reaching its climax.

[16] For the text of the Alliance of 1911 see MacMurray, pp. 900 ff.

stated that " the Government of Japan and the
Government of Great Britain having in view the
important changes which have taken place in the
situation since the conclusion of the Anglo-Japanese
Agreement of August 12, 1905, and believing that
the revision of that Agreement responding to such
changes would contribute to general stability and
repose, have agreed upon the following stipulations
to replace the Agreement above mentioned." Such
stipulations were to have the same objects as the
Agreement, namely: (1) The maintenance of the
general peace in the regions of Eastern Asia and
India. (2) The preservation of the independence
and integrity of China and the Open Door policy
therein. (3) The maintenance of the territorial
rights of the Contracting Parties in the regions of
Eastern Asia and India and their special interests
in those regions.

The language of the new treaty followed closely
that of the treaty of 1905. It provided for full and
frank communications between the contracting parties in regard to their interests in the regions covered by the agreement. The attack of any one power
was again to be sufficient cause for common action on
the part of the allies. The alliance was to last for
ten years, with the same self-extending provision
which we find in both the first and the second treaties
of the alliance. Thus we see that the provisions of
the treaty of 1905 were repeated. There were, however, several important changes. The alliance of

1905 had been concluded before Japan and Russia
signed their peace treaty at Portsmouth. It therefore provided, by Article VI, for the continuous
maintenance of neutrality by Great Britain, unless
some other Power should join in hostilities against
Japan. In 1911, six years after the conclusion of the
Portsmouth Treaty, such a provision, if repeated,
would have been not only unnecessary, but super-
fluous. So would have been a repetition of Article
III of the second Alliance by which Great Britain
recognised that Japan possessed paramount political, military and economical interests in Korea, since
Korea had already been annexed by Japan in 1910.
Again, the second Alliance provided, by Article IV,
for the security of the Indian frontier. The Anglo-
Russian entente of 1907 and the friendship between
these two countries developed since the conclusion of
the second Anglo-Japanese Alliance, deprived this
Article of its value. Consequently, all these provisions disappeared from the Alliance.

One all-important new element appeared. This
was Article IV in the new treaty, which provided:
" Should either of the High Contracting Parties
conclude a treaty of general arbitration with a third
Power, it is agreed that nothing in this Agreement
shall impose on such contracting party an obligation
to go to war with the Power with whom such an arbitration treaty is in force." This provision was
intended, of course, to make the alliance inapplicable

in case of an armed conflict between Japan and the United States.[17]

During the summer of 1911 England was much occupied with the bitter controversy concerning the powers of the House of Lords and the possibility of labor troubles. Little attention was therefore paid to the new alliance.[18] But, judging from the mild interest which the treaty aroused, we may safely conclude that England was very much in favour of the revision. Two days after its conclusion, the *Times* extended its welcome to the new treaty in the following words: " We welcome it in itself; we welcome it as a condition of the Arbitration Treaty; we welcome it because it is the common work of the responsible statesmen of the Empire; we welcome it, not least, because it is a gage of continuity for the future as it is an example of continuity in the past—because it discloses, to all eyes that can see, an additional element of permanence in our foreign affairs." [19]

[17] This was the most important reason for the revision of the old alliance. *Par. Deb.*, 5th Series, Commons, XXVIII, 1256. The Russian Ambassador in London to Neratov, July 4-17, 1911. Siebert, p. 32.

[18] The new edition of the treaty was concealed from the House till its conclusion. *Par. Deb.*, 5th Series, Commons, XXVIII, 1256.

[19] London *Times*, July 15, 1911. Commenting on the new treaty an article in the *Living Age* remarked: " If then, a treaty of general arbitration should happily be signed in the course of the present year with the United States, and some time afterwards a war should arise between Japan and the United States, in which (let us say) the United States is the aggressor, we shall not be bound to assist Japan, as we should have been at any time during the last six years. The

Two views of the revised treaty were taken in Japan, both being based upon the conviction that the new alliance was the direct outcome of the Anglo-American arbitration treaty which, it was expected, would soon become effective.[20] At one end of the scale of opinion there was the feeling that the new arrangement was distinctly unfavorable to Japan, because her principal rival in the Pacific was thereby expressly excluded from the scope of its operation. This feeling was best expressed in the words of the veteran Count Okuma who tersely said, " Japan must help England; but England, in a certain eventuality, need not help Japan."[21] " In short," remarked the *Hochi*, " the diplomatic slate of the Far East is wiped clean. As for Japan, the very foundations of her diplomatic policy have been swept away from under her."[22] She was to be, it was feared, left standing in the cold in " inglorious isolation."[23] Those of this opinion therefore believed " that the special interests which Japan had acquired in China,

mere contemplation of what might have happened, of the awful and ruinous consequences, not only to England and the United States, but also to Canada, of a mishap under the old treaty, will enable our readers to measure the value of the revised version." " Treaties of War and Peace," in the *Living Age*, CCLXX, 565.

[20] Adachi Kinnosuke, "Anglo-American Arbitration and the Far East," in the *Review of Reviews*, XLIV, 602 ff. Cf. *Japan Daily Mail*, July 17, 1911; *Japan Times*, July 18.

[21] Quoted in " Japan and the Monroe Doctrine," in the *Living Age*, CCLXXIV, 48.

[22] Quoted by Adachi Kinnosuke, "Anglo-American Arbitration and the Far East," in the *Review of Reviews*, XLIV, 602.

[23] Ibid., XLIV 602.

especially in Manchuria, would throw her into the arms of Russia, which had similar interests to protect. Germany was friendly to Russia after the Potsdam Conference. . . . . Therefore, the breakdown of the old Anglo-Japanese combination spelled the coming of the triple understanding with Russia, Germany and Japan."[24]

The second view took exactly the opposite stand. Its adherents thought the revised treaty advantageous to Japan, for it would release the tension between the United States and Japan, and work toward closer relations between the two countries. "The new treaty," they believed, "had brought about a new triple alliance, composed of Great Britain, the United States, and Japan. The Anglo-American arbitration treaty was in reality a treaty of alliance of the most effective kind. The solid and undivided support of the two peoples was back of it, to say nothing of the ties of kinship and commercial community of interests. Article IV of the new Anglo-Japanese treaty was nothing more than the recognition of this fundamental fact. Therefore, by her recognition of the above mentioned fact and through Great Britain's arbitration with America, Japan had become a party to the Anglo-American pact."[25]

The second view represents more nearly that of the Government at Tokio in 1911. The new arrange-

[24] Ibid., XLIV, 602.
[25] Ibid., XLIV, 603.

ment had been criticized as distinctly unfavorable
to Japan, because the United States was excluded
from its scope of operation, and the relations between Japan and the United States, at this time,
were none too cordial. The facts, upon which this
view was based, were correct; their interpretation
was wrong. If, in 1911, Japan were in a position to
fight the United States, their conclusion that the new
arrangement was distinctly unfavorable to Japan
would be correct, as it excluded the possibility that,
in the event of war between the United States and
Japan, England might be compelled, as she would
be under the terms of the old alliance, to join in hostilities against the United States. But this was not
the case, for in 1911, Japan was in no position to
fight the United States. In the first place, she could
not finance such a war. Her credit at the close of the
Russo-Japanese War was strained to the utmost.
Her loans were declining in value. Her war debts
were not yet paid. No investor of sane judgment
would advance money to a country, so hampered, to
fight so hopeless a contest. Furthermore, the great
war loans for her war with Russia were mostly made
to her by Jews in order to secure the punishment of
Russia, the persecutor of Jews. On the other hand,
the United States was a haven to the persecuted
Hebrews. Japan, in a war with the United States,
could not expect to raise any war loans among these
people. In the second place, the resources of Japan
were limited. Compared to that of the United States,

Japan's naval force was smaller, her population nowhere near as large, her wealth much smaller, the burden of her interest-bearing debt many times higher, and the yield of her taxation insignificant. In the third place, Japan could not find herself engaged in a war with the United States without imminent danger to her position in the Far East. While Japan was straining her resources in war with the United States, both China and Russia would promptly seize such an opportunity to regain what they had lost in the years 1895 and 1905. Therefore, a war with the United States in 1911 was out of the question for Japan.[26]

The far-sighted Japanese statesmen recognized this fact. They, therefore, sincerely wished to pacify the antagonistic feelings in America, and to come to more cordial relations with Washington. When, in 1907-1908, the United States battleship fleet, on its way around the world, visited Japan, Japan decided to treat the event as an honor, and gave a most generous reception to the officers and crews of the American fleet.[27] A few months later, on November 30, Baron Takahara, the Japanese Ambassador

[26] Cf. Jeremiah W. Jenks, " The Japanese in Manchuria," in The Outlook, March 11, 1911, XCVII, 549.

[27] President Roosevelt later remarked: " The most noteworthy incident of the cruise was the reception given to our fleet in Japan. . . . . The event even surpassed my expectations. I cannot too strongly express my appreciation of the generous courtesy the Japanese showed the officers and crews of our fleet; and I may add that every man of them came back a friend and admirer of the Japanese." Quoted by Payson J. Treat, *Japan and the United States, 1853-1921*, Boston, 1921, pp. 196-197.

at Washington, exchanged notes with Mr. Root, the American Secretary of State, on the policies of their Governments in Manchuria.[28] The purpose of this exchange was to make a frank avowal of the common aims, policies, and intentions of the two Governments in the region of the Pacific Ocean, in order to strengthen the relations of friendship and good neighborliness, which had immemorially existed between the two countries, and thus to contribute to the preservation of the general peace. It was the wish of the two Governments to encourage the free and peaceful development of their commerce on the Pacific. Their policy, uninfluenced by any aggressive tendencies, was to maintain the *status quo* in that region and to defend the Open Door policy in China. They pledged themselves to respect the territorial possessions belonging to each other, and to support the independence and integrity of China and the Open Door therein. " Should any event occur threatening the *status quo* above described or the principle of equal opportunity as above defined, it remains for the two Governments to communicate with each other in order to arrive at an understanding as to what measures they may consider it useful to take." [29]

[28] *Foreign Relations,* 1908, pp. 510-511.

[29] In May, 1908, an arbitration convention was concluded between the United States and Japan, providing that " differences which may arise of a legal nature, or relating to the interpretation of treaties existing between the two Contracting Parties, ... shall be referred to the Permanent Court of Arbitration established at the Hague by

In regard to the controversy over Japanese emigration to the United States, a marked moderation was seen in the Japanese policy. The treaty of November 22, 1894, between Japan and the United States, stipulated that Article II, which provided for reciprocal freedom of commerce and navigation, did not in any way affect the laws, ordinances and regulations with regard to trade, the immigration of laborers, police and public security which were in force or which might hereafter be enacted in either of the two countries.[30] On February 20, 1907, an immigration act was passed in the Congress, authorizing the President to refuse entrance to immigrants who, to obtain entrance to the mainland, were using passports originally issued to " any country other than the United States." [31] Under this authority, President Roosevelt issued the proclamation of March 14, 1907, which ordered that " Japanese or Korean laborers, skilled or unskilled, who have received passports to go to Mexico, Canada or Hawaii,

---

the Convention of July 29, 1899, provided, nevertheless, that they do not affect the vital interests, the independence, or the honor of the two Contracting States, and do not concern the interests of third parties." *Foreign Relations,* 1908, pp. 503 ff. In 1909, Japan gave the United States "assurances" that the Sino-Japanese Agreement of that year would not be construed to operate against the principle of the Open Door. The *American Magazine,* LXX, 423.

[30] For the text of the treaty see William M. Malloy, *Treaties, Conventions, International Acts, Protocols, and Agreements between the United States of America and Other Powers,* Washington, 1910, p. 1028.

[31] Sec. 1, 34 Stat. 898, ch. 1134.

and come therefrom, be refused permission to enter the continental territory of the United States." [32]

In view of this attitude of the American Government and the anti-Japanese agitation in the American States along the Pacific coast since 1900, the Japanese Government concluded the so-called Gentlemen's Agreement of 1907-8 with President Roosevelt. By this agreement, the Japanese Government pledged itself not to issue passports to laborers skilled or unskilled wishing to go to the continental United States,[33] and accepted the definition of " laborer " as given in the United States Executive Order of April 8, 1907. Thus, the Japanese Government voluntarily prohibited the immigration of Japanese laborers into the United States.[34]

On February 21, 1911, a new commercial treaty between Japan and the United States was signed.[35] Upon the insistence of the Japanese Government the provision in the treaty of 1894, which expressly stated that the laws with regard to the immigration of laborers in either of the two countries were not to be affected, was omitted. The treaty was ratified by the Senate, with the reservation, " That the treaty shall not be deemed to repeal or affect any

[32] Department Circular No. 147, March 26, 1907; and Rule 21, Immigration Regulations of July 1, 1907.

[33] With the exception of two main classes: (1) those who return to resume a formerly acquired domicile; (2) parents, wives and children, under twenty years of age, of laborers in the United States.

[34] Although Hawaii was not included in the agreement, the Japanese Government similarly limited immigration to that destination.

[35] For the text of the treaty, see *Foreign Relations,* 1911, pp. 315 ff.

of the provisions of the Act of Congress entitled
' An Act to regulate the Immigration of Aliens into
the United States,' approved February 20, 1907.''
Japan accepted this understanding, and the Japanese Government, through its representative at
Washington, in the official correspondence which accompanied the treaty, promised to maintain with
equal effectiveness the limitation and control which
it had exercised since 1908 in regulation of the emigration of laborers to the United States.[36]

The warm reception given to the American battleship fleet in 1908, the Root-Takahara Agreement
of the same year, the Gentlemen's Agreement regu-
lating Japanese immigration to the United States,
and similar acts on the part of the Japanese Government were all based on a general policy to pacify
the American public, and to avoid a war that might
mean the beginning of the end of the Japanese
power. It was, then, no wonder that the Japanese
Government, in 1911, was willing to have Article IV
included in the new Anglo-Japanese Treaty.[37] The

[36] Ibid., 1911, p. 319. For details in regard to Japanese immigration in the United States see Raymond L. Buell, " Japanese Immigration," *World Peace Foundation Pamphlets*, 1924, VII, Nos. 5-6,
pp. 281 ff.

[37] According to Viscount Ishii, Japan was the first to propose this
revision: " Let me tell you a little piece of secret history. When it
became known to us that the American and British Governments
were alike desirous of entering into a general treaty of arbitration,
but that they found the making of such a treaty was precluded by
the terms of the British alliance with Japan as they then stood, it
was not with the consent of Japan, but it was because of Japan's
spontaneous offer that the stipulations of the alliance were revised

revised treaty was, in fact, the crowning step of
Tokio's effort to pacify the American public and to
show its intention to maintain friendly relations with
the United States. The new arrangement was, therefore, not so disadvantageous to Japan as it might at
first seem to be.

To England, the new alliance was distinctly favorable. The new arrangement, besides strengthening
her friendship with Japan, and thus insuring her
position on the Pacific at a time when her relations
with Germany were tense, saved her from the em-
barrassing situation that would arise in case of a
war between her ally in the Far East and her broth-
erly country on the other side of the Atlantic.

Hardly three months afterwards the new alliance
came under a serious strain, for in October, 1911, a
revolution broke out in China, which overthrew the
then ruling dynasty and led to the establishment of
a Republic. Now, Japan's policy was to assist *sub
rosa* any attempt to split China and to establish a
republic in the south, in return for a suitable *quid
pro quo*. For years the Japanese authorities are believed to have connived at the plotting on Japanese
soil of Dr. Sun Yat-Sen and his colleagues against
the Chinese Government; and to have given large
funds to support the movement. There is ground
for believing, however, that Japan's real intention

---

so that no obstacle might be put in the way of the proposed treaty."
Speech by Viscount Ishii before the National Press Club at Washington, September 21, 1917, quoted by Wood, pp. 71-72.

was not to help the Chinese revolutionalists to establish a republic for all China, but to facilitate local disturbances and unrest in China such as would give Japan opportunities for intervention in order to obtain concessions. The fact that the uprising in 1911 developed into a national movement was a surprise to Japanese officialdom. The Japanese Government quickly realized its significance; and at once tried to intervene on the side of the Manchus.[38]

Tokio's policy of supporting the Manchus, or of limiting the republic to the south of China, would have succeeded had London stood aloof and acquiesced in the interference. But British interests involved on this occasion were too large for Downing Street to remain silent and to back up their political ally in the Far East. The London Government, through its representative Sir Claude Mac-Donald, then British Ambassador at Tokio, three times sharply sought to prevent Japan's taking un-neutral action which could only have ended, as it was intended to end, in the territorial disintegration of China.[39] The difference of opinion between the Governments of Japan and England was confessed to by

[38] For details concerning Japan's policy in China in 1911-12, see Pooley, ch. iii.

[39] The British Government protested at Tokio, first against M. Ijuin's statement to Yuan Shi-Kai to uphold the dynasty, secondly against a proposed loan by Japan to the Manchus, and thirdly against the proposed use of armed force. Subsequently it again protested against the Okura mortgage on the Ningpo Railway and against the negotiations for the acquisition of the "China Merchants" fleet, over which the Hongkong and Shanghai Bank had claims.

representatives of both countries. Sir Claude Mac-
Donald, in an interview with Mr. Andrew M. Pooley,
at the time, said:

> The Japanese authorities profess to believe that the revo-
> lution is a series of sporadic local affairs. We don't. We
> believe it is developing into a national movement. We say that
> it is like a river in spate; they say it is only a little stream
> which can be easily stopped.

The Japanese Government, in a statement issued
in Tokio, summed up the difference in the following
words:

> The Japanese Government from the first considered a
> monarchial system most suitable for the government of China,
> and on Yuan Shi-Kai taking the reins of government the
> Tokio Foreign Office believed that the trouble in China would
> come to an end with the adoption of a Monarchical Govern-
> ment. On receiving an invitation from the British Govern-
> ment to join in the mediation for peace negotiations, the
> Japanese Government suggested that mediation should be
> undertaken only on condition of the adoption of a Consti-
> tutional Monarchy. The British Government, however, was
> of a different opinion, and refused to agree to the condition
> stipulated by the Japanese.
> The Japanese Government, however, was confident that
> Yuan Shi-Kai would strongly and absolutely insist on a Con-
> stitutional Monarchy being established, and that the negotia-
> tions would be brought to a successful conclusion accordingly,
> without any special effort being made to direct the course of
> events. Now, however, the pendulum has swung in the other
> direction, and it appears that peace cannot be arrived at with-
> out establishing a Republic. The attitude of Yuan Shi-Kai,
> who, it was believed, would insist on a Monarchical Govern-
> ment, has now become suspicious, and the result of the negotia-

12

tions seems to be different from what the Japanese Government anticipated. Consequently, the Japanese Government is much perturbed at the turn events have taken, and is considering means for extricating itself from the awkward position.

Indeed, Japan was in an "awkward position." She had spent a large sum of money to finance the Chinese revolution, with the hope that she could obtain various concessions from a divided China. But China was soon united under a republican form of Government, and Japan had got nothing except a bundle of promissory notes issued by the revolutionary leaders.

Thus, the Chinese revolution of 1911 was a rather disastrous affair for Japan, and this was chiefly because the British Government refused to give its support to Tokio's policy.[40] The result was a general outbreak early in 1912 of anti-British feeling in Japan. The Japanese press united in expressing the belief that the Alliance between Great Britain and Japan had been deprived of its soul. Commenting on the Alliance on January 18, 1912, the *Osaka Mainichi* said:

The Alliance ended for all practical purposes last July, when it was revised. It no longer furnishes any guarantee for the protection of China's integrity. So far from Japan and

[40] Hitting at the failure of the British to back up their policy, Viscount Uchida said in the Diet on February 2, 1912, that the Government had extended all possible assistance to Japanese firms and individuals seeking concessions and interests in China, but that such action had to be stopped in view of the representation of other Powers that such action was contrary to neutrality. Pooley, p. 68.

Great Britain taking joint action when their rights and interests are threatened, no measures are taken at all. England is no longer faithful to the principles of the Alliance, and the Japanese Government would be well advised to make a definite declaration as to whether it is to be regarded as a live instrument or not.[41]

The *Kokumin Shimbun* took a more practical view, when it wrote on February 5, 1912:

The authorities hug with persistence the Anglo-Japanese Alliance. They desire only to walk in the footsteps of Great Britain. The Alliance, in our opinion, has already been deprived of its soul by the recently effected revision. It is the cast-off skin of the cicada (small lemon). We do not say that it is altogether useless, for even a scare-crow sometimes prevents the mischief of naughty birds. We do not object to its existence as long as the other party to it does not object. But we emphatically assert that to leave the matter of the Chinese revolution in the hands of Great Britain is a most unsafe policy. Britain is groaning under the overwhelming dimensions of her colonies, against which we have only gained a footing in Korea. Great Britain has more than enough to do in other parts of the world. Can she afford to stretch out to the Far East to meddle with China? Japan must do her own work in China without depending on Great Britain.[42]

But, Japan, standing alone, could not very well do her own work in China. Thus, she again turned to Russia. Since December, 1910, Russia had decided upon a program of consolidating her interests in China, especially in North Manchuria and Outer Mongolia, the execution of which, it was realized, de-

---

[41] *Osaka Mainichi,* January 18, 1912, quoted in Pooley, p. 70.
[42] *Kokumin Shimbun,* February 5, 1912, quoted in ibid., p. 71.

pended upon a previous understanding with England and Japan.[43] The motive which lay behind the
action of the Russian Government was to put a stop
to the Chinese activities in North Manchuria and
Mongolia, in order to forestall the possibility that
some day the Chinese might grow so strong as to
force the Russians to withdraw from these territories.[44] Japan, on the other hand, did not entertain such a fear. The only danger she could foresee
" would come from America whose fleet in the Pacific, on the completion of the Panama Canal, would
be so powerful that the Japanese fleet might undertake a defensive action, but certainly not attack."
She, therefore, also " believed that Russia and
Japan had to regulate definitely their position in
China before the beginning of this period." [45]

Thus, early in 1911, Japan and Russia found themselves negotiating with each other in order to reach
an agreement concerning their interests in China.[46]
The Chinese revolution, which broke out in the autumn of 1911, presented a most favorable oppor-

[43] Sazonov to the Russian Ambassador in London, November 27–
December 10, 1910, Siebert, p. 23. Protocol of an Extraordinary Meeting of the Ministerial Council at St. Petersburg, November 19–December 2, 1910, Siebert, pp. 24-27.

[44] Protocol of an Extraordinary Meeting of the Ministerial Council at St. Petersburg, November 19–December 2, 1910, Siebert, pp.
24-27. Neratov to the Russian Ambassador at Tokio, April 16-29,
1911, Siebert, pp. 31-32.

[45] Neratov to the Russian Ambassador at Tokio, April 16-29, 1911,
Siebert, pp. 31-32.

[46] Neratov to the Russian Ambassador at Tokio, April 16-29, 1911,
Siebert, pp. 31-32.

tunity for Russia to settle the whole series of questions in abeyance between Russia and China.[47] For this purpose Russia was more than ever anxious to reach an understanding with Japan.[48] This led to the conclusion of a secret convention in July, 1912.[49] The object of this agreement was " to define the respective spheres of interest of Russia in Outer Mongolia and North Manchuria, and of Japan in Inner Mongolia and South Manchuria." [50]

[47] In regard to (1) The Manchurian question; (2) The question of Mongolia's existence as an autonomic component part of the Chinese realm; and (3) The question of the revision of the St. Petersburg Commercial Treaty between Russia and China. Neratov to the Russian Ambassador in London, January 12-25, 1912, Siebert, p. 33. Memorandum by the Minister of Foreign Affairs, January 10-23, 1912, Siebert, pp. 33-35.

[48] Memorandum by the Minister of Foreign Affairs, January 10-23, 1912, Siebert, p. 34.

[49] Sazonov to the Russian Ambassador in London, June 19–July 2, 1912, Siebert, pp. 39-40. Pooley, pp. 76 ff.

[50] In an interview with Mr. Andrew M. Pooley on July 19, 1912, Mr. Kurachi, then Japanese Vice-Minister for Foreign Affairs, said: "These communiqués are supplementary to the Russo-Japanese Agreements of 1907 and 1910. Their object is to define the respective spheres of interest of Russia in Outer Mongolia and North Manchuria, and of Japan in Inner Mongolia and South Manchuria. By Inner Mongolia is meant that portion of Manchuria formerly known as Inner Mongolia. The exchange of these communiqués was necessitated by the recent revolution in China and by the subsequent negotiations for the supply of a loan to China by the Powers. The exchange of communiqués has resulted in the clearest understanding between the two Powers on the Chinese question, and has created an entente between Russia and Japan of the very greatest importance for the preservation of peace in the Far East. Indeed, the new entente may be described as second only to the Anglo-Japanese Alliance in its bearing on the Far Eastern situation." Pooley, p. 77.

From 1912 to 1914 the Russian and Japanese Governments, while trying to win the support of France and England, adopted a policy of working closely together in all matters concerning China.[51] The Six Power Consortium was a case in point.[52] In April, 1911, certain American, British, German and French banking interests signed an agreement with China, and loaned to her £10,000,000. After the conclusion of this loan, Japan and Russia asked that their respective banking interests be allowed to cooperate in future general loans to China. This was agreed to, and an agreement was signed on June 18, 1912, by the banking groups of the six countries. Russia

[51] In a Memorandum prepared on January 23, 1912, the Russian Minister of Foreign Affairs remarked: "As our interests in Manchuria coincide with those of Japan, and as we have concluded political agreements with this country in 1907 and 1910, our task will be greatly facilitated by cooperation with Japan." In the latter part of the same memorandum, he said: "If we proceed in agreement with Japan, we shall be able to reckon all the sooner upon the fulfillment of our wishes as we succeed in assuring ourselves of the support of our French ally, just as England might also give her support to Japan." Siebert, pp. 33-35. On December 9, 1913, Mr. Motono, the Japanese Ambassador to St. Petersburg, then at Tokio, was reported to have said that "Russia and Japan should make it perfectly plain to the Chinese Government and the other Powers that they both possess special interests in Manchuria and Mongolia, which they in no case intend to renounce." After expressing his opinion on the issue of further loans to China, he said: "In all other matters concerning China, Russia and Japan must act conjointly with France and England, but the two first-named Powers should arrive at a closer agreement between themselves in order to be constantly and fully informed as to their mutual intentions and views." The Russian Ambassador at Tokio to Sazonov, November 26–December 9, 1913, Siebert, pp. 40-41.

[52] Willoughby, II, 992 ff.

and Japan, however, acted together, and obtained certain reservations which were to protect the " special interests " which Japan and Russia claimed in North China, Manchuria and Mongolia.[53]

In 1911-12 Great Britain, by protesting against Japan's policy of interference in China, was working in harmony with the United States.[54] This, however, did not mean that Great Britain was ready to give up her alliance with Tokio. The situation in Europe in 1912 was grave: Great Britain could not afford to take extreme measures in the Far East to protect her own interests, lest her friendly relations with Russia and Japan be damaged.[55] Therefore,

[53] The reservations read as follows: " In the event of the Russian and/or Japanese Groups disapproving of any object for which any advance or loan under the agreement shall be intended to be made, then, if such advance or loan shall be concluded by the other groups or any of them and the Russian Government or the Japanese Government shall notify the other Governments concerned that the business proposed is contrary to the interests of Russia or Japan as the case may be, the Russian group or the Japanese group as the case may be shall be entitled to withdraw from the agreement, but the retiring group will remain bound by all financial engagements which it shall have entered into prior to such withdrawal. The withdrawal of the Russian or Japanese Group shall not affect the rights or liabilities of the other groups under the Agreement." For the text of the Inter-Bank Agreement, see MacMurray, II, 1021.

[54] *For. Rel.*, 1912, pp. 46 ff.

[55] On March 22, 1912, in a telegram to the Russian Ambassador in London, Mr. Sazonov, Russian Minister of Foreign Affairs, commenting on the International Syndicate which was then negotiating with China to grant her a loan, said: " We do not, however, refuse officially to join the Syndicate, but can only do this upon conditions that do not render it necessary for us to distract our attention from our interests in Europe and the Balkans in order to concentrate upon the defence of our position in the Far East. We are of the opinion

while cooperating with the United States to maintain the open door and integrity of China, she yielded in many respects to the wishes of Tokio and St. Petersburg.[56] Thus, in the case of the Six Power Consortium, she " admitted the special rights of Russia and Japan in the regions of Manchuria and Mongolia, but at the same time affirmed the policy of the open door." [57]

In 1914 the war broke out in Europe. On August 1 Sir Edward Grey, while considering that, under certain conditions, England might find it necessary to intervene, in a telegram to Sir C. Greene, then British Ambassador at Tokio, asked the latter to inform the Japanese Minister for Foreign Affairs that, if England did intervene, it would be on the side of France and Russia, and he therefore did not see that England was likely to have to apply to Japan under their alliance, or that the interests dealt with by the

that this is a matter of common interest to the powers of the Triple Entente." Siebert, p. 37. Cf. ibid., March 5-18, 1912, Siebert, p. 37. Sazanov evidently knew the telling effect such a statement would have upon the London Government.

[56] In 1912, in regard to the question of Manchuria and Mongolia, where Russia and Japan claimed special interests, Sir Edward Grey advised the Powers not to make any move until he heard from the Russian and Japanese Governments. The American Ambassador to Great Britain to the Secretary of State, *For. Rel.*, 1912, p. 137. He also traded with Russia for British preferential position in Tibet, by giving his acquiescence to Russia's project concerning Mongolia. Sazonov to the Russian Minister at Peking, February 24–March 9, 1914, Siebert, pp. 41-42.

[57] The American Ambassador to Great Britain to the Secretary of State, *Foreign Relations,* 1912, p. 80; ibid., p. 136.

alliance would be involved.[58] Two days later, upon
the recommendation of Sir William Tyrrell,[59] the
British Prime Minister instructed the British Ambassador at Tokio to communicate with the Japanese Government under Article I of the 1911 Agreement, and to warn them that, if hostilities spread to
the Far East, and an attack on Hong Kong or Wei-
Hai-Wei were to take place, Britain was to rely on
their support.[60]

The above-mentioned communications showed that
the British Government at the time was not at all
anxious to invoke their alliance with Japan, if Germany did not attack British possessions in the Far
East. This, the German Government did not attempt to do, for it did not want war in the Far East.
Answering the American inquiry as to its views
relative to circumscribing war in the Far East, the

[58] Sir Edward Grey to Sir C. Greene (Tokio), August, 1914, *Brit.
Doc.*, XI, 256.

[59] Sir William Tyrrell, upon the request of Sir Edward Grey, made
an inquiry into the question whether the war situation in any way
affected the Japanese under the 1911 Agreement and whether England had anything to ask them, and reached the conclusion: " The
only ways in which the Japanese could be brought in would be if
hostilities spread to the Far East, *e. g.*, an attack on Hong Kong
by the Germans, or if a rising in India were to take place. There
seems no reason to say anything about India, but it might be as
well to warn the Japanese Government that in the event of a war
with Germany there might be a possibility of an attack upon Hong
Kong or Wei-Hai-Wei when we should look to them for support.
The Japanese are no doubt quite alive to this possibility, but perhaps
under Article I of the agreement we should communicate with them."
Note by Sir William Tyrrell, *Brit Doc.*, August 3, XI, 292.

[60] Sir Edward Grey to Sir C. Greene (Tokio), August 3, *Brit. Doc.*,
XI, 298.

German Government made known to Washington its stand: [61]

1. Germany does not seek war with Japan.

2. If Japan, on account of the treaty with England, asks that Germany do nothing against English colonies, warships, or commerce in the East, Germany will assent in return for corresponding promise from England.

3. England and Germany to reciprocally agree that either all warships of both in the East leave eastern waters or remain inactive as against the other, if remaining there.

4. Japan, England, and Germany to agree that none of these three shall attack warships, colonies, territory, or commerce of any of the others in the East.

5. The East to mean all lands and seas between parallels London 90 east and all Pacific to Cape Horn. [62]

The war in Europe, therefore, would not need to extend to the Far East, at least in its early stage, if Japan should stand for peace and not seek an opportunity to enhance her own glory. But the Japanese Government had cherished a hope to strengthen Japan's foothold in China as far as possible, [63] and to seek an opportunity to occupy Kiao-

---

[61] The Ambassador in Germany (Gerard) to the Secretary of State, August 13, 1914, *For. Rel.*, 1914, pp. 169-170.

[62] To this was added " If this zone is too large, smaller limits will be accepted."

[63] In reply to an interpellation made in the lower House on December 8 whether Japan was content with the condition in which she then found herself in Manchuria and Mongolia, Baron Kato, the Japanese Minister for Foreign Affairs, said: " Of course there are still many things to be desired in Manchuria and Mongolia, but this state of affairs has not arisen to-day for the first time. It has constantly existed before and after the Russo-Japanese war, and still continues to exist. The present Cabinet, like its predecessors, when

chow, and, perhaps, South Manchuria, and Fukien as well.[64] That Government, therefore, made an offer of assistance to London, and wished to be invited to participate in the war.[65] The offer being politely refused by London,[66] Japan then, based upon the ostensible necessity of removing all causes of disturbance to the peace of the Far East and of safeguarding the general interests contemplated by the agreement of alliance between Japan and Great Britain, sent an ultimatum to the Imperial German Government and made the terms impossible for it to accept.[67] Con-

---

an available opportunity occurs, wishes to exert its best efforts, and to strengthen Japan's foothold there as far as possible. I wish you to understand that this is a hope cherished by this Cabinet." Extract from the Parliamentary Supplement to the "Official Gazette," December 9, 1914, reported by the Ambassador in Japan (Guthrie) to the Secretary of State, *For. Rel.*, 1914, pp. 206-207.

[64] The Chargé d'Affaires in China (MacMurray) to the Secretary of State, August 11, 1914, *For. Rel.*, 1914, p. 166; August 13, 1914, p. 169.

[65] Sir C. Greene to Sir Edward Grey, August 3, 1914, *Brit. Doc.*, XI, 305; August 4, XI, 327-328. Cf. Paul S. Reinsch, *An American Diplomat in China*, New York, 1923, p. 123.

[66] Sir Edward Grey, after expressing his most cordial thanks to Baron Kato for his generous offer of assistance, told the Japanese Ambassador at London on August 4, in the following words: " I had been impressed by the way in which Japan, during the Russo-Japanese war, demanded nothing of us under our alliance with her except what was strictly in accord with the Treaty of Alliance; indeed, she had asked almost less than at one time it seemed she might have been entitled to have from us. I had thought that a fine attitude of good faith and restraint; and now we in turn should avoid, if we could, drawing Japan into any trouble." Sir Edward Grey to Sir C. Greene, *Brit. Doc.*, XI, 329. Cf. Reinsch, p. 123.

[67] The Japanese Government demanded that the German Government should withdraw immediately from the Japanese and Chinese waters German men-of-war and armed vessels of all kinds and to

sidering the possibility of a war between Germany
and Japan, and that resistance on the part of Germany would be hopeless, the German Chargé d'Affaires at Peking opened discussions with China as
to the possibility of immediately retroceding Kiaochow directly to the Chinese Government.[68] This
project failed, because both Japan and Great Britain
warned China that they would refuse to recognize
such a transfer, even if carried out.[69] The war in
the Far East, being desired by Japan, was thus
precipitated by the Japanese Government, and a
state of war existed between Japan and Germany
from noon, August 23, 1914.[70]

The British Government, being unable to persuade
Japan to stand aloof, persuaded Japan to promise
that she would respect both the neutrality and the
integrity of China.[71] The Governments of Great
Britain and Japan, therefore, announced that they
were of the opinion that it was necessary for them

---

disarm at once those which could not be so withdrawn, and deliver, on
a date not later than September 15, 1914, to the Imperial Japanese
authorities without condition or compensation, the entire leased territory of Kiaochow, with a view to its eventual restoration to China.

[68] The Chargé d'Affaires in China (MacMurray) to the Secretary
of State, August 19. *For. Rel.*, 1914, pp. 172-173.

[69] Great Britain opposed the transfer, because she thought Kiaochow might be returned to Germany after the war. Ibid., 1914,
pp. 172-173. The Chargé d'Affaires in China (MacMurray) to the
Secretary of State, August 20, 1914. Ibid., 1914, pp. 173-174. Reinsch,
p. 123.

[70] The Japanese Minister of Foreign Affairs (Kato) to the Japanese Ambassador (Chinda), August 23, 1914. *For. Rel.*, 1914, p. 174.

[71] The Ambassador in Great Britain (Page) to the Secretary of
State, August 11, 1914. Ibid., 1914, pp. 167-168.

to act in the protection of their general interests in
the Far East contemplated by the Anglo-Japanese
Alliance. They, nevertheless, kept specially in view
the independence and integrity of China as provided
for in that agreement. The announcement further
stated: " It is understood that the action of Japan
will not extend to the Pacific Ocean beyond the China
Seas, except in so far as it may be necessary to protect Japanese shipping lines in the Pacific, nor beyond Asiatic waters westward of the China Seas,
nor to any foreign territory except in German occupation on the continent of eastern Asia." [72]

The course of events later proved that all the
pledges and assurances which Japan gave were
made to be violated, rather than to be kept. The
Japanese, acting conjointly with the British, not
long afterwards took military action in disregard
of the declared neutrality of Chinese territory in
their war against Germany in Shantung.[73] The
Japanese Government also claimed reversionary
rights as to German railway concessions in the entire province.[74] Southward, they also violated their
pledges by acting well beyond the area of the China

[72] The British Chargé d'Affaires (Barclay) to the Secretary of
State, August 18, 1914. Ibid., 1914, p. 171.

[73] The Chargé d'Affaires in China (MacMurray) to the Secretary
of State, September 3, 1914. Ibid., 1914, p. 177; September 10, 1914,
pp. 186-189. Extract from the *Peking Gazette*, October 6, 1914, reported by the Minister in China (Reinsch) to the Secretary of State,
October 12, 1914. *For. Rel.*, 1914, pp. 194 ff.

[74] The Chargé d'Affaires in China (MacMurray) to the Secretary
of State, September 29, 1914. *For. Rel.*, 1914, p. 181; see also ibid.,
1914, pp. 181, 182, 201, 202, 206, and 207.

Seas, and seized the Marshall Islands and other
German outposts in the Pacific.[75] The clearest vio-
lations of international law and morality on the part
of Japan were, however, exhibited in her relations
with China, for, in January, 1915, four months after
Japan's declaration of war against Germany, the
purpose of which Japan claimed to be entirely un-
selfish, Japan opened negotiations with Peking which
led directly to the signing by the Japanese and Chinese Governments on May 25, of various agreements
that gave to Japan a greatly strengthened position
in China.[76]

In order to safeguard the interests thus obtained,
Japan approached Russia and concluded a convention with her on July 3, 1916, providing for the general cooperation of the two Powers in the Far
East.[77] Under the cover of the open convention was
a secret agreement of the same date, by which Japan
and Russia engaged to safeguard China from the
political domination of any third hostile Power, and
therefore mutually obligated themselves to cooperate to this end.[78] The Agreement was to run for five

[75] The Ambassador in Japan (Gutherie) to the Secretary of State,
October 6, 1914, ibid., 1914, pp. 183-184; also see ibid., 1914, pp. 185,
190, 207-210. From a military point of view, the Anglo-Japanese
Alliance was beneficial to the allies' cause.

[76] (A) Treaty, and exchanges of notes, respecting the Province of
Shantung; (B) Treaty, and exchange of notes, respecting South Manchuria and Eastern Inner Mongolia; (C) Exchange of notes respecting the matter of Hanyehping; and (D) Exchange of notes respecting the Fukien question. MacMurray, II, 1216 ff.

[77] Ibid., II, 1327-28.

[78] The secret Treaty of July 3, 1916, between Russia and Japan,
practically had the effect of an alliance. Article II of this treaty

years, with provision for continuation beyond that
date, and was to remain " profoundly secret except
to both of the High Contracting Parties." [79]

The treaty respecting the Province of Shantung
of May 25, 1915, between China and Japan, provided,
by Article I: " The Chinese Government agrees to
give full assent to all matters upon which the Japanese Government may hereafter agree with the German Government relating to the disposition of all
rights, interests and concessions which Germany, by
virtue of treaties or otherwise possesses in relation
to the Province of Shantung." [80] The Japanese,
being anxious as to her eventual share of the spoils
at the peace conference, naturally disliked the idea
that China should participate in the war and become
one of the victorious Powers.

---

provided: "In the event, in consequences of measures taken by
mutual consent of Russia and Japan, on the basis of the preceding
article, a declaration of war is made by any third Power, contemplated by Article I of this Agreement, against one of the contracting parties, the other party, at the first demand of its ally, must
come to its aid. Each of the high-contracting parties herewith
covenants in the event such a condition arises, not to conclude peace
with the same enemy, without preliminary consent therefor from its
ally." The obligations on the part of the allies thus provided for,
however, were limited by Article IV of the same Treaty, which Provided: "It is requisite to have in view that neither one nor the
other of the high-contracting parties must consider itself bound by
Article II of this agreement to lend armed aid to its ally, unless it
be given guarantees by its ally that the latter will give it assistance
corresponding in character to the importance of the approaching
conflict."

[79] For the text of this secret agreement, see MacMurray, II, 1328.
[80] Ibid., p. 1216.

From 1914 to 1917, Japan had succeeded in pre-
venting China from joining in the hostilities against
the Central Powers.[81] But early in 1917 the United
States severed her relations with Germany, and on
February 9 secured from China a promise that Peking would follow the example of Washington.[82]
Japan, being unable to prevent China's entry into
the war on this occasion, resorted to another means
to insure her share of the spoils at the conclusion of
peace. In the latter part of February she secured
from England, France, Russia, and Italy the signature of secret agreements, in the form of exchanges
of notes, in regard to the disposal of Germany's
rights in Shantung and possession of the islands
north of the equator.[83] These secret agreements, together with the notes exchanged between Secretary
Lansing and Viscount Ishii in November,[84] prepared
the way for Section VIII of the Treaty of Versailles
of 1919, which provided for the transfer of German
interests in Shantung to Japan.[85]

During the years 1914-1918, England, wholly occupied by her war with the Central Powers, could spare
little attention to affairs in the Far East. This situation gave Japan opportunities for consolidation and

[81] Cf. Dennis, pp. 47 ff.

[82] China broke her diplomatic relations with Germany in March,
1917, and on August 14 formally declared war. MacMurray, II, 1361.

[83] Ibid., pp. 1167 ff. Thomas F. Millard, *Conflict of Policies in
Asia*, New York, 1924, pp. 57-63.

[84] The Lansing-Ishii Agreement was reached on November 2, 1917.
See below, ch. vii.

[85] MacMurray, II, 1488.

expansion of her interests in China, backed up by
the influence and prestige of the British Empire, but
directly in contradiction to the principles embodied
in the Anglo-Japanese Alliance. Failing to prevent
Japan's entry into the war, Great Britain, in consideration of her own interest, was forced to act
with Japan in 1914 in warning China that a direct
retrocession of Kiaochow by Germany to the Chinese
Government would not be permitted.[86] A year later,
when Japan was pressing upon China her Twenty-
One Demands, the British Minister, acting conjointly
with the Ministers of the Entente Powers, gave
advice to the Chinese Government not to attempt
armed resistance to Japan.[87] In 1917, when Japan
wanted to have assurance from the Allied Powers
in regard to the disposal of Germany's interests
in Shantung and North Pacific Islands, it was again
Great Britain which came out first in giving the
assurance.[88]

But not all the actions which the British Government undertook during the years 1914-18, in sup-

[86] Great Britain also acted with Japan in violating China's neutrality by her military operations in Shantung.

[87] Reinsch, pp. 144-145.

[88] The British assurance was given on February 16, 1917. The
message, after professing to "accede with pleasure to request of the
Japanese Government for an assurance that they will support Japan's
claims in regard to the disposal of Germany's rights in Shantung
and possessions in the islands north of the equator on occasion of
the Peace Conference," stated that "it being understood that the
Japanese Government will in the eventual peace settlement treat
in the same spirit Great Britain's claims to the German islands south
of the equator." MacMurray, II, 1167-68.

13

porting of Japan's diplomacy, were willingly taken. On the contrary, most of the actions were forced upon it by the circumstances then existing.[89] In 1914-18 Great Britain was engaged in a war which demanded her full attention and the entire strength of the nation. She had to sacrifice her interests in the Far East, in order to retain Japan's cooperation. After the war, the British naturally resented what Japan had done at a time when they were preoccupied with events in Europe. In fact, many had expressed their resentment even before the war was over. For instance, Mr. Putnam Weale wrote:

Though Englishmen believe that the gallant Japanese are entitled to a recompense just as much now as they were in 1905 for what they have done, Englishmen do not and cannot subscribe to the doctrine that Japan is to dominate China by extorting a whole ring-fence of industrial concessions and administrative privileges which will ultimately shut out even allies from obtaining equal opportunities. . . . . In China, though they are willing to be reduced to second place and even driven out by fair competition, they will fight in a way your correspondents do not yet dream of to secure that no diplomacy of the jiujitsu order injures them or their Chinese friends.[90]

In 1921, the German menace, which was the principal reason for the continuation of the Anglo-Japa-

[89] For instance, Japan's request for an assurance from the British Government in regard to Shantung and North Pacific Islands, came "at a very serious moment of the Allied cause. The submarine campaign was reaching its height in European waters; conditions in Russia were becoming very critical; the United States had not as yet entered the war; and the Allied fortunes were desperately threatened." Dennis, p. 46.

[90] Quoted in Reinsch, p. 136.

nese Alliance in 1911, no longer existed. There were, however, other considerations that still claimed the attention of the British Government.[91] British diplomacy feared the possibility that Japan might become an enemy of the Empire, if the alliance were discontinued. Not only the bad treatment of the Japanese in the British Dominions, but the anti-Japanese attitude maintained by the British residents in the Far East, might lead to serious friction between the two countries.[92] In such case Japan might attack Australia, or she might intrigue against British interests in India.[93] Also, there was the pos-

[91] Cf. Millard, *Conflict of Policies in Asia*, pp. 176-177.

[92] There were still other grievances on the side of Japan against Great Britain. Professor Dennis, in summing up the anti-British campaign in the Japanese Press in 1916-17, classified these attacks under five main headings: (1) discrimination against Japanese in British colonies; (2) the obstruction of Japanese economic expansion in the South Sea Islands; (3) the efforts to exclude Japanese interests from south China; (4) the British share in the defeat of the fifth group of Japanese demands on China in 1915; and (5) the declaration that Russia and Germany need no longer be feared, while in any case the United States threatened to nullify the usefulness of the Anglo-Japanese Alliance. Dennis, p. 51.

[93] The *Nippon-oyobi-Nipponjin,* in March, 1916, declared: "The Anglo-Japanese Alliance mainly relates to China, and the greater the consideration paid by Japan to India, the more should be the British concessions to Japan as regards China." Pooley, p. 29. Such were the words of leading Japanese journals, written for the digestion of the British statesmen. In 1920, Colonel Misumachi, in his statement to the Canadian missionaries in Chientao, warned them that if the missionaries actually do "give assistance, material or immaterial, to either the independence movement in Korea or to anti-Japanese sentiment, the Buddhists in Japan would be able to find a legal reason for giving anti-British assistance to those behind the noncooperation movement in India." *Japan Advertiser,* December 3, 1920.

sibility of a Russo-German-Japanese alliance.[94] Such a combination, if formed, would make it difficult for England to protect her interests in India and in the Pacific.

The British power of resistance in 1921, only three years after her life-and-death struggle with Germany, was particularly weak. A continuation of the Japanese alliance would not only mean a guarantee against Japan's ill-will, but would also serve as an insurance policy in the Far East. It was true that since the opening of China, Great Britain had always stood for the Open Door, but in 1921, owing to the rising industry and the growing competition of the other countries, that policy was no longer as decisively favorable to her as it had been in the old days. England, therefore, though still preferring fair competition and equal opportunities for commerce and industry, was not loath to take up the alternative policy of exclusive concessions and mo-

[94] In 1916-17, a wide-spread pro-German campaign took place in Japan. Pooley, pp. 23 ff. From the documents published after the Russian Revolution it is manifest that efforts towards the conclusion of a separate peace and an alliance between Germany, Russia and Japan were made by the German Government in March, 1916, through the Japanese Ambassador (Ujida Uchida); and from the official files of Central Soviet Papers, secured at Perm on February 2, 1919, it is equally reliable that the Japanese Government at the end of October, through the Japanese Extraordinary Representative Oda, had approached the German Government for the conclusion of a German-Japanese secret treaty to which Russia should be subordinated, and a treaty to embody the principles agreed upon was actually drafted. See Putnam Weale, *The Truth about China and Japan*, New York, 1919, pp. 205 ff.

nopolistic sources of trade, if political expediency should require.[95]

Finally, the Alliance "had been in existence within a few days of twenty years. It had served a great purpose in two great wars. It had stood the strain of common sacrifices, common anxieties, common efforts, common triumphs."[96] British conservatism naturally could not lightly give up the alliance.

When two nations have been united in that fiery ordeal, they cannot at the end of it take off their hats one to the other and politely part as two strangers part who travel together for a few hours in a railway train. Something more, something closer, unites them than the mere words of the treaty; and, as it were, gratuitously and without a course to tear up the written contract, although it serves no longer any valid or effective purpose, may lead to misunderstandings in one nation just as much as the maintenance of that treaty had led to misunderstandings in another.[97]

If England hesitated to give up the alliance, Japan was even more unwilling to do so.[98] The alliance,

[95] Professor Raymond L. Buell goes so far as to declare: " England was apparently deserting the policy of the Open Door, to which she owes her mercantile greatness, to engage in an undignified scamble for exclusive concessions and monopolistic sources of trade." *The Washington Conference*, New York, 1922, pp. 125 ff.

[96] Mr. Balfour in a speech at the Fourth Plenary Session of the Washington Conference, December 10, 1921, 67th Cong., 2d Sess., S. Doc. No. 126, *Conference on the Limitation of Armament*, 1921-22, p. 172.

[97] Ibid., p. 172.

[98] Cf. Buell, ch. iv. Willoughby, *China at the Conference*, Baltimore, 1922, pp. 5 ff. Millard, *Conflict of Policies in Asia*, p. 176.

during its life-time, had effectually prevented foreign opposition; it had fostered Japanese military activities abroad; and it had increased its prestige at home. It was still the foundation of Japan's foreign policy in 1921, as it had been since its formation twenty years before. The discontinuance of the British alliance might mean an " inglorious isolation " for Japan, which the Tokio Government had exerted its best efforts to avoid ever since its diplomatic defeat after the Sino-Japanese War.

On July 8, 1920, Lord Curzon and Baron Chinda presented a joint declaration to the League of Nations. This declaration stated that the Governments of Great Britain and Japan had reached the conclusion that the 1911 Agreement, " though in harmony with the spirit of the Covenant of the League of Nations," was " not entirely consistent with the letter of the Covenant." They accordingly jointly informed the League that " they recognized the principle that if the said agreement be continued after July, 1921, it must be in a form which is not inconsistent with that Covenant." [99] This indicated the desire of both Governments to continue the Alliance after July, 1921, though in a modified form. Indeed, according to Mr. Putnam Weale, tentative

[99] League of Nations, Treaty Series, September, 1920, No. 1. Article II of the alliance which provided for immediate military action in common against a common foe, was directly in contradiction to Articles XIII and XIV of the Covenant which provided for a system of investigation, mediation, etc.

drafts of a renewed Anglo-Japanese Alliance were already in existence in the spring of the next year.[100]

That the alliance would be renewed in 1921, if opposition from other quarters did not come in time, there was not the slightest doubt. In 1921, however, the Chinese people protested vehemently against a renewal of the alliance.[101] Then, also, there were the British residents in China and the Far East, who, owing to the increasing competition of Japanese commerce in China, objected to a continuance of the Japanese alliance.[102] In America, it was felt that the Anglo-Japanese treaty was a menace to American interests and, therefore, should not be continued.[103]

[100] B. L. Putnam Weale, *An Indiscreet Chronicle from the Pacific,* New York, 1922, p. 52.

[101] Below, ch. vi.

[102] " Such general feeling of opposition to the alliance appeared, however, as early as 1918 in the protests of various British chambers of commerce in China. By the beginning of 1921 it had taken such definite form that an analysis of the Far Eastern press shows the main British reasons for opposing the alliance to be: (1) it no longer has any object; (2) Japanese policies in China are opposed to the alliance and to British interests in China; (3) British and Japanese interests in China are incompatible; (4) Chinese resentment is increasing against Japan and hence indirectly against the British; and (5) opposition exists in Australasia and in Canada to certain features of the alliance." Dennis, pp. 63-64. Cf. Millard, *Conflict of Policies in Asia,* pp. 195-196. For extracts illustrating the view of the British in the Far East in 1920-21 toward the Anglo-Japanese Alliance, see Millard, *Conflict of Policies in Asia,* pp. 452-469.

[103] Lord Bryce recognized this fact in the following words: " Nine men out of ten in the United States continue to repeat that England is the ally—the exclusive ally of Japan, and that the effect of the treaty has been and is to make Japan think she has a comparatively free hand and may adopt policies of aggression on which she would

The opposition which weighed heavier than any other in the mind of the British statesmen, came, of course, from the Dominions.

It will be remembered that, in 1911, the Dominions had opposed a renewal of the alliance, and that their opposition was not withdrawn until a provision had been made in the new treaty to exclude the United States from the scope of its operation. In 1921, the war clouds hovered over Japan and the United States more darkly than ever before.[104] The Dominions reasoned, therefore, in this way:

No treaty can be called a Treaty of Alliance unless it can be invoked against some one. Even if the new Treaty is so worded that it exempts Britain specifically and absolutely from participation in an American-Japanese struggle, it will have to apply against China if she throws in her lot with the United States. [In view of the relations then existing between China and the United States, this was more than a possibility.] And thus sooner or later it would in effect bring Britain and the United States into collision with one another, first on Chinese soil and then by natural processes everywhere on the Pacific.[105]

Nevertheless, Australia, New Zealand and India, owing to their geographical propinquity to Japan, and their inability to defend themselves in case of an attack from that country, took the view that, to

otherwise fear to embark. No explanations seem likely to remove this impression from the American mind." *New York Times*, October 19, 1921.

[104] Buell, ch. ii.

[105] Memorandum prepared by Mr. Putnam Weale for the Canadian Prime Minister, *An Indiscreet Chronicle from the Pacific*, p. 58.

hold the hands of Japan, a renewal of the alliance, with its terms greatly modified, would not be entirely undesirable.[106] Canada and the Union of South Africa were uncompromising; they sternly opposed a continuation of the alliance.

"America is the nation," declared General Smuts, " that is closest to us in all the human ties. The Dominions look upon her as the oldest of them. She is the nation with whom we most closely agree, and with whom we can most cordially work together. . . . . To my mind it seems clear that the only path of safety for the British Empire is a path on which she can walk together with America." [107]

General Smuts was not opposing the Japanese Alliance alone, when he uttered these words, nor was he advocating an alliance with America. He was opposed to all " exclusive alliances." Thus, he said: " The British Empire is not in need of exclusive alliances. It emerged from the War quite the greatest Power in the world, and it is only unwisdom or unsound policy that could rob her of that great position. She does not want exclusive alliances. What she wants to see established is more universal friendship in the world." [108]

With Canada, the reason lay much deeper. The Canadians feared that, sooner or later, the alliance

[106] The position of the Dominions in regard to the renewal of the alliance was made clear by remarks of their representatives inside and outside of the Imperial Conference.

[107] *Parl. P.,* 1921, XIV, Imperial Conference, 1921, p. 24.

[108] Ibid., p. 24.

would compel Great Britain to fight on the side of
its ally in a war between Japan and the United
States. Should this happen, " what in such circumstances would be the fate of Canadian territory, with
all the ex-soldiers of Canada influenced by geographical and racial propinquity pouring in tens of
thousands into the United States to assist her?
There was only one answer. The Anglo-Japanese
Alliance, as it stood, was a symbol of the break-up
of the British empire." [109]

In view of the diversity of opinion which existed
in the Dominions, the London Government considered it wise to postpone the answer to the question
as to the renewal of the Anglo-Japanese treaty in
order that the matter might be dealt with by the
Prime Ministers of the Dominions. The first question the Imperial Cabinet [110] had to consider was
whether, as contended by some, the joint declaration
by the British and Japanese Governments to the
League of Nations on July 8, 1920, constituted a
denunciation of the Agreement in the sense of Clause
VI. The Japanese Government took the view that

[109] For Canadian position with reference to the renewal of the
alliance, see Weale, *An Indiscreet Chronicle from the Pacific*, Part II.

[110] The official title of the meeting, which met in London June–
August, 1921, was " Conference of the Prime Ministers and Representatives of the United Kingdom, the Dominions, and India." By
popular usage, it has taken up the title " The Imperial Conference,"
although strictly speaking it was not an Imperial Conference, as
that term was used before. The conference was at first scheduled
for 1922, but later events proved that such a conference should be
called a year earlier in order to decide upon all the important questions then pending for solution.

no notice of denunciation had been given. This view was shared by the British Secretary of State for Foreign Affairs. The Imperial Cabinet, after consulting the Lord Chancellor and the Law Officers of the Crown, definitely held that the declaration to the League of July, 1920, was not a denunciation of the Alliance.[111]

It followed, therefore, that the alliance would remain in force unless it should be denounced, and would lapse only at the expiration of twelve months from the time notice of denunciation was given. In view of this decision, the British and Japanese Governments, on July 7, 1921, dispatched a second communication to the League, supplementary to that of the first on July 8, 1920, to the following effect:

They hereby notify the League pending further action that they are agreed that if any situation arises whilst the Agreement remains in force in which the procedure prescribed by the terms of the Agreement is inconsistent with the procedure prescribed by the Covenant of the League, then the procedure prescribed by the said Covenant shall be adopted and shall prevail over that prescribed by the Agreement.[112]

After careful deliberation, taking into consideration the general political situation on the Pacific, and the international relations between the Pacific Powers, the Imperial Conference of 1921 came to the conclusion that the best policy would be to communicate " with complete frankness to the United States,

[111] *Par. Deb.,* 1921, 5th Series, Commons, CXLIV, 916.
[112] *Monthly Summary of the League of Nations,* August, 1921, p. 64.

Japan and China, with the object of securing an exchange of views which might lead to more formal discussion and conference,"[113] in order to solve all the problems of the Pacific and the Far East. Mr. Lloyd George, summarizing the situation in the House on July 11, 1921, said:

The broad lines of Imperial policy in the Pacific and the Far East were the very first subjects to which we addressed ourselves at the meetings of the Imperial Cabinet, having a special regard to the Anglo-Japanese Agreement, the future of China, and the bearing of both those questions on the relations of the British Empire with the United States. We were guided in our deliberations by three main considerations. In Japan, we have an old and proved ally. The agreement of twenty years' standing between us has been of very great benefit, not only to ourselves and her, but to the peace of the Far East. In China there is a very numerous people, with great potentialities, who esteem our friendship highly, and whose interests we, on our side, desire to assist and advance. In the United States we see to-day, as we have always seen, the people closest to our aims and ideals with whom it is for us, not merely a desire and an interest, but a deeprooted instinct to consult and co-operate. Those were the main considerations in our meetings, and upon them we were unanimous. The object of our discussions was to find a method combining all these three factors in a policy which would remove the danger of heavy naval expenditure in the Pacific, with all the evils which such an expenditure entails, and would ensure the development of all legitimate national interests of the Far East.[114]

[113] Lloyd George's speech in the House of Commons, July 11, 1921, *Par. Deb.*, 1921, 5th Series, Commons, CXLIV, 917.
[114] Ibid., CXLIV, 915.

In view, however, of the conflict of interests between China and Japan on the one side, and the
United States and Japan on the other, a policy which
would safeguard British interests on the Pacific,
and, at the same time be agreeable to the United
States, Japan and China, was not easily to be found
unless the four Powers could be brought together in
a conference in order to reach a common understanding. It was thus no wonder that " President
Harding's invitation to a Conference on Disarmament was warmly welcomed by all the members of
the (Imperial) Conference." [115]   *doubtful*

Japan, on the other hand, did not enter the Washington Conference willingly. The Japanese Government feared that, " so far as the discussion of Pacific and Far Eastern questions was concerned, it
might be called upon to give justifications of certain of its acts which it would be difficult to give
and that from the Conference might result policies or determinations which would not be agreeable
to itself." [116] Nevertheless, the Japanese Government realized that a refusal to participate in the
Conference would hurt the feelings of both London
and Washington. Hence, she accepted the invitation,
but with the understanding that the main object of
discussing the Pacific and Far Eastern problems in
the proposed conference, the original and principal

---

[115] Imperial Conference, 1921, *Parl. P.,* 1921, XIV, 3. Cf. *Par. Deb.,*
1921, 5th Series, Commons, CXLIV, 917.
[116] Willoughby, *China at the Conference,* p. 7.

aim of which was the limitation of armament, was
" to reach a common understanding in regard to
general principles and policies in the Pacific and the
Far East," and that the introduction therein of problems of " sole concern to certain particular Powers or of such matters as might be regarded accomplished facts should be scrupulously avoided." [117]

The Conference met at Washington during November and December, 1921, and January and February, 1922, and was attended by nine Powers.
Besides concluding a treaty between the United
States of America, the British Empire, France,
Italy, and Japan, limiting naval armaments, a treaty
between the same Powers in relation to the use of
submarines and noxious gases in warfare, a treaty
between all nine Powers relating to principles and
policies to be followed in matters concerning China,
a treaty between the nine Powers relating to Chinese
customs tariff, and other resolutions, the Conference
had, as one of its results, a treaty relating to the
signatories' possessions and insular dominions in
the Pacific Ocean, signed by the United States of
America, the British Empire, France, and Japan on
December 13, 1921, which was to take the place of
the 1911 agreement between Japan and Great
Britain.

[117] Japanese reply of July 27 to the American memorandum which
was delivered at Tokio by the American Chargé d'Affaires, and was
made public on July 23. Also see Millard, *Conflict of Policies in
Asia,* pp. 221-224.

In its preamble, the Four-Power Treaty declares:

The United States of America, the British Empire, France, and Japan, with a view to the preservation of the general peace and the maintenance of their rights in relation to their insular possessions and insular dominions in the region of the Pacific Ocean, have determined to conclude a Treaty to this effect:

I. The High Contracting Parties agree as between themselves to respect their rights in relation to their insular possessions and insular dominions in the region of the Pacific Ocean. If there should develop between any of the High Contracting Parties a controversy arising out of any Pacific question and involving their said rights which is not satisfactorily settled by diplomacy and is likely to affect the harmonious accord now happily subsisting between them, they shall invite the other High Contracting Parties to a joint conference to which the whole subject will be referred for consideration and adjustment.

II. If the said rights are threatened by the aggressive action of any other Power, the High Contracting Parties shall communicate with one another fully and frankly in order to arrive at an understanding as to the most efficient measures to be taken, jointly or separately, to meet the exigencies of the particular situation.

III. The Treaty shall remain in force for ten years from the time it shall take effect, and after the expiration of the said period it shall continue to be in force subject to the right of any of the High Contracting Parties to terminate it upon twelve months' notice.

IV. This Treaty shall be ratified as soon as possible in accordance with the constitutional methods of the High Contracting Parties and shall take effect on the deposit of ratifications, which shall take place at Washington, and thereupon the agreement between Great Britain and Japan, which was concluded at London on July 13, 1911, shall terminate.[118]

In conformity with Article IV of the Four-Power Treaty, the representatives of the United States of America, the British Empire, France and Japan met at the Department of State at Washington on August 17, 1923, and deposited with the Government of the United States the instruments of the ratification by the Governments they represented. The instrument of ratification by the United States was deposited with the reservation that " The United States understands that under the statement in the preamble or under the terms of this Treaty there is no commitment to armed force, no alliance, no obligation to join in any defence." [119] With the deposit of ratifications the Four-Power Treaty took effect, and the Anglo-Japanese Treaty of Alliance of July 13, 1911, was thereupon terminated.

The third alliance was a mere continuation of the 1905 agreement between Great Britain and Japan. The treaty was rewritten in 1911 in order to exempt the United States from its scope of operation. Dur-

[118] For the text of the Treaty, see the Declaration accompanying it, and the supplementary Treaty of February 6, 1922, *Conference on the Limitation of Armament,* pp. 889 ff. For a general treatise on the Washington Conference, see Buell, *The Washington Conference,* 1922.

[119] For the text of the Protocol of Deposit of Ratifications of the Four-Power Treaty, concluded at Washington December 13, 1921, see *State Papers,* 1923, CXVII, 472. Deposit of Ratifications of the supplementary Treaty of February 6, 1922, was also made on the same date, August 17, 1923, *State Papers,* 1923, CXVII, 473-474.

ing the life time of the new treaty, from 1911 to
1921, the close harmony between the allies had been
disturbed on several occasions—all in connection
with China. But, on the whole, the alliance had been
profitable to both parties. For Great Britain, the
alliance of 1911 had relieved her from anxiety as to
her interests in India and the Far East during the
trying days of 1914-18. For Japan, it had served as
a support for her aggressive policy on the Asian
continent, and had encouraged the Japanese military party to launch upon a program of political
domination of China without fear of intervention by
other Powers.

14

CHAPTER VI

Korea, China and the Alliance

Covered by the Alliance but not parties to it, affected by the same alliance and yet not consulted, were several countries, namely, China, Korea, and India. As to India, it was not included in the first treaty. The second treaty, besides including among its objects the consolidation and maintenance of the general peace in the region of India, the maintenance of the territorial rights of Great Britain, and the defence of British special rights in that country, stipulated Japanese recognition of Great Britain's special interests in all that concerned the security of the Indian frontier, and the right of Great Britain to take such measures in the proximity of that frontier as she might find necessary for safeguarding her Indian possessions. In the third treaty, this specific provision was dropped, and only the general reference to India made in the preamble was retained. Throughout its life-time, the Alliance, besides effecting, in the mind of the British statesmen, a feeling of security about their Indian possessions, and besides restraining the hand of Japan in intrigue against British interests in that region, produced no effect of great importance upon India.[1]

[1] The Japanese assistance rendered in aiding the suppression of mutiny by a British Indian regiment in 1915, took place in Singapore, outside of the region of India.

With Korea, the case was totally different. The original and principal reason for the conclusion of the Alliance, so far as Japan was concerned, was the protection of Korea against Russian aggression and the establishment of a Japanese preponderance and ultimate protectorate over that peninsula. Thus, the first treaty stipulated that Japan, in addition to the interests which she possessed in China, was interested in a peculiar degree politically as well as commercially and industrially in Korea, and, therefore, would be permitted to take such measures as might be indispensable in order to safeguard those interests if threatened either by the aggressive action of any other Power, or by disturbances arising in the country. This provision had the immediate effect of strengthening Japan's position at Seul, and, shortly after the conclusion of the alliance, the Russian Minister notified the Tokio Cabinet that, so far as his Government was concerned, Japan was at liberty to have a free hand in Korean affairs. A year later, however, when the Russian military party gained ascendency at St. Petersburg, the Russian Government again looked to a forward policy, both in China and Korea, which directly led to the war between Japan and Russia in 1904-05.[2]

Ever since the Sino-Japanese War and the elimination of the Chinese influence at Seul in 1894-95, Russia and Japan had been fighting for control over Korea, which country, owing to her military weak-

[2] See above, ch. iii.

ness, was entirely helpless, and at the mercy of her strong neighbors. The first Anglo-Japanese Treaty, though recognizing Japan's special interest in Korea, had as one of its avowed objects the maintenance of the independence and territorial integrity of the Empire of Korea, and of the principle of the Open Door therein. Both of the high contracting parties declared themselves to be entirely uninfluenced by any aggressive tendencies in that country. Korea, at the time, placed faith in the allies' adherence to their promises.[3] This explains the statement of the Korean Government that it " regarded with much satisfaction the agreement concluded on the 30th January " between Great Britain and Japan.[4]

When hostilities broke out between Japan and Russia early in 1904, the Korean Emperor, placing faith in Japan's adherence to the promise to main-

[3] The Korean Government believed at the time that Japan and Great Britain, especially the latter country, sincerely wished to maintain the Open Door, and the independence and integrity of Korea. They were, therefore, most anxious to show themselves worthy of the support which the agreement would give them, and placed great reliance on the advice of the British Minister at Seul. Cf. the Marquess of Lansdowne's account of his own conversation with the Korean Minister: " I expressed the pleasure with which I had listened to the Minister's statement, and my hope that strengthened by the existence of the new agreement, the Korean Government would have the courage to resist any insidious advances which might be made to them with the object of undermining their independence or obtaining concessions inconsistent with the interests of Korea and the just rights of other Powers." The Marquess of Lansdowne to Mr. Jordan, February 15, 1902. *Brit. Doc.*, II, 129.

[4] Ibid.

tain the independence of the country,[5] immediately
concluded an alliance with Japan, and gave the Japanese army the use of Korean territory as a base of
military operations against Russia.[6] But, during the
war, Japan made use of the treaty to obtain various
privileges and concessions, at variance with the
principles which she had several times promised to
observe.[7] As a result, the Koreans realized that
neither of the parties to the Anglo-Japanese treaty
was sincere in standing by the principles which were
embodied in that document. They therefore turned,
at the close of the Russo-Japanese war, to America
in addressing their grievances and seeking assistance.[8]

On August 12, 1905, three days after the opening
of the peace conference at Portsmouth, the second
Anglo-Japanese treaty was signed at London, in

[5] See the conversation between the Korean Emperor and Marquis
Ito on November 15, 1905, as recorded in Henry Chung, *The Case
of Korea*, New York, 1921, p. 52.

[6] Henry Chung, *The Case of Korea*, p. 49.

[7] The *Korean Daily News*, September 4, 6, 12, 1905, etc.

[8] Early in August 1905, two Koreans, Rev. P. K. Yoon and Mr.
Singman Rhse, representing a powerful Korean society, the Il Chin
Hoi, which, translated, means "the Daily Progress," arrived in
America, with the declared purpose to petition President Roosevelt
to use his good offices to prevent their country from being parti-
tioned off or gobbled up entirely by the warring powers in the East.
The *Korean Daily News*, September 9, 1905. Cf. ibid., September
22, 1905. About the same time, the Korean Emperor dispatched
Professor Hulbert, an American educationalist in the employment
of the Korean Government, to Washington with a letter from the
Emperor himself, calling attention to the great evils Japan was in-
flicting upon Korea, and asking for American aid. McKenzie, pp.
130-131.

which Korea was relegated to a subordinate position, and no reference was made to the independence
and territorial integrity of the country. Article III
of the document provided:

Japan possessing paramount political, military, and economical interest in Korea, Great Britain recognises the right
of Japan to take such measures of guidance, control, and protection in Korea as she may deem proper and necessary to
safeguard and advance those interests, provided always such
measures are not contrary to the principle of equal opportunities for the commerce and industry of all nations.

Following closely the language of this provision,
the Portsmouth Treaty provided:

The Imperial Russian Government, acknowledging that
Japan possesses in Korea paramount political, military and
economical interests, engage neither to obstruct nor interfere
with the measures of guidance, protection and control which
the Imperial Government of Japan may find it necessary to
take in Korea.[9]

The exact construction to be put on Article III of
the 1905 agreement between Great Britain and
Japan depended, of course, very much upon the
spirit in which it was read. In view of the later
events, we can, however, safely conclude that by this
agreement Great Britain had consented to stand
aside and leave Japan a free hand in Korea. It is
true that Great Britain's promise was merely of
non-interference and not of active assistance as to
this part of the programme. But, in 1905, any effec-

[9] Article II, Treaty of Peace between Russia and Japan, September 5, 1905, MacMurray, I, 523.

tive objection to Japan's absorption of Korea could have come only from three nations, namely, Russia, Great Britain, and the United States. Russia was naturally eliminated, as she just had been defeated. The British assent to Japan's action in Korea left the United States alone with a free hand, which the Washington Government was not only reluctant, but actually afraid, to use for the protection of Korea.[10] For, since both Great Britain and Russia were bound to stand aloof, any serious obstruction to Japan's policy in Korea might mean a war with Japan to whose assistance Great Britain would come by virtue of the 1905 agreement.

This was just what Japan aimed at, for the Tokio Government knew that, by cutting off all hope of appeal on the part of Seul to the outside world, they could get the Korean Government under absolute control, and take whatever step towards the absorption of the country they might want to take. Thus, in November, 1905, only three months after the conclusion of the Anglo-Japanese treaty, Japan forced Korea to assign to Japan the control and direction of her external relations.[11] Two years later, the Korean Emperor was forced to abdicate,

[10] "So far from pleading the case of Korea with Japan, America was the first to fall in with and give its open assent to the destruction of the old administration. On the first intimation from Japan, it agreed, without inquiry and with almost indecent haste, to withdraw its Minister from Seul." McKenzie, p. 131.

[11] By the Treaty between Japan and Korea, signed November 17, 1905.

and finally, in 1910, the country was formally annexed to the Japanese Empire.[12] In the new Anglo-Japanese treaty, which was renewed in 1911, no mention whatsoever was made of Korea, thus leaving it to be understood that it was only a part of the Japanese Empire, giving a formal recognition, though tacit, to the fact that Korea as an independent country no longer existed.

It cannot be said that Japan's ambition to absorb Korea was of a recent origin. Indeed, her plans for the final absorption of the country were laid as early as immediately after the " Restoration." [13] Nevertheless, if the alliance had not existed, Japan would not have dared—and could not if she did dare—to effect the annexation so early as 1910. The Anglo-Japanese treaty, by giving tacit acquiescence to Japan's policy in Korea, and by recognizing Japan's right to have a free hand in that country, prevented all possibilities of foreign interference in Korea's favor, and actually encouraged Japan to take definite steps in destroying the sovereignty of Korea. Therefore, so far as Japan was concerned, the desire to establish a protectorate over Korea, and to effect ultimately the annexation of that country, sup-

[12] By the Treaty between Japan and Korea, signed August 29, 1910. For details on the establishment of the Japanese protectorate over Korea, and the annexation of that country to the Japanese Empire, see McKenzie; Homer B. Hulbert, *The Passing of Korea,* New York, 1906; Park-In Sick, *The Tragic History of Korea,* Chinese Edition, Shanghai, 1915.

[13] Henry Chung, *The Case of Korea,* pp. 42-43.

plied the principal motive for Japan to conclude
the alliance with London. As to Great Britain,
Korea was at first Great Britain's bait to Tokio in
order to induce Japan to fight Russia, and then the
price Great Britain had to pay to Japan—though
she had no right to do so—for her ally's gallant
victory over the Northern Colossus.

Still another country was covered and intimately
affected by the Anglo-Japanese Alliance. This was
China. Before 1902, and especially in the years immediately preceding that date, the attitude of the
Peking Government toward England was cordial and
friendly. This was because England, though not
hesitating to pursue now and then the policy of the
" sphere of influence," was, on the whole, standing
by the principle of the Open Door, and the independence and integrity of China.[14] As to Japan, the
Chinese were, of course, hostile to that country during the Sino-Japanese War. But during, and in the
years immediately following the period of the
" scramble for concessions," China saw in Japan a
check to Russia's policy in Manchuria, and the Chinese Emperor looked to Japan for assistance in his
programme of reformation.[15] The Peking Government believed that, for the purpose of preserving the
independence and territorial integrity of their coun-

[14] Mingchien J. Bau, *The Foreign Relations of China,* new ed.,
New York, 1922, ch. viii.

[15] Cf. A. R. Colquhoun, " The Yellow Peril," in the *Independent,*
April 14, 1904, LVI, 825 ff.

try, only three Powers could be trusted: the United States, Japan, and Great Britain.[16]

The United States, however, at the time had no desire to be involved in an entangling alliance in the Far East, nor was she strong enough, so far as her military power in that region was concerned, to render China much help. Peking officialdom well understood this fact. They, therefore, looked to Great Britain and Japan as the only two countries from which they could draw material assistance. In March, 1898, the Chinese Privy Council sounded Sir C. MacDonald, then British Minister at Peking, as to an alliance between Great Britain, Japan, and

[16] In 1902, on being asked by the Empress Dowager what foreign Power he thought could be most trusted by China, H. E. Hu Yu-fen, one of the Directors of the Northern Railway, replied, the United States. "The United States," said he, "from the highest to the lowest, cared not for the lands of other people; this being a principle with them when first that country acquired independence. As for Japan, that Power came next, although she went to war with China in 1894, yet ever since peace had been declared between the two countries Japan had never swerved from her anxiety to prove her friendship to China on the ground of being related to each other as kindred Empires occupying the same Continent. With regard to Great Britain, her sole ambition was to trade in peace and therefore she cared not to enter lightly into war with China or with any other nation. The above three Powers could therefore be trusted. As to Russia, however, her words are sweet, but her sole ambition has always been earth-hunger and the encroaching upon the territories of others, hence Russia must always be guarded against." It was also reported that the Empress Dowager appeared to approve H. E.'s words. "Sinwenpao," quoted in the *North China Herald* (The Weekly Edition of the *North-China Daily News*), New Series, February 19, 1902, LXVIII, 314. This represented the general view of the Chinese officialdom at the time.

China.[17] Failing to receive a satisfactory answer
from the British representative, China turned to
Japan, and sent two delegates to that country in the
summer of 1899, with the concealed, but none the
less real, purpose of effecting an alliance between
China and Japan.[18] During the time of the negotiation with Russia over Manchuria, after the North
China campaign, it was again these three Powers,
to wit, the United States, Great Britain, and Japan,
to which Peking turned and asked for assistance.[19]

It was, therefore, only natural that in 1902, when
the alliance between Great Britain and Japan, with
the avowed objects of maintaining the *status quo*
and general peace in the Extreme East, and the
independence and territorial integrity of the Empire
of China, was made public, the *North China Daily
News* should report that every enlightened Chinese
welcomed this agreement.[20]

[17] In a telegram to the Marquess of Salisbury on March 18, 1898,
Sir C. MacDonald, British Minister at Peking, remarked: " The
idea of an alliance between Great Britain, Japan, and China with
regard to which I was privately sounded by the Privy Council, seems
to have originated with the Hankow Viceroy, Chang Chih-tung. It
has met with much favour, the fact that China contributes nothing
to the strength of the alliance being left out of account." *Brit. Doc.*,
I, 21.

[18] London *Times*, July 24, 1899, p. 7; July 27, p. 5; July 28, p. 5;
August 12, p. 3; August 26, p. 3; October 25, p. 6. Also see Paul S.
Reinsch, *World Politics at the End of Nineteenth Century*, N. Y.,
1900, p. 181.

[19] *Parl. P.*, China, No. 2 (1904), Nos. 16, 17, 18, 24, 32, 33, 35.

[20] According to an article appearing in the *North China Daily
News*, Yuan Shih-kai, the powerful Viceroy in China, and his colleagues had, it was no secret, been for some time urging on Great

When hostilities broke out between Japan and
Russia, China's sympathy with her eastern neighbor
was undivided.[21] At the time the peace conference
met at Portsmouth China naturally desired to be
represented in so far as the negotiations affected her
rights and interests. But she was promptly silenced
by Japan, the victorious belligerent. After the peace
treaty was concluded, China protested against certain of its terms regarding Manchuria, and pointed
out " that eighteen months was a longer time than
was needed to get the two armies away from Manchuria, that there was nothing in the state of the
country to warrant so large a railway guard as was
provided by the treaty, and that while the contracting Powers obligated themselves to restore the ad-

---

Britain the conclusion of such an agreement with Japan as was signed
on January 30, 1902. They had throughout been strenuous in their
opposition to the Manchurian Convention; it was certain, therefore, that to them the agreement was most welcome. The *North
China Herald, New Series,* February 19, 1902, LXVIII, 314. Prince
Ching thought that the Anglo-Japanese Agreement " will considerably facilitate his negotiations for the evacuation of Manchuria."
Brit. Doc., II, 126. For the attitude of the Hankow Viceroy, see
Brit. Doc., II, 136.

[21] This was recognised by the Japanese. Even before the war broke
out, on July 29, 1903, Lieutenant-Colonel Wingate in a report to
the British War Office, could make the following observation:
" The Japanese place reliance on the assistance which might be
afforded them by the Chinese in Manchuria." *Brit. Doc.,* II, 211.
When the war was about to break out, Japan advised China to maintain neutrality which, for several reasons, in the opinion of the Japanese Government, was more desirable than China's joining hostilities on the side of Japan. *Brit. Doc.,* II, 232-233. For the attitude
of China toward the war and China's part during the war, see Cassell, ch. xxiv.

ministration of Manchuria to China, no date for this promised restoration was fixed." To China's surprise, Japan instead of listening to this reasonable protest, acted conjointly with Russia, so far as they noticed China's protest at all, and let it be known " that it was for them to decide these matters, and the tone of these statements conveyed the impression that China was, or would be, lucky in getting Manchuria under any terms." [22]

The attitude thus taken by the Japanese Government, together with the action of the Japanese military administration at Mukden,[23] created, naturally, no small amount of apprehension among the Chinese officials. Some of them began to suspect the intention of Japan with regard to the three Eastern provinces.[24] They felt that China was now completely isolated, and could not rely even on the Anglo-Japanese Alliance.[25] Nevertheless, the intention of Japan was not yet at the time sufficiently demonstrated. Nor did the Peking Government thoroughly understand the true significance of the Anglo-

[22] Thomas F. Millard, " The Powers and the Settlement," in *Scribners Magazine,* New York, January 1906, XXXIX, 114. Cf. *The North China Herald,* September 29, 1905, LXXVI, 706.

[23] On October 8, 1905, H. E. Chao Erh-hsun, Military Governor of Shengking, wired to Peking to the following effect: The Japanese Military administration at Mukden put obstacles in the way of the Chinese administration. The *North China Herald,* October 13, 1905, LXXVII, 59.

[24] See the *North China Daily News,* September 8, 14, 1905, in the *North China Herald,* September 15, 1905, LXXVI, 591 and 635 respectively. Cf. *North China Herald,* September 8, 1905, LXXVI, 534.

[25] *North China Herald,* October 13, 1905, LXXVII, 102.

Japanese treaty. Therefore, despite the suspicion
which many Peking officials entertained of Japan's
intention, when the second Anglo-Japanese Agreement was published, " their Majesties, the Emperor
and the Empress Dowager, were quite satisfied with
the Treaty, and Prince Ching thought that by the new
Alliance China had been saved from the incessant
intrigue and aggression which Russia, Germany and
France had hitherto cast around her, and that from
now the integrity of her territory and the protection
of China's interest were guaranteed." Even " H. E.
Viceroy Yuan Shih-Kai was impressed by the bene-
fits the Alliance between Great Britain and Japan
would confer upon China." [26]

It did not take long, however, for the Chinese
statesmen fully to appreciate the true significance of
Japan's post-war policy, for Japan's dealings with
China in the years following the Russo-Japanese
conflict, and her settlement of differences with Russia, the ambition of which country had always been
to encroach upon the territories of China, proved
beyond any doubt that the aim of Japan's post-war
policy was China, and not Russia, and that Japan
was as dangerous as any other aggressive Power.
Great Britain, being allied with Japan and friendly
toward Russia, could not, of course, be depended
upon for assistance in checking the advance of the
very Power with whom she was allied. The only
country left, which still had a free hand and could

[26] *North China Herald,* October 6, 1905, LXXVII, 4.

be trusted, was the United States. From 1907 on, the relations between China and the United States became, therefore, more and more cordial.[27]

In 1911, when the alliance was again renewed, China was too much occupied by internal troubles to pay attention to the new treaty.[28] The events during the years 1914-18, and at the peace conference, proved conclusively to China what injuries the Anglo-Japanese treaty had done to the country. Thus, early in 1920, when the question of the renewal or termination of the alliance began to appear in the world's press, a strong feeling arose in China that " one at least of the stipulations of the Treaty had not been carried out in practice—the clause referred to was that for the preservation of the common interests of all Powers in China by ensuring the independence and integrity of the Chinese Empire and the principle of equal opportunities for the commerce and industry of all nations in China." [29] Throughout the Republic there was a growing public sentiment against the renewal of the Anglo-Japanese Treaty, at least in its old form.[30] The Chinese

[27] Bau, ch. ix.

[28] Only three months later, on October 10, 1911, the Chinese Revolution broke out in Wuchang.

[29] Letter from the China Association of London to the British Foreign Office, June 21, 1921.

[30] Dr. Sun Yat-sen, Father of the Republic of China, in an interview with a representative of the *North China Herald* on June 10, 1920, declared: " I am deadly opposed to any renewal of the Anglo-Japanese Alliance. Because it will be detrimental to China. When Japan is taking aggressive measures, why does England wish to

reasons were best embodied in a memorandum presented by ten representative organisations in Shanghai to Sir Beilby Alston, then British Minister to China, who was on his way to London on furlough, July, 1920.[31] In the memorandum the Chinese representatives said:

During the last two decades there has developed the practice among the Powers of treating China as a semi-dependent country. Instead of treating directly with China concerning her affairs and welfare, they treated among themselves as if China were a mere diplomatic appendage. The Chinese people cannot but regard such practice with apprehension and resentment, especially in the case where a certain Power assumes a paternal diplomatic relationship to China and pretends to exercise a right to intervene in the diplomatic intercourse between China and any other country.

In conclusion the representatives of China stated:

In presenting this memorandum to the British Government we merely voice the sentiment of the people. In our humble opinion the changed conditions of the world to-day do not call for any further renewal of the Anglo-Japanese Alliance.

The motives of the alliance, so far as they concern China, do not exist to-day. The aggressive and imperialistic policy

---

assist her? . . . . All the Chinese are against Japan and if the Anglo-Japanese Alliance is concluded we will be against England as well." *North China Herald*, June 12, 1920, CXXXV, 642.

[31] These organisations are the Educational Association of Kiangsu Province, the Shanghai City Chamber of Commerce, the Chinese Bankers' Association, the Chinese Cotton Mill Owners' Association, the Shanghai Educational Association, the Western Returned Students' Union, the World's Chinese Students' Federation, the Overseas Federation, the Chinese Christian Union, and the National Association of Vocational Education of China.

of Russia and Germany has passed away and there is no further menace from any other Power.

The violation of the objects of the alliance by Japan has seriously embarrassed Great Britain. The renewal of the alliance, at least under the existing or similar terms, tends only to irritate China on the one hand and to cause Great Britain to share the distrust of the Chinese people so widely and deeply entertained towards Japan.

Besides, a renewal of the alliance will only cause the Chinese people strongly to suspect Great Britain's having some other motives, as the Covenant of the League of Nations covers the ground of the alliance, and China is an original member of the League.[32]

Nor did the Peking Government remain inactive. Early in 1920

instructions were . . . . sent to the Chinese Minister in London to make formal enquiries regarding the reports appearing in the press and to point out that while obviously the international arrangements of other Powers did not in the ordinary course of events concern others than the High Contracting Parties, the treatment of China merely as a territorial entity in the written text of any such agreements would no longer be tolerated by the public opinion of the country and would indeed be viewed by all as an unfriendly act.

To these first enquiries China received the following verbal reply: first, that the question of the renewal or the termination of the Anglo-Japanese alliance had not yet come up for consideration; secondly, that inasmuch as the successive agreements have been couched in the same language, it would naturally follow that if the alliance were renewed it must follow the same lines.[33]

[32] Reproduced in Wood, pp. 160-169. Also see *North China Herald*, July 10, 1920, CXXXVI, 79-80.

[33] Chinese Official Statement to the Press, June 6, 1920. For a full text, see *North China Herald*, June 12, 1920, CXXXV, 642.

15

In consequence of this reply an official memorandum was sent to the British Government, through the British Minister at Peking, in May, 1920, to the following effect:

The whole question of the Anglo-Japanese alliance affects the destiny of the Far East in general and of China in particular. The Chinese people view the proposed renewal of the alliance with deep concern and strong misgivings. Fortunately it has been an established international usage that when two friendly nations conclude a treaty, it can cover only those rights and interests which intimately belong to the nations who are parties to the agreement.

This usage has acquired fresh strength as a result of the European War, out of which has been developed the doctrine of equality of nations. The treaty of alliance in question contains reference to China and her integrity. Such reference, without China's actual participation in the conclusion of the treaty, will seriously impair the dignity and good name of her people as an independent nation. The Government and the people of China, therefore, cannot allow the matter to pass without expressing their emphatic protest.[34]

These representations of the Chinese Government and people were not without force, for China, though a weak nation in the military sense, still had one strong weapon in her possession, the economic boycott. During and following the peace conference at Paris a boycott of Japanese goods existed in China. Considerable talk of a proposed boycott against British goods appeared in 1920-21 in the native

[34] Quoted in Wood, pp. 116-117. This memorandum had also been sent to the Japanese Government. Millard, *Conflict of Policies in Asia,* p. 201.

press: the Chinese threatened to carry out the proposal in case Great Britain disregarded their wishes and renewed her alliance with Japan.

As a result, when the Conference of Prime Ministers and Representatives of the United Kingdom, the Dominions, and India, met in London during June, July, and August, 1921, to deliberate upon the Pacific and other Imperial questions, due consideration was given to China and the Chinese. " We also aim," remarked the British Prime Minister in the House of Commons when he was asked to make a statement about the position of the Anglo-Japanese Treaty as seen by the Imperial Cabinet, " at preserving the open door in China, and at giving the Chinese people every opportunity of peaceful progress and development." [35] When all the representatives of the Empire agreed that their standpoint on the Pacific and Far Eastern questions should be communicated with complete frankness to the interested Powers, with the object of securing an exchange of views which might lead to more formal discussion and conference, China was included in the list of interested Powers, and was given an opportunity, which she was entitled to have as an independent country, to express her own will over matters concerning her national welfare.[36]

Upon the same date, August 11, 1921, when the principal allied and associated Powers were invited

[35] *Par. Deb.*, 5th Series, Commons, July 11, 1921, CXLIV, 917.
[36] Ibid., July 11, 1921, CXLIV, 917; also 915.

by the President of the United States to attend " a conference on the subject of Limitation of Armament, in connection with which Pacific and Far Eastern questions should also be discussed," an invitation was sent to the Chinese Government to " participate in the discussion of Pacific and Far Eastern questions, in connection with the Conference on the subject of Limitation of Armament." [37] This invitation was promptly accepted by the Chinese Government. " It is with special satisfaction that the Government of the Republic of China makes known its desires to co-operate on a footing of equality with other governments in this beneficent movement." [38]

Four days after the opening session, when the Committee on Pacific and Far Eastern questions met for the first time, on November 16, 1921, the Chinese Delegation, headed by Dr. Alfred Sze, presented what has since been known as " China's Ten Points " which, in the opinion of the Chinese Delegation, should guide the conference in its determinations. The Third Point read:

With a view to strengthening mutual confidence and maintaining peace in the Pacific and Far East, the Powers agree not to conclude between themselves any treaty or agreement

[37] China was invited to participate only in the discussion of Pacific and Far Eastern questions. The language of the invitation was, therefore, different. Otherwise, the wording of the invitation was similar to that sent to the other Powers.

[38] Chinese reply to the American invitation to participate in the Washington Conference, August 17, 1921. For a brief discussion of the convening of the Conference, see Willoughby, *China at the Conference,* Baltimore, 1922, ch. i.

directly affecting China or the general peace in these regions
without previously notifying China and giving her an opportunity to participate.[39]

At the fourteenth meeting of the committee on
December 8, Dr. Koo of the Chinese Delegation
made a strong attack upon those agreements which
" had in the past frequently been made relating
to the Far East or to China particularly without
participation on the part of China or previous notice to the Chinese Government ";[40] and the Chinese Delegation subsequently submitted a tentative
list of Inter-Power Agreements that had, in the past,
been entered into with reference to China and asked
their cancellation. In this list the Anglo-Japanese
Treaty was included.[41]

If the Third Point proposed by the Chinese Delegation had been accepted, it would have prevented
the Powers thereafter from entering into any treaty
or agreement relating to the Far East generally and
to China in particular. It would also have prevented the extension, in any form, of the Anglo-
Japanese Alliance. It was, therefore, only natural

[39] 67th Cong., 2d Sess., S. Doc. No. 126, *Conference on the Limitation of Armament,* 1922, p. 444. At the 14th meeting of the Committee on December 8 Dr. Koo of the Chinese Delegation said that
" the essential principle laid down therein was that the Chinese
Government should have previous notification of the negotiation of
any treaty or agreement which would affect Chinese interests." *Conference on the Limitation of Armament,* p. 561.

[40] Ibid., pp. 561 ff.

[41] The tentative list was read at the sixteenth meeting of the Committee, held December 14, by Dr. Chung-Hui Wang of the Chinese
Delegation. Ibid., pp. 584 ff.

that both Mr. Balfour of the British Delegation and Mr. Hanihara of the Japanese Delegation should have vigorously opposed the adoption of the principle.[42] The resolution finally approved by the Committee, and adopted by the Conference at its fourth plenary session, held December 10, in regard to the Chinese demands in this respect, was originally proposed by Sir Auckland Geddes, and ran, in its adopted form, as follows:

That the powers attending this conference, hereinafter mentioned, to wit, the United States of America, Belgium, the British Empire, China, France, Italy, Japan, the Netherlands, and Portugal declare that it is their intention not to enter into any treaty, agreement, arrangement, or understanding, either with one another, or individually or collectively with any power or powers, which would infringe or impair the principles which have been declared by the resolution adopted November 21 by this Committee.[43]

[42] Secretary Hughes also thought that, although there should be no treaty affecting China adversely, or secret engagements between the Powers, each Power should be left free to make agreements necessary for the preservation of its own proper interests. Any general proposition going so far as to derogate or limit the right to make agreements relative to fundamental, legitimate interests, he said, would be one not easily defended. *Conference on the Limitation of Armament*, pp. 563 ff.

[43] Ibid., p. 570. "The resolution adopted November 21 by this Committee" referred to the Root principles which reads: "It is the firm intention of the Powers attending this conference hereinafter mentioned, to wit, the United States of America, Belgium, the British Empire, France, Italy, Japan, the Netherlands, and Portugal:

"(1) To respect the sovereignty, the independence and the territorial and administrative integrity of China;

"(2) To provide the fullest and most unembarrassed opportunity to China to develop and maintain for herself an effective and stable government;

This resolution as later substantially incorporated in Article II of the Nine Power Treaty relating to principles and policies to be followed in matters concerning China, read:

The Contracting Powers agree not to enter into any treaty, agreement, arrangement, or understanding, either with one another, or individually or collectively, with any Power or Powers, which would infringe or impair the principles stated in Article 1.[44]

All of the three treaties of alliance between Great Britain and Japan covered the Far East in general and China in particular. Yet, in concluding these treaties China was never once consulted; nor was she once notified after these treaties were concluded, although countries whose rights and interests were much less intimately connected with the alliance were extended this courtesy.[45] In 1902 both Japan and Great Britain were pursuing a policy which supported China's independence and integrity, and the

---

"(3) To use their influence for the purpose of effectually establishing and maintaining the principle of equal opportunity for the commerce and industry of all nations throughout the territory of China;

"(4) To refrain from taking advantage of the present conditions in order to seek special rights or privileges which would abridge the rights of the subjects or citizens of friendly States and from countenancing action inimical to the security of such States." *Conference on the Limitations of Armament,* pp. 459-460.

[44] For the full text of the Treaty, see *Conference on the Limitation of Armament,* pp. 893 ff. Article I of this Treaty embodies the four Root principles.

[45] The substance of the first agreement was communicated, before its publication, to the United States and German Governments. The second agreement was communicated to the United States, French, and Russian Governments.

Open Door doctrine in that country.[46] Thus, when
the alliance was concluded for the first time, although
the High Contracting parties mutually recognised in
the agreement each other's right to take necessary
measures for the safeguarding of their interests
within the Chinese Empire—a provision which,
when carried to its logical conclusion, would impair
China's sovereignty—the Chinese authorities welcomed the arrangement. For, in the same document
the British and Japanese Governments declared that
they were entirely uninfluenced by any aggressive
tendencies, and that they desired to maintain the
independence and integrity of China as well as the
principle of the Open Door. In 1902, everybody
understood that Russia, and not China, was the principal aim of the combination. As a result of the ever
increasing Russian menace in Manchuria, China naturally welcomed every move that had the purpose of
checking the advance of her northern neighbor.

In 1905, when the first alliance was renewed, Japan
was just beginning to pursue an aggressive policy
on the Continent, the true significance of which was
not yet well understood at Peking. The new alliance
stipulated that two of the objects of the alliance
were " the consolidation and maintenance of the general peace in the regions of Eastern Asia and India,"

[46] During the period from the Sino-Japanese War in 1894-95 to the
Russo-Japanese War in 1904-05, Japan's policy was centered on the
coming struggle with Russia. She therefore abandoned her old hostility toward China and espoused the Open Door policy in that
country. See Bau, ch. x, "The Development of Japan's Policy in
China."

and "the preservation of the common interests of all Powers in China by insuring the independence and integrity of the Chinese Empire and the principle of equal opportunities for the commerce and industry of all nations in China." These were the very objects the Chinese themselves desired. The second alliance was, therefore, on the whole, well received in China.

But the treaty of 1905 had still another object: "the maintenance of the territorial rights of the high contracting parties in the regions of Eastern Asia and of India, and the defence of their special interests in the said regions." By interpreting this clause liberally, Japan was able, under the cover of the alliance, to launch upon a career of continental expansion, to violate the Open Door doctrine, and to menace the integrity of China.[47] After the Peking Treaty of December 22, 1905, which confirmed the transfer of Russia's interests in Manchuria to Japan made by the Peace Treaty at Portsmouth, China became fully aware of the danger of Japan's aggression. After 1907, when both Russia and Great Britain were on good terms with Japan, China had leaned towards the United States.

The 1911 Anglo-Japanese agreement changed nothing, so far as the parts of the treaty relating to China were concerned.[48] Preoccupied with serious

[47] For Japan's policy in China after the Russo-Japanese War, see ibid., ch. x. Pooley, ch. ii.

[48] Those parts of the 1905 agreement relating to China were simply repeated in the 1911 treaty between Japan and Great Britain.

internal troubles at the time, China paid little attention to the new agreement. The events during the World War and at the Paris Conference, especially the controversy over Shantung, made her fully realize what harm an on-the-surface self-denying ordinance could do, and caused her to put up, therefore, a stern opposition to any renewal of the agreement. The Chinese opposition, together with the opposition of the United States, and above all, of Canada, forced the British Government to delay her decision as to the renewal of the alliance, and finally to conclude at the Washington Conference the Four-Power pact as a substitute.

It has been argued that, without the conclusion of the Anglo-Japanese Alliance, Japan would not have gone to war with Russia, and without Japan's defeat of Russia, China could not have been relieved of the Russian incubus. But it must be remembered that Japan fought primarily for her own existence, and that it was only incidentally that she fought to relieve China of the Russian nightmare. Moreover, the position of Russia in China was immediately taken up by Japan. Thereafter, she did many things to impair China's integrity, and to injure her sovereignty to a degree which even the Russians never dreamed of. The Anglo-Japanese Alliance, by holding the hand of Great Britain, encouraged Japan's aggression in China, and prevented from being effective any foreign intervention in China's favor.

CHAPTER VII

The United States and the Alliance

One country that was neither a party to the Alliance, nor covered by it, and yet whose interests were closely involved, was the United States. The interest of the United States in the Far East has always been a purely commercial one. She has never sought for special privileges; she has always tried to maintain the most friendly relations with the Eastern countries.[1]

When the Sino-Japanese relations became strained in 1894, the United States pursued a " policy of scrupulous fairness," in order to retain the confidence which both China and Japan had in its goodwill.[2] During the war, both belligerents trusted the interests of their nationals in the enemy country to the care of the United States representatives.[3]

---

[1] For American relations with the Eastern countries during the 19th century see John W. Foster, *American Diplomacy in the Orient,* Boston, 1903. For American policy in China, see Bau, ch. ix. For the relations between the United States and Japan, see Treat.

[2] In the course of the interviews with both the Chinese and Japanese Ministers, the Secretary of State, Mr. Gresham " had made it clear to them that the United States had no policy in Asia to be endangered by the war, and that thus occupying a position of absolute and impartial neutrality toward the belligerents, the President, however solicitous to see the restoration of peace, would in no event go beyond acting as a mere peacemaker upon the request of both parties." *For. Rel.,* 1894, App. I, p. 92. See also, p. 76.

[3] Ibid., pp. 95, 97, 98, 99, 100. App. I, pp. 37, 42, 43, 50.

Throughout the period of hostilities, the Government of the United States had acted quite independently, and had abstained from even a friendly intervention,[4] although it had promised to tender its good offices if they would be acceptable to both belligerents.[5]

[4] On being asked to " adjust the difficulty and avert a conflict," the American Secretary of State, Mr. Gresham, told the Korean Minister that " while the United States sympathized with his Government and desired to see its sovereignty respected, we must maintain toward it and the other powers an attitude of impartial neutrality; that our influence could be exerted with Japan only in a friendly way, and that in no event could we intervene jointly with other powers." Ibid., 1894, App. I, p. 37. See also pp. 31, 38, 39, 70, 74, 77, 81.

[5] On November 6, 1894, Mr. Dun, American Minister at Tokio, was instructed to " ascertain whether a tender of his [the American President's] good offices in the interests of a peace alike honorable to both nations would be acceptable to the Government at Tokio." Ibid., App. I, p. 76. See also ibid., pp. 77, 78. On November 17, Japan declined the offer and gave the reason that China had not yet approached Japan directly. Ibid., 1894, App. I, p. 79. See also p. 80. For America's part as a peacemaker, during the war of 1894-95, see ibid., pp. 22, 23, 80, 81, 84. After the conclusion of peace, the Emperor of Japan addressed a personal letter to the President of the United States. It read:

" Great and Good Friend: During the war between our Empire and that of China, which has now happily been brought to an end by the conclusion of a treaty of peace, the diplomatic and consular officers of the United States in China, with Your Excellency's gracious permission and acting under Your Excellency's wise direction, extended their friendly offices to our subjects in China and on many occasions afforded them succor and assistance.

"Again, as the war was nearing its final stage, the representatives of the United States at Tokio and Peking, by Your Excellency's authorization, provided the way whereby China was able to approach directly our Government, and it was through the facilities afforded by those two representatives by direct reciprocal communication between the Governments of Japan and China that all the prelimi-

After the Treaty of Shimonoseki, a period of great activity on the part of the Continental Powers, with Russia taking the lead, began in China. This period " was marked, from the first, by complete disregard on the part of the great European nations of China's integrity, a period characterized by a general scramble to gain particular concessions and counter concessions and to establish ' spheres of influence.' " [6] The United States Government, with great commercial interests in China to look after, was, quite naturally, keenly interested in these developments. During this period, it had not only to protect the American economic interests against foreign aggression; it had also to protect American citizens against the anti-foreign riots in China. In both, the Department of State had maintained a policy of acting independently as far as possible, and had always kept in view that American policy had as its aim only the protection of American interests.

---

naries looking to the opening of negotiations for the definite termination of hostilities were adjusted. The manner in which those delicate services in the interest of peace were performed left nothing to be desired.

"And we take this opportunity to express to Your Excellency our high appreciation of those acts on the part of Your Excellency as well as on the part of Your Excellency's officers, acting under Your Excellency's wise directions, which not only tended to mitigate the severities and hardships of the war and finally to promote the successful issue of the negotiations for peace, but served to draw still closer the bonds of friendship and good neighborhood which happily unite our two countries." Quoted in Treat, pp. 156-157.

[6] Stanley K. Hornbeck, *Contemporary Politics in the Far East*, New York, 1916, p. 221.

In 1895, since the beginning of June, serious anti-foreign riots had broken out in China. On August 12, Mr. Denby, American Minister at Peking, was instructed to " consult with the minister of Great Britain and co-operate so far as conducive to security and welfare of the United States citizens." Otherwise he should " act independently and carefully; abstain from joining in any course or policy which, however important to British interests, did not concern those of the United States." [7] Following a massacre of missionaries in Kutien, an investigation was made concurrently by China, Great Britain, and the United States. Upon the request of the Chinese Government that Minister Denby should be instructed " not to unite with the British Minister at Peking in causing difficulties to the Chinese Government, and thus hamper its action and seriously hinder the execution of its good intentions," the Department of State gave in reply the positive assurance that " this Government was investigating the Kutien riots concurrently with Great Britain only so far as was necessary to protect American interests of person and property, and not to assist that power in any supposed ulterior political object." [8]

If the United States Government, in protecting its citizens in China, had adopted a policy of avoiding interference or connection with European complications, it certainly had no more desire to bind her-

[7] *For. Rel.*, 1895, part I, pp. 102-103.
[8] Ibid., p. 122.

self to, or to get entangled with the policies of, foreign Powers in China by taking joint actions with those Powers, though such actions might protect America's economic interests. In December, 1896, the American Minister at Peking had already been instructed to " employ all proper methods for the extension of American commercial interests in China." [9] The drastic actions taken by Germany and Russia early in 1898 affected American trade interests as well as those of other commercial countries. Anxiety was thus aroused at Washington as to future Russian and German policies with respect to trade in those regions of China which they had practically annexed by means of leases, and Secretary Sherman, in a dispatch to Mr. White, American Ambassador in Berlin, wrote:

The subject [of trade] is naturally one of interest to the United States, this Government having been among the first to bring about the opening of China to foreign commerce and the relations of the United States with the Chinese Empire having been since that time of large and growing importance. [10]

Nevertheless, when, on March 8, 1898, the British Ambassador, by a confidential and unofficial memorandum, inquired " whether the British Government could count on the co-operation of the United States in opposing action by foreign Powers which might tend to restrict freedom of commerce of

[9] December 19, 1896, Olney to Denby, ibid., 1897, p. 56.
[10] (Department of State) D. S., To Germany, XX, No. 347, Feb. 11, 1898, Sherman to White, quoted in Alfred L. P. Dennis, *Adventures in American Diplomacy*, 1896-1906, N. Y., 1928, p. 182.

all nations in China either by imposing preferential conditions or by obtaining actual cession of Chinese coast territory,'' the Secretary of State answered that '' the President was in sympathy with the policy which should maintain open trade in China, that all his advices up to . . . . [that] time indicated no foreign occupation which interfered with that trade or aimed at exclusive commercial privileges, and that he did not see any . . . . reason for the departure of the United States from our traditional policy of respecting (sic) foreign alliances and so far as practicable avoiding interference or connection with European complications.'' [11]

In 1898 Great Britain was beginning to feel the danger of her '' splendid isolation,'' and certain British statesmen were earnestly desirous of concluding an alliance with the United States regarding the Far Eastern situation. On March 25, in a report to Secretary Sherman, Ambassador Hay remarked:

I may add that in my conversation during the last few days with men connected with public affairs, the situation of things on the Pacific Coast is regarded with utmost concern. They seem to think there is an understanding between Russia, France and Germany to exclude, as far as possible, the trade of England and America from the Far East, and to divide and reduce China to a system of tributary provinces.[12]

It was with this in mind that the British statesmen were trying to build up an alliance between the

[11] (Hay Papers) H. P., March 17, 1898, Sherman to White, quoted in Dennis, pp. 170-171.

[12] D. S., From London, CXCI, No. 325, March 25, 1898, Hay to Sherman, quoted in Dennis, p. 198.

United States and Great Britain. On May 13, in a speech at Birmingham, Mr. Chamberlain, British Colonial Secretary, after trying to impress upon his audience the possibility that Great Britain might be " confronted at any moment with a combination of Great Powers so powerful that not even the most extreme, the most hotheaded politician would be able to contemplate it without a certain sense of uneasiness," advocated an alliance with the United States:

What is our next duty? It is to establish and to maintain bonds of permanent amity with our kinsman across the Atlantic. They are a powerful and a generous nation. They speak our language, they are bred of our race. Their laws, their literature, their standpoint upon every question are the same as ours; their feeling, their interest in the cause of humanity and the peaceful development of the world are identical with ours. I do not know what the future has in store for us. I do not know what arrangements may be possible with us, but this I know and feel—that the closer, the more cordial, the fuller, and the more definite these arrangements are, with the consent of both peoples, the better it will be for both and for the world. And I even go so far as to say that, terrible as war may be, even war itself would be cheaply purchased if in a great and noble cause the Stars and Stripes and the Union Jack should wave together over the Anglo-Saxon alliance. Now, it is one of the most satisfactory results of Lord Salisbury's policy that at the present time these two great nations understand each other better than they have ever done since more than a century ago. They were separated by the blunder of the British Government.[13]

[13] London *Times,* May 14, 1898, p. 12.

16

To the same end Mr. A. R. Colquhoun, the special correspondent of the London *Times,* wrote:

The result of my journey in the north—through Siberia to Peking—has been to strengthen the views held by me; and unless steps be taken by Britain to assert herself in the Yangtze Valley, so as to prevent it passing into the hands of some Power that will not allow the open door, she will be squeezed out in Central China, as she has been in the North.

The process of partition is in full operation, and Britain and the United States should make up their minds which of the two policies they will press for; to couple the two—"open door" and "sphere" (as Lord Charles Beresford is doing I believe) will lead to failure.

I view with increasing apprehension the growing influence of Russia in China, and there is one aspect of the question which deserves attention; viz. that Russia has not only acquired an important coast line on the Pacific, but has now the command of first class and cheap material (men and coal) for building up her sea port, for which she is at present dependent upon France.

I trust that the United States will give full consideration to the Chinese question, and that action will be taken while there is time.[14]

To these writings and public utterances the United States turned a deaf ear.[15] In January, 1899, both the British and American Governments were protesting at Peking against the extension of French concessions at Shanghai. Lord Salisbury seized this opportunity and made overtures to Washington to the

---

[14] A letter of Mr. Colquhoun of January 12, 1899, quoted in Dennis, p. 198.

[15] These discussions were reported by the American Ambassador at London to the Department of State.

effect that " if these protests were made conjointly their force would thereby be much increased." [16] The British suggestion was rejected by Washington, and Secretary Hay made it clear in his reply that Mr. Conger, the new American Minister in China, was " only to act regarding American interests." [17]

In the year 1898 Lord Charles Beresford, a member of British Parliament, in his trip to China, had preached the doctrine of the Open Door. He based " all his hopes of keeping the door open by enlisting the sympathies of America during his trip across the continent." [18] In November, in a letter to Secretary Hay, he wrote:

I am glad to tell you that nothing could exceed the cordiality that I have met with from every American citizen out here and the interest they take in my mission is most gratifying. They have all been in sympathy with the views I communicated to you before I left England. As America has got over 50 per cent. of the important trade into the north of China, it is imperative for American interests as well as our own, that the policy of the " open door " should be maintained. I have every hope that in the near future the suggested commercial alliance

[16] H. P., January 8, 1899, Pauncefote to Hay, quoted in Dennis, p. 199. According to John Hay, Lord Salisbury had proposed to him an Anglo-American Agreement to defend the integrity of China and the Open Door, before he left England, and he had rejected the proposal. Hay to his Wife, Oct. 29, 1900, Hay, Letters, etc., III, 199, Dennis, p. 251.

[17] D. S., To French Embassy, X, No. 226, June 12, 1899, Hay to Cambon; From London, CXCV, No. 647, January 19, White to Hay; For. Rel., 1899, pp. 143-50. Dennis, p. 199.

[18] H. P., January 6, 1899, Wildman (American Consul General at Hongkong) to Hay, quoted in Dennis, p. 199.

between Great Britain and America with reference to the " open door " in China, may become an absolute fact.[19]

Subsequently, he published his book *The Break-up of China,* in which he sought to prove the identity of interests of Great Britain and the United States and the necessity of an Anglo-American policy in China.[20] By this book, and by his speeches made in the United States, Lord Charles Beresford greatly aroused public opinion in the States on the Chinese question. Early in 1899, the reports from the American Minister at Peking also suggested that some immediate action should be taken by Washington to protect American commerce. In a report on the Italian attempt to secure a lease of the bay of San Moon, Mr. Conger, American Minister at Peking, observed:

This action of the Italian Government is only additional evidence of the general belief that China is going to pieces and the purpose of another of the powers to make a preemption before it is too late, the title to which can be more easily perfected when the break up comes.

I do not know what the desire of the Department is upon this question nor its proposed policy; but if it shall deem it advisable to own or control a good coaling station on the Chinese coast, or if it wishes to be a party to the division and a sharer in the assets, then it is necessary the place be selected and its session or lease demanded at once; even now it may be too late.

[19] H. P., November 29, 1898, Beresford to Hay, quoted in Dennis, p. 186.
[20] Charles Beresford, *The Break-up of China,* London, 1899.

[His own opinion, however, was that] a permanent ownership of territory (except for a coaling station if that was
needed) in China was not desirable. But if all China was
to fall into the hands of European powers, a strong foothold
here by the United States, with something tangible to offer
them, might compel them to keep permanently open doors for
our commerce.[21]

It was then evident that the United States had to
take some action to keep the Chinese door open before it was too late. Mr. W. W. Rockhill, the distin-
guished American diplomat, on being asked by Secretary Hay to express his views on the matter, presented a memorandum, on August 28. In his covering letter to the Secretary of State, he said:

In view of the great weight which Beresford's book seems
to have with the American public I have reviewed in the
Memorandum the principal points of his work. This shows—
if it is necessary to show it—that the policy suggested as
that best suited to our interests is not a British one—for
England is as great an offender in China as Russia itself.[22]

In the memorandum Mr. Rockhill thus criticized
Beresford's plan:

That the existence of a strong and well officered and disci-
plined army and navy in China might assist that country to
ward off the attacks of a foreign foe, is likely; that, in the
absence of such a force, and with the present aggressive policy
of some of the Treaty Powers, the creation of " Spheres of
interest " (or influence) easily reached by rail or by sea by

[21] D. S., From China, CVI, No. 155, March 1, 1899, Conger to
Hay, quoted in Dennis, pp. 207-208.
[22] H. P., Holland House, New York, August 28, 1899, Rockhill to
Hay, quoted in Dennis, p. 186.

the interested Powers from their own territory, should be held
to be the only way of insuring China against complete partition, is comprehensible; but that the United States should
lend a hand to the carrying out of either of these two policies
seems absolutely suicidal to our vast and growing interests
in that part of the world.[23]

He suggested:

In view of the probability of complications soon arising
between the interested powers in China, whereby it will become difficult, if not impossible, for the United States to
retain the rights guaranteed them by treaties with China,
. . . . we should at once initiate negotiations to obtain from
those Powers who have acquired zones of interest in China
formal assurance that (1) they will in no way interfere within
their so-called spheres of interest with any treaty port or
with vested rights in it of any nature; (2) that all ports
they may open in their respective spheres shall either be free
ports, or that the Chinese treaty tariff at the time in force
shall apply to all merchandise landed or shipped, no matter
to what nationality belonging, and that the dues and duties
provided for by treaty shall be collected by the Chinese Government; and (3) that they will levy no higher harbor dues on
vessels of other nationalities frequenting their ports in such
spheres, than shall be levied on their national vessels, and that
they will also levy no higher railroad charges on merchandise
belonging to or destined for subjects of other powers transported through their spheres than shall be levied on similar
merchandise belonging to its own nationality.[24]

As a result, despite the British representations
and the public utterances of the British statesmen
urging that the two Anglo-Saxon countries should

---

[23] H. P., August 28, 1899, Rockhill to Hay, quoted in Dennis, p. 211.
[24] Ibid., p. 212.

work together in China, the Washington Government rejected the idea of an Anglo-American policy and adopted a policy along an entirely different line.[25] Following the recommendations of Mr. Rockhill the Secretary of State sent his famous note to the interested powers—to Great Britain, Germany, and Russia on September 6, to Japan on November 13, to Italy on the 17th, and to France on the 21st—and asked them to give formal assurances that they would adhere to the principle of equal opportunity of trade in the Chinese Empire.[26] To this request Italy alone gave an unconditional assent.[27] All the other powers replied that they would assent if the others would.[28] The replies of Germany, Russia and France, in fact, hardly did more than promise to apply most favored nation treatment. The Secretary then made a clever stroke, announcing, on March 20, 1900, that the condition originally attached to the acceptance of the Hay note " that all other powers concerned should likewise accept the proposals of the United States

[25] Secretary Hay was in favor of an alliance with England and Japan to check the aggressions of the powers on China, but President McKinley preferred adopting an independent policy and requesting the other powers to consent to it. John H. Latané, *A History of American Foreign Policy,* New York, 1927, p. 565.

[26] *For. Rel.,* 1899; To London, p. 131; To Berlin, p. 129; To St. Petersburg, p. 140; To Japan, p. 138; To Italy, p. 136, and To France, p. 128.

[27] Ibid., 1899, January 7, 1900, p. 138.

[28] Ibid., 1899, From France, December 16, 1899, p. 128; From Germany, February 19, 1900, p. 131; From Great Britain, November 30, 1899, p. 136. Cf. September 29, p. 135; From Japan, December 26, p. 139; From Russia, December 18-30, p. 141.

. . . . having been complied with, this Government
will therefore consider the assent given to it . . . .
as final and definitive.''[29] In this way the United
States secured an open approval of the Open Door
policy in China from each of the interested powers,
and yet incurred no treaty obligations, thus avoiding foreign complications.

Then came the North China campaign in which
American troops took a prominent part with those
of England, Russia, France, and Japan in the march
to Peking for the relief of the legations. Yet,
throughout the crisis and during the negotiations
which followed, the United States Government,
while cooperating with the other powers, maintained, on the whole, a free and independent position. Early in 1900 Mr. Conger, American Minister
at Peking, had sent to the Tsungli Yamen an identic
note with the French, English, and German Minister urging that '' an imperial decree be published
and promulgated, ordering by name the complete
suppression and abolition '' of the Boxer societies.[30]
In a dispatch on March 22, Secretary Hay com-
mented on the identical note and said:

While the Department finds no objection to the general
terms of this paper, it would have preferred if you had made
separate representation on the question instead of the mode
adopted, as the position of the United States in relation to
China makes it expedient that, while circumstances may

[29] Ibid., 1899, p. 142.
[30] Ibid., 1900, pp. 93-94 and 96.

sometimes require that it act on lines similar to those other
treaty powers follow, it should do so singly and without the
cooperation of other powers.[31]

On June 8, when the Boxer movement had become
more serious, Mr. Hay instructed Mr. Conger by a
telegram to—

Act independently in protection of American interests where
practicable, and concurrently with representatives of other
powers [only] if necessity arise.[32]

Two days later the Secretary again emphasized
this policy and instructed Mr. Conger:

We have no policy in China except to protect with energy
American interests, and especially American citizens and the
legations. There must be nothing done which would commit
us to future action inconsistent with your standing instructions. There must be no alliances.[33]

This policy of the United States was carried out.
On July 3, the American Government made a statement of its policy in a circular telegram to the powers. As thus declared, the policy of the United States
was " to seek a solution which may bring about permanent safety and peace to China, preserve Chinese
territorial and administrative entity, protect all
rights guaranteed to friendly powers by treaty and
international law, and safeguard for the world the
principle of equal and impartial trade with all parts
of the Chinese Empire." [34] To this all the powers

[31] Ibid., 1900, p. 111.
[32] Ibid., 1900, p. 143.
[33] Ibid., 1900, p. 143.
[34] Ibid., 1901, App. 12.

concurred, nominally at least, and on September 7, 1907, the final protocol for the settlement of the disturbances of 1900 was signed.[35]

But the question of Manchuria was not settled. Russia was not only reluctant to withdraw her troops from that region; she was actively engaged in a policy which would have made Manchuria a Russian protectorate. In November, 1900, a secret agreement was signed between Admiral Alexiev and the Tartar General of Mukden.[36] This secret convention, if ratified, would have given Russia the right to close Manchuria to all foreign trade. Naturally, it was opposed by all the commercial powers.[37] Taking this opportunity, the Japanese Government made inquiry to the United States Government as to what the policy of the United States would be in view of this violation by Russia of her pledges and promises. To this the Secretary of State replied that " we were not at present prepared to attempt singly, or in concert with other Powers, to enforce these views as to the integrity of China in the east by any demonstration which could present a character of hostility to any other Power." [38]

As a result, Japan and Great Britain reached an agreement alone, and in no stage of the negotiations

[35] MacMurray, I, 278 ff.

[36] Above, ch. ii.

[37] Great Britain, Japan, the United States, and Germany warned China of the danger of negotiating with one power while she was trying to restore friendly relations with all. Treat, p. 177.

[38] D. S., Numerical File, DXLVII, memorandum, February 1, 1901, quoted in Dennis, p. 242.

was the United States consulted. Secretary Hay
assured Count Sassini, the Russian Ambassador, on
March 6, 1902, " that the Government of the United
States was entirely foreign to the recent agreement
[the Anglo-Japanese Alliance]; that it was not even
approached in regard to it; and that since its negotiation the Government of the United States has
never been asked to give its adhesion to the agreement." [39]

Communication of the substance of the Anglo-
Japanese alliance was, however, made to the United
States Government before its publication, but the
United States Government did not announce its
opinion upon it until the text of the treaty was published.[40] It then expressed its gratification that the
alliance had as its aim the preservation of the independence of China, but reserved liberty of action on
the part of the United States with regard to the protection of its own interests in China and Korea.[41]
There is no doubt that the United States was pleased
to see other powers making alliances to do the chores
for her.[42] This feeling was abundantly reflected in

[39] D. S., Numerical File, DXLVII, memo., March 6, 1902, Dennis,
pp. 374-376. Cf. ibid., DXLVII, memo., January 16, 1902.

[40] *Par. Deb.*, 4th Series, CII, 1246-47.

[41] Dennis, p. 352.

[42] On the occasion of the conclusion of the Anglo-German Agreement of 1900, Secretary Hay wrote to Adams: " Our position was a
matter of course. We can't make alliances, but we can't object to
other powers making all alliances to do our chores for us." Hay,
Letters, etc., III, 201, quoted in Dennis, pp. 238-239.

the press. An extract from the New York *Evening Sun* is worthy of being quoted:

> The new dual alliance . . . . will result in the carrying out of an American theory in practice. It must be all the more satisfactory to us when we consider that the thing has been done without this country's breaking through the rule to avoid all entangling alliances. China, with her teeming millions, will be open to our trade and commerce. We alone of the nations will not pay for the privilege. Each of the other Powers will be restricted in some way as the result of this new arrangement.[43]

From 1902 to the outbreak of hostilities between Japan and Russia, the United States continued to act independently,[44] despite the fact that Lord Lansdowne still thought it most important that an understanding should be reached between the United

[43] Quoted in London *Times* February 13, 1902, p. 5. For brief summaries of the United States press opinion, see also ibid., February 14, p. 3; February 15, p. 7. Cf. the *Nation*, New York, February 20, 1902, LXXIV, 144. Dennis, p. 352.

[44] Indeed Count Cassini was almost fulsome in his tribute to the skill which Secretary Hay had shown in making his inquiry yet at the same time avoiding anything like the appearance of joint action with Great Britain and Japan. Dennis, p. 353. The policy of the United States in the Far East in 1902-04 was defined clearly in a letter which Secretary Hay wrote to President Roosevelt on May 1, 1902: "We are not in any attitude of hostility towards Russia in Manchuria. On the contrary, we recognize her exceptional position in northern China. What we have been working for two years to accomplish, if assurances are to count for anything, is that, no matter what happens eventually in northern China and Manchuria, the United States shall not be placed in any worse position than while the country was under the unquestioned dominion of China." Quoted in Tyler Dennett, *Roosevelt and the Russo-Japanese War*, New York, 1925, pp. 135-136.

States, Great Britain and Japan with regard to the action which they should take in dealing with the Manchurian question.[45]

The war between Russia and Japan broke out on February 9, 1904, and Japan immediately made known that she was fighting for the Open Door and the integrity of China.[46] The United States believed that Japan was fighting a battle for all the commercial countries, and, naturally, public opinion in America was strongly favorable to Japan during the conflict.[47] After the destruction of the Russian fleet in the Sea of Japan at the end of May, 1905, President Roosevelt, with the help of the German Kaiser, mediated, and the treaty of peace between Russia and Japan was finally signed on September 5 at Portsmouth, New Hampshire.[48]

While the plenipotentiaries of Russia and Japan were negotiating peace at Portsmouth, the new alliance between Great Britain and Japan was signed at

[45] *Brit. Doc.*, XI, 207. Cf. ibid., p. 199.

[46] Japanese Imperial Rescript Comprising Declaration of War Against Russia, February 10, 1904, quoted in Dennett, pp. 145-146.

[47] Treat, p. 180. Jacob H. Schiff, "Japan after the War," in the *North American Review*, Aug., 1906, CLXXXIII, 161 ff. The Russo-Japanese conflict was essentially a war, not for the integrity or independence of either Korea or China but for the control of both. According to Mr. Dennett, " it is not perfectly clear whether President Roosevelt realized this aspect of the situation. We incline, however, to believe that he did realize it. The choice presented to him was not between the independence of these states and their dependence, but between their dependence on Russia and their dependence on Japan. President Roosevelt preferred Japan to Russia." Dennett, pp. 143-144.

[48] Ibid., chs. viii and ix.

London. The second Anglo-Japanese treaty of alliance, besides having as it objects the maintenance of the general peace in the regions of Eastern Asia, and the preservation of the Open Door and integrity of China, by relieving Japan of all apprehension of vindictive action on the part of Russia in the future, made it easier for Japan to moderate her demands, and thus facilitated the negotiations of peace at Portsmouth.

As the new alliance would greatly influence the terms of the Russo-Japanese treaty of peace, the nature of its terms was communicated by the British Government to President Roosevelt even before the alliance itself was signed.[49] When the alliance was published, all the British papers admitted that " the new alliance made Great Britain and Japan absolute arbiters in the Far East." " Lords of Asia " was the way the *Evening Mail* put it, adding: " By virtue of their armaments Great Britain and Japan are able to overmatch any possible combination of the Powers, and to do it with such palpable ease that hereafter in that theater it will be necessary for them, in order to accomplish any joint object, merely to show their hands, not to play them."[50] The United States, or at least Government circles in Washington, however, failed to see that the Anglo-Japanese treaty was in a very few years to operate greatly to her disadvantage. Thus, we

---

[49] Ibid., p. 257.
[50] London *Times*, September 28, 1905, p. 3.

find that " satisfaction was expressed in Government circles in Washington with the new Anglo-Japanese Treaty," and that " the absolute assurance of the maintenance of the policy of the open door in China established by the late Mr. Hay was considered especially gratifying." [51]

This was because the American statesmen failed to foresee that Japan was soon to adopt an imperialistic policy in both China and Korea, a policy which was no less threatening to the commercial interest of the United States than had been the policy which Russia had pursued before the war.[52]

[51] London *Times*, September 29, 1905, p. 3. Certain Americans, including President Roosevelt, believed in the desirability of an Anglo-American-Japanese Alliance in 1905. But the constitutional provision that no treaty with foreign countries could be valid without the consent of the Senate prevented even an understanding amounting to a confidential informal agreement. Dennett, pp. 113-116. On July 29, 1905, Count Katsura, Japanese Premier and Minister for Foreign Affairs, had a conversation with a personal representative of President Roosevelt. The American, after saying that it was impossible for the United States Government to conclude an alliance with Great Britain and Japan, said that " he felt sure that without any agreement at all the people of the United States was [*sic*] so fully in accord with the people of Japan and Great Britain in the maintenance of peace in the Far East that whatever occasion arose appropriate action of the Government of the United States, in conjunction with Japan and Great Britain, for such a purpose could be counted on by them quite as confidently as if the United States were under treaty obligation to take [it.] " This view on behalf of President Roosevelt was later confirmed by the President. An agreed memorandum of this conversation was drawn up. This memorandum was quoted in part in Dennett, pp. 112-114.

[52] In June (16th), 1905, Roosevelt remarked: " I do not believe that she [Japan] will look toward the Philippines until affairs are settled on the mainland of Asia in connection with China, even if she ever looks toward them, and on the mainland in China her policy is the policy to which we are already committed," quoted in ibid., p. 166.

With regard to Korea, Roosevelt took, early in 1905, the attitude that " we cannot possibly interfere for the Koreans against Japan," for " they could not strike one blow in their own defence." [53] With such a low estimate of the Koreans, the President naturally refused to receive Mr. Hulbert when he arrived at Washington on a mission to ask for American aid, by virtue of the first article of the treaty of 1882 between Korea and the United States, on behalf of the Korean Emperor. " So far from pleading the case of Korea [54] with Japan, America was the first to fall in with and give its open assent to the destruction of the old administration. On the first intimation from Japan it agreed, without inquiry and with almost indecent haste, to withdraw its Minister from Seul." [55]

With China, the case was entirely different. The United States could not so light-heartedly give up

[53] Roosevelt to Hay, January 28, 1905, quoted in ibid., p. 110.

[54] The first Article of the American-Korean Treaty of 1882 read: " If other Powers deal unjustly or oppressively with either government the other will exert their good offices, on being informed of the case, to bring about an amicable arrangement, thus showing their friendly feelings."

[55] F. A. McKenzie, pp. 130-131. In fact, on July 29, 1905, the representative of President Roosevelt, in his conversation with Count Katsura, had already " fully admitted the justness of the Count's observations that Korea should be put under Japanese control, and remarked to the effect that, in his personal opinion, the establishment by Japanese troops of a suzerainty over Korea to the extent of requiring that Korea enter into no foreign treaties without the consent of Japan was the logical result of the present war and would directly contribute to permanent peace in the East," quoted in Dennett, p. 114.

the Chinese market, with its tremendous possibilities. In April, 1905, when President Roosevelt was mediating between Russia and Japan, he had imposed upon Japan the restriction that she should give a full pledge to respect the Open Door in Manchuria and to restore Manchuria to China.[56] Five days later, on April 25, Baron Komura, Japanese Minister for Foreign Affairs, replied: "Japan adheres to the position of maintaining Open Door in Manchuria and of restoring that province to China."[57] The events in the years following, however, proved that Japan, despite her pledges to respect the Open Door and integrity of China, had adopted a policy injurious to China's integrity as well as to the Open Door. On July 30, 1907, Japan reached an agreement with Russia to divide the Chinese spoils, and it then became clear that Japan had abandoned her pre-war policy in China.

In 1907, Mr. Taft was visiting the Far East. At a banquet given in his honor under the auspices of the American Association of Shanghai, on the 8th of October, the American Secretary of War observed that

for our present purpose the attitude of the United States toward China must be regarded not alone as a country interested in the trade of China, but also as a Power owning territory in China's immediate neighborhood. . . . . the trade,

[56] Roosevelt to Taft, April 20, 1905, quoted in Dennett, p. 178.

[57] Barnes to Wm. Loeb, Jr., April 25, 1905, transmitting a telegram from the Japanese Minister for Foreign Affairs, quoted in Dennett, pp. 179-180.

17

both exports and imports, between China and the United
States is second only to that of Great Britain. . . . . It is
certain, therefore, that the American Chinese trade is sufficiently great to require the Government of the United States
to take every legitimate means to protect it against diminu-
tion or injury by the political preference of any of its competitors. It cannot, of course, complain of loss of trade effected
by the use of greater enterprise, greater ingenuity, greater
attention to the demands of the Chinese market and greater
business acumen by its competitors, but it would have the right
to protest against exclusion from Chinese trade by a departure from the policy of the open door. The acquiescence
in this policy by all interested nations was so unhesitating and
emphatic that it is hardly worth while to speculate as to the
probable attitude of the United States were its merchants'
interests injured by a violation of it. How far the United
States would go in the protection of its Chinese trade no one
of course could say. This much is clear, however, that the
merchants of the United States are being roused to the importance of their Chinese export trade, that they would view
political obstacles to its expansion with deep concern, and
that this feeling of theirs would be likely to find expression in
the attitude of the American government. . . . . While we
have been slow in rousing ourselves to the importance of a
trade which has grown without government encouragement
and almost without business effort to its present important
proportions, I feel sure that in the future there will be no
reason to complain of seeming government indifference to it.[58]

Inoffensive and pacific in tone as this utterance
was, and containing no specific reference to Japan,
it was nevertheless a direct warning to Tokio, and
indicated that an energetic and forward policy in

[58] *North China Herald,* October 11, 1907, pp. 100 ff.

China was contemplated by the Washington Government.[59] To allay the growing excitement in America with regard to Japanese policy in Manchuria, the Japanese Ambassador at Washington, Baron Takahara, exchanged notes on November 30, 1908, with Mr. Root, the American Secretary of State, to the effect that the policy of both Governments was " to encourage the free and peaceful development of their commerce on the Pacific," to maintain " the existing *status quo* in the region above mentioned," to defend " the principle of equal opportunity for commerce and industry in China," to respect reciprocally " the territorial possessions belonging to each other," and " to preserve the common interest of all powers in China by supporting by all pacific means at their disposal the independence and integrity of China," and the principle of the Open Door. Finally, the notes provided for mutual communication in order to arrive at a common understanding should any event occur threatening the *status quo* and the Open Door as above defined.[60]

In 1909, the United States, taking the opportunity of the joint enterprise of American and British firms to construct the Chinchou-Aigun Railway, proposed the famous Knox plan of " neutralization " of all

[59] According to Mr. Thomas F. Millard, the new Japanese-American relations may be said to have begun on the date of the delivery of Mr. Taft's speech of October 8, 1907, at Shanghai. Thomas F. Millard, " Our Blundering Diplomacy in the Far East," in the *American Magazine*, July. 1910, LXX, 417.

[60] MacMurray, 1, pp. 769-771.

the railways of Manchuria.[61] Both Japan and Russia opposed the scheme. England, being an ally of Japan and friend of Russia, refused to give any support to the American plan. The project thus fell through.[62]

The conflict of interests in Manchuria, however, did not form the only cause of ill feelings between Japan and the United States. From the opening of Japan to the beginning of the Russo-Japanese war the relations between the United States and Japan had been uniformly friendly, but in 1905 a sudden change in public opinion occurred in both countries. Hardly had the Portsmouth Treaty been concluded, when an effort was made by a certain section of the American Press, led by the New York *Times,* to lessen the popular admiration for the Japanese. The reason for this *volte face* was, apparently, to be found in the alarm of the commercial interests of the United States at the expected great extension of Japan's trade with China and other parts of the Orient.[63]

In Japan, there were many who believed that the terms of peace were humiliating to Japan, and that

[61] The neutralization plan of Secretary Knox in 1909 was foreshadowed by the suggestion of Mr. Conger, the American Minister at Peking, on March 31, 1905, on behalf of the Chinese Government, that the Manchurian railway be transferred to China after the war under an international guarantee both for its protection and for whatever payment might be necessary either to Russia or to Japan. Dennett, pp. 157-158.

[62] Above, ch. v.

[63] Cf. London *Times,* September 12, 1905, p. 3.

the United States, being the mediator of peace, was responsible for such humiliating terms. There was also the immigration question which came to the front in the following years. The action taken by the Western States of the United States on the immigration problem and the school question stung the sensitive Japanese to the quick, and largely destroyed whatever good feeling there still remained in the two countries toward each other. Consequently, after 1905, there were alarming statements regarding American-Japanese relations and much talk of an American-Japanese war.[64]

In 1911, the United States was negotiating a treaty of general arbitration with Great Britain. To make the general arbitration treaty effective and to satisfy the opposition in the Dominions, the British Government began negotiations with Japan and revised their treaty of alliance of 1905. In the new treaty a provision was made to exclude from the scope of its operation any Power which had concluded a treaty of general arbitration with either of the high contracting parties. The Anglo-American general arbitration treaty failed, however, when it came up in the United States Senate for approval.[65] In September, 1914, a " peace commission " treaty was signed by Great Britain and the United States, and this treaty both Great Britain and Japan ac-

---

[64] Treat, ch. x.

[65] See Arbitration and the United States (*World Peace Foundation Pamphlets*), Boston, 1926, IX, Nos. 6-7, pp. 524-535.

cepted as equivalent to a treaty of general arbitration.[66] But the position which the British and the Japanese Governments took in regard to this treaty was not formally made known to the United States.[67]

From 1911 to 1921 the relations between Japan and the United States grew from bad to worse. The Japanese action in China in 1911, during the Chinese Revolution, and in 1915, were occasions for criticisms in the United States. In 1917 the United States was at war with the Central Powers. On November 2 Secretary Lansing reached an agreement, in the form of exchange of notes with Viscount Ishii, former Japanese Minister for Foreign Affairs and then on a special mission to the United States, which, it was declared, was " to silence mischievous reports that have from time to time circulated." In the agreement the two Governments denied that they had " any purpose to infringe in any way the independence or territorial integrity of China," and they declared, furthermore, that they would always " adhere to the principle of the so-called ' Open Door ' or equal opportunity for commerce and industry in China." One portion of the notes read: " The Governments of the United States and Japan

[66] Japanese Foreign Minister Uchida's address to the Diet, Japan Advertiser, February 5, 1921. London Times, December 30, 1920; ibid., December 31, Treat, p. 203. Buell, p. 128.

[67] On March 3, 1921, the British Under-Secretary of Foreign Affairs, Mr. Kellaway, admitted in the House that no official communication (had) been made to the United States of America. Par. Deb., 5th Series, Commons, March 3, 1921, CXXXVIII, 1574. See also ibid., CXLIII, 1792. New York Times, June 23, 1921.

recognize that territorial propinquity creates special relations between countries, and, consequently,
the Government of the United States recognizes that
Japan has special interests in China, particularly in
the part to which her possessions are contiguous.'' [68]

Though the agreement was to silence mischievous
reports that had from time to time circulated, differences which had their root in the vital interests
of the two countries could not be so easily patched
up. Furthermore, an occasion was soon to arise
which demonstrated the insincerity of one of the parties, for at the Paris Conference of 1919, Japan insisted on succeeding to the former German rights in
Shantung. Bound by the secret agreements of February and March, 1917, to award the German rights
in Shantung to Japan, the principal Allied Powers,
led by Great Britain, supported the Japanese claim.[69]
In view of this situation, President Wilson had to
yield to the Japanese contention and to accept the
decision of the Council of Three which, on April 30,
1919, awarded Japan all the German rights in Shantung, and, in addition, the right to officer the railway
police along the Kiaochow-Chinan Railway, and to
establish a permanent concession in Tsingtao.[70]

[68] MacMurray, II, 1394-96.

[69] For the secret agreements, see *Millard's Review,* Supp., July 17,
1920, pp. 1-3.

[70] Articles 156, 157, 158 of the Treaty of Peace with Germany,
signed at Versailles on June 28, 1919. This Treaty was not signed by
the Chinese Delegation, nor ratified by the American Senate. For
the reasons why President Wilson acceded to Japan's demand in

Such happenings naturally did not relieve the United States of her suspicion regarding Japan's foreign policies. In 1921 the war clouds hovered over Japan and the United States more darkly than ever before. With their experience at the Paris Conference fresh in mind,[71] the Americans felt that the Anglo-Japanese Alliance had encouraged Japan's aggressive policy abroad, and, being ignorant of the interpretation put upon the Anglo-American '' peace commission '' treaty, feared that, should a war break out between the United States and Japan, Great Britain, by force of the alliance, might be found on the side of Japan.[72] Thus, in 1921 nine men out of ten in the United States were opposed to the alliance between Japan and Great Britain.[73] The fear of the Americans that Great Britain might be drawn into an American-Japanese conflict by force of the alliance was shared by the people of the British Dominions, especially that of Canada, who strongly opposed the alliance, particularly in its unmodified form. These oppositions—from the United States and the Dominions—together with the opposition in

---

regard to Shantung, see Millard, *Conflict of Policies in Asia,* ch. ii. Charles Hodges, '' President Wilson's Japan '' in the *Far Eastern Fortnightly* (The Bulletin of the Far Eastern Bureau), New York, March 15, 1920, VII, No. 6, p. 55.

[71] Indeed it was then believed that a tri-power entente regarding all Asia had been reached by the British, French and Japanese Governments. Thomas F. Millard, *Asia,* August, 1919.

[72] See Millard, p. 214. Also, see *The Anglo-Japanese Alliance and the Future of American British Relations,* a confidential memorandum, printed for private circulation only, Hongkong, March 30, 1921.

[73] Observation of Lord Bryce, New York *Times,* October 19, 1921.

China, forced the British Imperial Cabinet to postpone its decision on the question of the renewal of
the alliance until the Washington Conference.

In 1921 there was a necessity for disarmament as
a result particularly of the naval competition between the United States, Great Britain and Japan.
The Senate, on May 26, and the House on June 29,
adopted a resolution which had been introduced by
Senator Borah on December 14, 1920, inviting the
president of the United States to convoke a conference on naval disarmament of the powers concerned.[74] On August 11, the United States formally
invited Great Britain, Japan, France and Italy to
attend " a conference on the subject of Limitation of
Armament, in connection with which Pacific and Far
Eastern questions should also be discussed." [75] As
China, Holland, Belgium and Portugal all had interests in the Pacific and the Far East, they also were
invited to participate in the Conference so far as it
was to deal with questions in these regions.[76]

As the Anglo-Japanese Alliance was not a subject
which the Conference proper could deal with, it was
not discussed in the Conference committees. All the
negotiations regarding the alliance were carried on
between the British, American and Japanese Dele-
gations. The British Delegation proposed at first an

[74] Buell, pp. 137-150.

[75] *Conference on the Limitation of Armament,* pp. 17-18.

[76] China was invited on August 11, on the same date that the American invitation was sent to the principal Allied Powers. Belgium,
Holland and Portugal were not invited till October 4. Ibid., pp. 18-19.

agreement between Great Britain, the United States, and Japan which would guarantee their respective interests in the Far East. The United States opposed this proposal because it would appear that the United States, by this agreement, had joined the Anglo-Japanese Alliance.[77] Instead, a four-power pact, including France, and abolishing entirely the guaranty relating to their respective interests in the Far East was suggested, and this suggestion by Mr. Hughes was finally adopted. The Four-Power Pact was signed on December 13, 1921.[78]

The United States was neither a party to the alliance, nor covered by it. Nor was she aimed at by any of the three treaties. Yet there was no nation, besides the contracting parties and China and Korea, whose interests were more intimately affected by this agreement. Even the interests of Russia and Germany were not so closely involved. This was because the United States had tremendous economic interests in the Far East in general and in China particularly. Furthermore, she was a Power owning territory not only on the Pacific, but immediately in China's neighborhood.

The traditional policy of the United States in the Eastern countries, especially in China, was to maintain the Open Door or equal opportunities for the commerce and industry of all nations. In 1902, Rus-

[77] Buell, pp. 174-177.

[78] The United States had also used her influence in effecting the different treaties and resolutions relating to China adopted by the Conference.

sia was violating the Open Door whilst Great Britain and Japan were defending it. Consequently, the alliance was hailed in the United States as the best means to keep the Chinese door open to the American trade, without obligating the United States to pay for the privilege. In the 1905 agreement the allies again pledged their support to China's integrity and the principle of the Open Door. The American statesmen at the time did not foresee that Japan was soon to change her policy in China and to adopt one to which the United States was wholly opposed. Furthermore, in September, 1905, when the alliance was concluded, President Roosevelt was mediating between Russia and Japan, and was anxious to see an agreement reached on the terms of peace. The Anglo-Japanese Treaty, by relieving Japan of all apprehension of vindictive action on the part of Russia in the future, made it easier for Japan to moderate her demands, and thus facilitated the negotiations for peace at Portsmouth. Thus, the new treaty was welcomed by the Government circles at Washington as well as by the American public.

The events in the following years soon proved that Japan's post-war policy in China had undergone a radical change. After her war with Russia, she was no longer a staunch defender of the Open Door. Instead, she became its worst enemy. Furthermore, since 1905 the general relations between the United States and Japan were becoming daily more unsatisfactory. Fearing that an American-Japanese conflict would necessarily, by virtue of the Anglo-Japanese Alliance, draw Great Britain into the war on the side of Japan, the United States, taking the opportunity of the negotiations of the Anglo-American general arbitration treaty, caused Great Britain to revise her treaty with Japan in 1911, in order to exclude the United States from its scope of operation.

Unhappily, the treaty of general arbitration between the United States and Great Britain failed in the United States Senate. In 1914 a " peace commission " treaty was signed by the American and British Governments. Both Great Britain and Japan accepted this as equivalent to a treaty of general arbitration. Unfortunately, for some reason, the British and Japanese interpretation of this treaty was not made known until 1921, and the American Government was kept ignorant of this broad interpretation. From 1911 to 1921 the American-Japanese relations grew from bad to worse. Japan's policy in China during the war period, and the position she took at the Peace Conference of 1919, were repugnant to the American mind and particularly injurious to American interests. Fearing that a conflict with Japan might mean a war with both Japan and Great Britain, the United States opposed any renewal of the alliance when the question came up in 1921. This attitude of the United States had its influence on the British Dominions, particularly Canada. Thus, the British Government

was forced, by the opposition in Canada, in the
United States, and in China, to delay her decision on
the renewal of the alliance, and finally, to conclude
at the Washington Conference the Four-Power pact
as its substitute.

In 1902-05 the United States had believed that the
Anglo-Japanese Alliance would result in the carrying out of an American theory in practice—that was
the Open Door in China. But the events since 1905
have proved beyond any doubt that the alliance in its
practical application was exactly opposed to the
American traditional policy. On the one hand, it
had encouraged Japan's aggression in China. On
the other hand, by taking away Great Britain from
the list of countries which would maintain the Open
Door in China, it had caused the United States to
stand alone, and had thus prevented any of her protests in favor of the principle of the Open Door
from being effective.

CHAPTER VIII

Conclusion

We are now in a position to summarize the conclusions to be reached from the facts set forth in the preceding pages.

Before the Sino-Japanese War, Great Britain had desired an alliance with China in order to protect British interests in India and the Far East against the menace of Franco-Russian combination. The War of 1894-95 exposed the military weakness of China. After that, China could no longer be looked upon as a possible ally for the purpose of checking the joint advance of France and Russia. The very weakness of the Chinese Empire was a temptation to the aggressive Powers. Among them, Russia stood foremost. The success of the Three-Power intervention, led by Russia, which forced Japan to return the Liaotung Peninsula to China, had turned Russia's attention toward the Far East, after which she had adopted a " forward policy " in both China and Korea.

Russia's aggressive acts in the Far East after 1895, supported by France and Germany, had alarmed both Great Britain and Japan. Since her " Reformation " Japan had looked upon East Asia, particularly Manchuria and Korea, as a supply region for raw materials and food products, and a field for immigration. Russia's activities in these regions had necessarily affected adversely the Japanese program of expansion, for the realization of which only two ways were open: to reach an understanding with Russia to share the common spoils or to conclude an agreement with Great Britain to check the Russian advance.

As it seemed to be easier to effect a Russo-Japanese understanding than to obtain an Anglo-Japanese Alliance, the Japanese Government at first sought to follow the seemingly easier course. The Japanese further reasoned that, even granting that an alliance with England could be effected, the Japanese position in the Far East would still be precarious in the face of a hostile Russia. Finally, an alliance might call forth a war with Russia for which Japan was not yet prepared. Thus, Japan tried hard in these years to persuade Russia to reach an understanding with her on the basis of Russian preponderance in Manchuria in return for a Japanese protectorate over Korea. But Russia refused to stay out of the Peninsula upon which, in the opinion of the Japanese, Japan's fate as a nation depended. This attitude of the Government at St. Petersburg prevented the conclusion of any satisfactory agreement between Japan and Russia.

For more than half a century England had occupied a leading position in the councils of the Western Powers in China. There she had maintained a high prestige and developed great commercial interests. The aggressive steps taken in China by the Continental Powers, particularly Russia, in the years following the Sino-Japanese War, directly threatened, in the opinion of the British, their position in China and indirectly the safety of their colonies in the Far East and of the British Indian empire. Standing alone and unable to check the advance of Russia, of France, and of Germany, the British Government resorted to the " policy of compensation." For every grant made by China to the continental Powers, Great Britain secured certain concessions. But British interests in China were principally commercial. She wanted an " open door " and, as a corollary of this, the maintenance of the independence and integrity of China. It was only after unsuccessful attempts to oppose the Powers' demands upon China that the British Government resorted to a policy of counter-demand. Every compensation granted was therefore an indication of failure, rather than success, of the British policy. As a result, not only was her commercial interest seriously threatened, but her prestige was affected.

Early in 1898, a group of British statesmen began to feel the danger of their isolated position, not only in the Far East, but in all parts of the world as well. Certain influential members of the London Cabinet began to desire a policy of alliances as a substitute for the traditional principle of " splendid isolation." In the Far East, Great Britain could either (1) ally herself with Japan, (2) with Germany, with the adherence of Japan and, perhaps, the United States, or (3) come to an understanding with Russia.

Although it seemed that Japan was a " natural ally " of Great Britain in the Far East, there were, nevertheless, certain practical difficulties on the way to an Anglo-Japanese Alliance. First, the foreign policy of a country could not be segregated into water-tight compartments. It was therefore impossible for England to be the enemy of Russia in Asia, and, at the same time, the friend of Russia in Europe and elsewhere. An alliance with Japan would mean that England had to be prepared to wage incessant war all over the world with Russia and her allies. Japan, though a rising Power, did not possess worldwide interests. It was not wise, therefore, for England to ally herself with Japan in the Far East, and thus incur the enmity of Russia, and perhaps be obliged to fight her alone, in all parts of the world. Second, British interests in the Far East were principally commercial, and therefore demanded peace. An alliance with Japan might provoke a war, and thus disturb the peace so valuable to the British trade. Finally, there existed in British high quarters a prejudice against an alliance with a non-Christian and Yellow race.

Thus, early in 1898 the British Government turned to Russia for a friendly understanding. Her statesmen reasoned that Russia and Great Britain, especially in the Far East, had to meet, but that they need not meet in anger. China was large

18

enough for both. If Russia banished the elements of
territorial designs and of trade restrictions from her
policy, Russia's undertakings in Manchuria and her
project of coming down to an ice-free port on the
Pacific would not be injurious to British interests
and therefore could not be seriously objectionable
to England. Accordingly, on January 17, 1898, the
British Ambassador at St. Petersburg was instructed
to sound the St. Petersburg Government as to
whether it was not possible for England and Russia
to work together in China, and suggested that an
understanding, if reached, should be extended to the
general area of their respective interests. With regard to China, the British Government proposed a
" partition of preponderance " as the basis of
agreement—that the valley of Huang-Ho and the
territory to the north of it should be regarded as
subject to Russian influence, and the Yangtze Valley
as subject to British influence. As the Russian Government refused to pursue the discussion of the
broad questions, the negotiations had to be dropped.

As soon as the Anglo-Russian rapprochement
seemed to have reached an *impasse,* Mr. Chamberlain, the powerful Colonial Secretary of the British Cabinet, opened negotiations with the German
Ambassador at London for an Anglo-German alliance. The negotiations lasted, with intervals,
throughout the year 1898, and did not entirely drop
until the end of the following year.

Unable to reach a general and lasting understanding with either Russia or Germany, the British Gov-

ernment adopted a policy of partial and temporary agreements in the Far East. Great Britain and Russia agreed, in 1899, on a " partition of spheres for concessions for the construction and workings of railways in China," that is, Russia to the north of the Great Wall, and Great Britain in the basin of the Yangtze. In October, 1900, in view of the Boxer uprising and the Russian aggression in China, Great Britain and Germany reached an agreement in the form of exchange of Notes, in which both Governments declared their respect for the open door and integrity of China, and prescribed the circumstances under which they were to discuss common actions.

It was soon discovered at London, however, that these partial agreements would not be effective for the attainment of the ends desired from them, for, following the Boxer uprising, Russia occupied Manchuria, disregarded property rights of British subjects in North China, and threatened British potential interests in the Chinese Empire. When Russia was pressing Peking in the spring of 1901 for the ratification of a secret treaty between Alexiev, the Russian commander-in-chief in the Far East, and the Tartar General of Mukden, which would make Manchuria virtually a Russian protectorate, Lord Lansdowne, by force of the Anglo-German Agreement of October 16, 1900, asked the Berlin Government to cooperate with England and Japan to oppose the Russian demand. The reply was that the agreement in question did not include Manchuria. But despite the difference between the German and British interpretations of the Anglo-German Agreement regarding Manchuria, the British Government did not abandon its project of a general alliance with Germany. It was not until the end of October that the London Government finally realized that an Anglo-German general understanding was impossible.

Standing alone, with prestige greatly prejudiced by the events in Asia as well as in Africa, and with her troops occupied in the Boer War, Great Britain was practically helpless against Russian encroachment in Manchuria. Her position in 1901 was one of dangerous even if " splendid " isolation. If Great Britain ever needed an ally, it was at this time. Both Russia and Germany had refused to come to a general understanding with her. The United States, though her commercial interests in Eastern Asia were great, did not wish to depart from her traditional policy of avoiding European complications. The only country with which Great Britain could ally herself was, therefore, Japan.

Ever since the Sino-Japanese War, Russian activity in Korea had been the nightmare of the Japanese statesmen. Time and again they had approached the Russian Government for a solution, but nothing had resulted except two pointless conventions which neither satisfied the Japanese, nor were promptly complied with by the Russian agents in Korea. By 1901, most Japanese writers and statesmen were definitely convinced that a Russo-

Japanese agreement was impossible, and that a war between the two countries could not be avoided.

The Russian encroachment in Manchuria in 1900 and 1901 did not directly concern Japan, and was not so considered, but the Japanese feared that Manchuria, under the military and political control of Russia, might become the Russian stepping-stone to Korea. The growing strength in Japan and her part in the North China campaign had inspired the Japanese with greater confidence in their country's ability to protect her own interests. They were therefore willing to fight Russia over the question of the Manchuria agreement before the Siberian railway was completed. They believed that they could beat Russia on the field in a single-handed combat; they only desired an ally to hold the ring for her—to prevent France from joining in the hostilities on the side of Russia.

With a view to preparing for open conflict with Russia, the Japanese Government instructed its Ministers at Washington, at Berlin, and at London, to sound the respective Governments to which they were accredited. From the American Secretary of State, Japan received the reply that " we were not at present prepared to attempt singly, or in concert with other Powers, to enforce these views [as to the integrity of China] in the east by any demonstration which could present a character of hostility to any other Powers." [1] The German answer was that

[1] D. S., Numerical File, DXLVII, memo., Feb. 1, 1901.

"Germany will observe benevolent neutrality in case matters should come to a crisis." [2] The Japanese inquiry at London alone received a serious consideration. Mr. Bertie, in his memorandum drawn up for the British Foreign Office, advised the British Government "to encourage Japan to look to us as a friend and a possible ally against Russia and France." [3]

Early in 1901 the German and British Governments were discussing a general alliance between the two countries. During the negotiation, Baron von Eckardstein, then First Secretary of the German Embassy, made the suggestion of an Anglo-German-Japanese pact. This served as the starting point of the negotiations between Lord Lansdowne and Mr. Hayashi, then Japanese Minister to the Court of St. James's, which resulted in the signing of the Anglo-Japanese Alliance on January 30, 1902.

Thus, it was the unconciliatory attitude of St. Petersburg which made impossible either a Russo-Japanese or a Russo-British understanding. And it was the same attitude of the Russian Government, combined with the international situation and the political events of the years 1894-1902, which forced Japan and Great Britain into the arms of each other. Had the German Government been sincere in its negotiations for a general understanding with Great Britain, and had the United States not wanted to

[2] *Brit.* Doc., II, 41.
[3] Ibid., II, 43.

stand aloof, the alliance of January 30, 1902, might have been an Anglo-German-American-Japanese alliance. Since both Berlin and Washington, though for different reasons, stood aloof, the result was the Anglo-Japanese Alliance of 1902.

A political alliance between nations is a living matter; its purposes are not necessarily only those specifically mentioned in the document. The exact operation and effect of a political alliance depends upon the interpretation which the contracting parties give to the terms of the agreement. To this general rule the Anglo-Japanese Alliance was no exception. Furthermore, during the twenty years [4] or more which the Alliance lasted, international relations had undergone important changes. These changes naturally had their effect upon the interpretation which the two parties put upon the terms of the Alliance. Not only this, the terms of the agreement had actually been twice altered in order to fit the changing circumstances.

First concluded in 1902, the alliance was directed against Russia. It was to protect the interests of the allies in the Far East—Britain's in China and Japan's in Korea. At the time when the first alliance was concluded, Russia had maintained a " forward policy " which threatened to upset the *status quo* in the Far East and to debase the independence

---

[4] From the conclusion of the first Alliance on January 30, 1902, to the date of deposit of ratifications of the Washington Conference on August 17, 1923.

and integrity of both China and Korea. It was, however, to the Allies' interest to maintain the *status quo* in the Far East, and the independence and territorial integrity of the Empires of China and Korea, and the Open Door therein. Nevertheless, the allies did not forget their true purpose—the safeguarding of their special interests in China and Korea. They therefore mutually recognized their right to take indispensable measures and to intervene in China and Korea in order to protect those interests.

Failure on the part of Russia to carry out her promised evacuation of Manchuria gave Japan an opportunity, in the autumn of 1904, to open direct negotiations with Russia. Diplomacy having failed, Japan hurled her naval and military forces against Russia. The success of Japanese arms gave great confidence to the military party at Tokio, consequently they took immediate steps to establish a protectorate over Korea and embarked on an ambitious program of continental expansion.

Being unwilling to incur the lasting resentment of the Japanese, the British Government agreed to all the transfers and concessions which Japan forced China and Korea to make to her. Thus, when the treaty was rewritten in August, 1905, the declared objects of the contracting parties were: " the consolidation and maintenance of the general peace in the regions of Eastern Asia and of India," " the preservation of the common interests of all Powers in China by insuring her independence and integrity and the principle of the ' Open door,' '' and '' the maintenance of the territorial rights of the high contracting parties in Eastern Asia and India, and the defence of their special interests in the said regions.'' The independence and territorial integrity of Korea was no longer envisaged. On the contrary, Article III expressly recognized Japan's paramount political, military, and economic interests in Korea, and her right to take necessary measures of guidance, control and protection in that country.

The main purpose of the first alliance was to hold the ring for Japan in her war against Russia. The second alliance, so far as Great Britain was concerned, was a part of her policy of seeking the Empire's security in alliances. It was to secure for her the friendship of Japan and thus the protection of her interests in India and the Far East. The treaty, by depriving Russia of any hope of success in her future aggressive policy toward India and Eastern Asia, was to force Russia to turn her attention once again toward Europe, and thus to bring her ultimately to the side of Great Britain. For Japan, the second alliance was to provide for any contingency resulting from a Russian come-back, and to guarantee to her an opportunity for a peaceful development of her commerce and industry and economic penetration of the Asian continent. Thus, the provision which constituted the basis of the alliance was so altered as to establish the obligation of each party to come to the immediate assistance of the other in the event of an unprovoked attack on the part of a third Power upon the rights and interests of either party to the treaty.

Only two years later, Russia came to separate agreements with Great Britain and Japan. As Japan had adopted an aggressive policy in China after the war of 1904-05, the significance of the Russo-Japanese agreement was that, thenceforth, the two aggressive Powers in the Far East—Russia and Japan—would work together in the Chinese Empire. This they did. Great Britain, being Japan's ally and Russia's friend, remained passive and silent, not only when China's interests were threatened, but even when the interests of British citizens were jeopardized. The London Government had placed their European policy above their interests in the Far East; they feared lest Japan and Russia would go over to the Central Powers, thus menacing the safety of the British Empire.

One country, however, had a free hand in the Far East. That was the United States. Since 1907 Washington had decided upon a more energetic policy, and in 1909 proposed the Knox plan of " neutralizing " the Manchurian railways. This project failed because both Japan and Russia opposed it and the British Government refused to give to it the necessary support. One result of the American intervention was that Japan and Russia reached a new agreement in 1910 " in order to reinforce their mutual relations and to preserve the position proper to them in Manchuria from all interference on the part of the other Powers." [5]

The conflict of interests and policies between the United States and Japan in China, the school question in the Western States of America, and the immigration question in the United States, all led to antagonism between Japan and the United States. The result was that the relations between the two countries from 1905 to 1911 were far from satisfactory. But Great Britain had no reason to quarrel with Japan, and in 1911 London and Washington were negotiating a general arbitration treaty. The alliance was therefore revised in order that the agreement should not be applicable in case of an armed conflict between the United States and Japan. As Korea had been formally annexed by Japan in 1910, and the Anglo-Russian entente of 1907 made provision for the security of the Indian frontier unnecessary, both India and Korea no longer required special provision in the new treaty. Otherwise, the language of the new agreement closely followed that of its immediate predecessor.

During the lifetime of the third alliance, on one important occasion at least, the British Government openly differed from the attitude of Tokio. That was in 1911 during the time of the Chinese Revolution, scarcely three months after the alliance was revised for the second time. But at the time, the

[5] Iswolsky to the Russian Ambassador at London, June 11-24, 1910, Siebert, p. 16.

situation in Europe was pressing, and Great Britain could not afford to take extreme measures in the Far East to protect her own interests, lest her friendly relations with Japan and Russia be damaged. Thus, while cooperating with the United States in the maintenance of the open door and integrity of China, she yielded in many respects to the wishes of Tokio and St. Petersburg. Already, early in 1912, a general outbreak of anti-British feeling had taken place in Japan as a result of British protests against Japan's unneutral action in China. In July, 1912, Russia and Japan again concluded a convention so that they could work closely together in all matters concerning China.

Two years later, war broke out in Europe. By Japan, this was regarded as " the most opportune moment for Japan to quickly solve the Chinese question." [6] She therefore, with characteristic energy, took steps toward a Japanese domination over China. Based upon the pretext of the Anglo-Japanese treaty of 1911 she declared war against Germany, and captured Tsingtao from that country. A few months later she presented directly to President Yuan Shih-Kai the notorious Twenty-One Demands, and forced China, by a direct threat of war, to sign, on May 25, 1915, the treaties respecting Shantung, South Manchuria and Inner Mongolia. In addition, notes were exchanged on the same date respect-

[6] Memorandum of the Black Dragon Society of Japan, Putnam Weale, *The Fight for the Republic in China*, New York, 1917, p. 128.

ing the Hanyehping and Fukien questions. In order to safeguard the interests thus obtained, Japan concluded with Russia another convention, July 3, 1916, for closer relations between the two countries in China, and in 1917 secured from Great Britain, France, Italy and Russia, the secret agreements by which these Powers bound themselves to support at the Peace Conference Japan's claim with regard to Shantung. By a decision of the " Council of Three," Japan was awarded all the German rights in Shantung. But, as China refused to sign the Versailles Treaty, the Shantung question was not settled until the Washington Conference.

Before 1905 Russia was intractable. The alliance of 1902 was concluded by Great Britain in order to hold the ring for Japan so that the latter could beat Russia on the field. Moreover, Japan's interest in China during this period was the same as that of Great Britain. She was interested in China's integrity and the Open Door. From 1905 to 1921 Japan was no longer interested in the same things in China. Her victory over Russia encouraged her to adopt an aggressive policy in China as well as in Korea. To the absorption of Korea Great Britain gracefully consented. As to Japan's aggression in China, the British Government, with their eyes fixed on *Weltpolitik* and the situation in Europe, remained passive and silent, though with reluctance.

After the World War both Russia and Germany could no longer seriously threaten the interests of

Great Britain. Yet the fear that Japan could create trouble in India and threaten the safety and security of Australia caused the conservative London Government to be reluctant to abolish the Japanese alliance. However, the opposition from China, from the United States, from the British residents in the Far East, and, above all, from the Dominions, especially Canada, forced the British Government to delay its decision on the question of the renewal of the alliance till the Washington Conference.

As the alliance had been, since the making of the agreement in 1902, the foundation of Japanese foreign policy, Tokio naturally was anxious to continue the alliance with Great Britain. But in 1921 the relations between the United States and Japan were so unsatisfactory that it was impossible for Great Britain to continue her alliance with Japan without offending the United States. The situation at the time showed that it was impossible for Great Britain to have the friendship of both of these countries at one and the same time. " It is the question for her [Great Britain]," as Mr. Sidney Osborne put it " of whether she is to chose the friendship of Japan or the friendship of America."[7] At the Washington Conference Great Britain chose the friendship of the latter country. To save the face of Japan, Great Britain, the United States, France and Japan signed the agreement of December 13, 1921, by which the contracting parties pledged them-

[7] Sidney Osborne, *The New Japanese Peril*, London, 1921, p. 142.

selves to respect the rights of one another in relation
to their insular possessions and insular dominions in
the region of the Pacific Ocean. For the cancellation of the Anglo-Japanese alliance Japan was com-
pensated by the provision, in the treaty limiting
naval armaments, that " The United States, the
British Empire and Japan agree that the *status quo*
at the time of the signing of the present Treaty,
with regard to fortifications and naval bases [in the
Pacific Ocean, with certain exceptions], shall be
maintained." [8]

The Four-Power Agreement, unlike the Anglo-
Japanese Treaty, is not an alliance. Under the agreement there is no commitment to armed force. Taken
together with the Five-Power Treaty limiting naval
armaments and the Nine-Power Treaty relating to
principles and policies to be followed in matters concerning China, the Four-Power Pact merely indicates the pacific intention of the contracting Powers
in their relations with one another.

Since the termination of the Anglo-Japanese Alliance by the conclusion and subsequent ratifications
of the Four-Power Treaty, rumors of a renewal of
the alliance have twice appeared in the press. [9] It is

[8] Article XIX of the Five-Power Treaty limiting naval armament,
concluded on February 6, 1922, at the Washington Conference.

[9] It appeared in the press first in the summer of 1927, following on
the breakdown of the Geneva Naval Conference, and then in the
winter of 1928, after the crisis between Great Britain and the United
States over the disclosure of the Anglo-French Naval-Military Agreement of July, 1928. See New York *Times,* June 28, 29, 1927, August

impossible at present to say how much truth there is in these reports.[10] It is safe, however, to say that Japan is, as she has always been, willing to revive the alliance. Since the Washington Conference Japan's policy in China has for the most part been a conciliatory one.[11] But this does not mean that she has given up the major object of her policy toward China—the domination of that country. She is only awaiting her time. She knows that, standing alone, she cannot push her policy to the extreme, especially in view of the fact that Washington is pursuing a different policy in China. It has been suggested by some Japanese that Tokio should seek support in a new direction from Russia and Germany. But there are certain difficulties in the way of such a combination. Granting that such a combination could be effected, it is extremely doubtful whether Russia and Germany can, at present, render much service to Japan. The best ally for Japan is still Great Britain.

British traditional policy in China has been the maintenance of the Open Door principle of equal

27. *London Times,* July 22, 1927. *The China Weekly Review,* December 8, 1928, XCVII, No. 2, pp. 43-45; January 5, 1929, XCVII, No. 6, pp. 227-230.

[10] It is quite possible that a temporary and local agreement concerning China between Great Britain and Japan has been reached. But it is very unlikely that the Anglo-Japanese Alliance has been revived.

[11] See " Japan keeps Faith," in the *Literary Digest,* December 23, 1922, LXXV, 9-10. " British and Japanese Policy in China," *China Weekly Review.* November 20, 1926.

opportunities for the commerce and industry of all nations, but this has not prevented her from adopting, at times, the alternative policy of " sphere of influences." During the period of the " scramble for concessions " in China, Great Britain was as guilty as the continental Powers of Europe in violating China's open door and integrity. During the life time of the Anglo-Japanese alliance, Great Britain acquiesced in many measures taken by Tokio which were injurious to China's integrity and sovereignty. But it should not be forgotten that, in adopting the policy of " spheres of influence," Great Britain was only compromising. Britain's interest and policy in China cannot, therefore, be said to be the same as that of Japan.[12] If the alliance is to be renewed, it surely will not be for reasons relating purely to China.

In 1921 Great Britain had desired to continue the alliance in order to restrain Japan's hands in India and to pacify the ill-feeling entertained by the Japanese against the British Dominions. But, since the alliance has been terminated, to say that Great Britain will renew it again merely for these reasons

[12] On December 18, 1926, in pursuance of Article VII of the Nine-Power Treaty signed at the Washington Conference, February 6, 1922, relating to the general principles and policies concerning China, the British representative presented a memorandum to the signatories of the Washington treaties, which embodies the essentials of the new British policy of "friendship" toward China. For a fair discussion of the new British policy and a text of the memorandum of December 18, 1926, see Bau, *China and World Peace,* New York, 1928, pp. 166-174 and ch. iv.

19

does not seem very probable. The first treaty of alliance was concluded to defeat Russia. The second and third treaties of alliance were concluded with the German menace in view. Is it not safe, therefore, to say that Great Britain will not renew her alliance with Japan unless her larger interests are again threatened? The only country which can threaten the larger interests of Great Britain at present is the United States.

The United States emerged from the World War as a great world Power. " In all the leading directions of trade, in South America, in Canada, in Australia, in Europe, in India and China, the growth of the American percentage of trade and the decline of the British percentage of trade can be traced." [13] In the Washington Conference Great Britain was compelled to accept in principle naval equality with the United States. Since the Washington Conference the expansion of the American navy has continued to challenge British supremacy on the sea. Over against these differences between the two Anglo-Saxon countries can be recorded the fact that they are of kin to each other not only in blood, but in language, in customs and in social heritage. Undoubtedly there exists a willingness on the part of both Governments to work together. As to whether

---

[13] R. Palme Dutt, " Dangers of War," in *Current History*, May, 1929, p. 193. This article by Mr. Dutt, together with another written by Mr. P. W. Wilson, appeared in the same issue of *Current History*, presenting opposed British points of view on " The Causes of Anglo-American Differences."

the two Anglo-Saxon countries will always maintain amicable relations toward each other, or whether they will eventually fall out the author does not venture to foretell.

To the credit—or discredit—of the Anglo-Japanese Alliance, during the twenty-one and one-half years of its existence, the following important developments may be directly or indirectly credited: The Russo-Japanese War; the absorption of Korea by Japan; the Russo-Japanese rapprochement and the substitution of Japan and Russia for Russia alone in Manchuria; the establishment and development of Japan's fivefold policy in China—economic exploitation, territorial expansion, paramount influence, political control, and the "Asiatic" Monroe Doctrine.

The question whether the alliance will be revived in the future depends, in my opinion, upon the attitude of the British Empire; and the attitude of the British Empire depends upon its relations with the United States. The alliance was concluded first in 1902 to make a war possible; it was terminated by the Four-Power Treaty in Washington Conference. It is safe to say that it will not be renewed unless a war is again decided upon—in this case, between Great Britain and the United States.

APPENDIX A[1]

GREAT BRITAIN AND JAPAN

AGREEMENT RELATIVE TO CHINA AND KOREA, JANUARY 30, 1902

The governments of Great Britain and Japan, actuated solely by a desire to maintain the *status quo* and general peace in the Extreme East, being moreover specially interested in maintaining the independence and territorial integrity of the Empire of China and the Empire of Korea, and in securing equal opportunities in those countries for the commerce and industry of all nations, hereby agree as follows:

ARTICLE I

The High Contracting Parties, having mutually recognised the independence of China and Korea, declare themselves to be entirely uninfluenced by any aggressive tendencies in either country. Having in view, however, their special interests of which those of Great Britain relate principally to China, while Japan, in addition to the interests which she possesses in China, is interested in a peculiar degree politically as well as commercially and industrially in Korea, the High Contracting Parties recognise that it will be admissible for either of them to take such measures as may be indispensable in order to safeguard those interests if threatened either by the aggressive action of any other Power, or by disturbances arising in China or Korea, and necessitating the intervention of

[1] MacMurray, I, 324-325.

either of the High Contracting Parties for the protection of the lives and property of its subjects.

ARTICLE II

If either Great Britain or Japan, in the defence of their respective interests as above described, should become involved in war with another Power, the other High Contracting Party will maintain a strict neutrality, and use its efforts to prevent other Powers from joining in hostilities against its ally.

ARTICLE III

If, in the above event, any other Power or Powers should join in hostilities against that ally, the other High Contracting Party will come to its assistance, and will conduct the war in common, and make peace in mutual agreement with it.

ARTICLE IV

The High Contracting Parties agree that neither of them will, without consulting the other, enter into separate arrangements with another Power to the prejudice of the interests above described.

ARTICLE V

Whenever, in opinion of either Great Britain or Japan, the above-mentioned interests are in jeopardy, the two Governments will communicate with one another fully and frankly.

ARTICLE VI

The present Agreement shall come into effect immediately after the date of its signature, and remain in force for five years from that date.

In case neither of the High Contracting Parties should have notified twelve months before the expiration of the said five years the intention of terminating it, it shall remain binding until the expiration of one year from the day on which either of the High Contracting Parties shall have denounced it. But if, when the date fixed for its expiration arrives, either ally is actually engaged in war, the alliance, shall, *ipso facto,* continue until peace is concluded.

In faith whereof the Undersigned, duly authorised by their respective Governments, have signed this Agreement, and have affixed thereto their seals.

Done in duplicate at London, the 30th of January, 1902.

(L. S.) LANSDOWNE, His Britannic Majesty's Principal Secretary of State for Foreign Affairs.

(L. S.) HAYASHI, Envoy Extraordinary and Minister Plenipotentiary of His Majesty the Emperor of Japan at the Court of St. James.

APPENDIX B [1]

GREAT BRITAIN AND JAPAN

AGREEMENT RESPECTING THE INTEGRITY OF CHINA, THE
GENERAL PEACE OF EASTERN ASIA AND INDIA, AND
THE TERRITORIAL RIGHTS AND SPECIAL INTERESTS OF
THE PARTIES IN THOSE REGIONS, AUGUST 12, 1905

Preamble

The Governments of Great Britain and Japan, being desirous of replacing the Agreement concluded between them on the 30th of January, 1902, by fresh stipulations, have agreed upon the following Articles, which have for their object:

(a) The consolidation and maintenance of the general peace in the regions of Eastern Asia and of India.

(b) The preservation of the common interests of all Powers in China by insuring the independence and integrity of the Chinese Empire and the principle of equal opportunities for the commerce and industry of all nations in China.

(c) The maintenance of the territorial rights of the High contracting parties in the regions of Eastern Asia and of India, and the defence of their special interests in the said regions.

ARTICLE I

It is agreed that whenever, in the opinion of either Great Britain or Japan, any of the rights and interests referred to in the preamble of this Agreement are in jeopardy, the two

[1] MacMurray, I, 516-518.

Governments will communicate with one another fully and frankly, and will consider in common the measures which should be taken to safeguard those menaced rights or interests.

ARTICLE II

If by reason of unprovoked attack or aggressive action, whenever arising, on the part of any other Power or Powers, either contracting party should be involved in war in defence of its territorial rights or special interests mentioned in the preamble of this Agreement, the other contracting party will at once come to the assistance of its ally, and will conduct the war in common, and make peace in mutual agreement with it.

ARTICLE III

Japan possessing paramount political, military, and economic interests in Korea, Great Britain recognises the right of Japan to take such measures of guidance, control, and protection in Korea as she may deem proper and necessary to safeguard and advance those interests, provided always such measures are not contrary to the principle of equal opportunities for the commerce and industry of all nations.

ARTICLE IV

Great Britain having a special interest in all that concerns the security of the Indian frontier, Japan recognises her rights to take such measures in the proximity of that frontier as she may find necessary for safeguarding her Indian possessions.

ARTICLE V

The high contracting parties agree that neither of them will, without consulting the other, enter into separate arrangements with another Power to the prejudice of the objects described in the preamble of this Agreement.

ARTICLE VI

As regards the present war between Japan and Russia,
Great Britain will continue to maintain strict neutrality unless
some other Power or Powers should join in hostilities against
Japan, in which case Great Britain will come to the assistance
of Japan, and will conduct the war in common, and make
peace in mutual agreement with Japan.

ARTICLE VII

The conditions under which armed assistance shall be afforded by either Power to the other in the circumstances mentioned in the present Agreement, and the means by which
such assistance is to be made available, will be arranged by
naval and military authorities of the contracting parties, who
will from time to time consult one another fully and freely
upon all questions of mutual interest.

ARTICLE VIII

The present Agreement shall, subject to the provisions of
Article VI, come into effect immediately after the date of its
signature, and remain in force for ten years from that date.

In case neither of the high contracting parties should have
notified twelve months before the expiration of the said ten
years the intention of terminating it, it shall remain binding
until the expiration of one year from the day on which either
of the high contracting parties shall have denounced it. But
if, when the date fixed for its expiration arrives, either ally
is actually engaged in war, the alliance shall, *ipso facto,* continue until peace is concluded.

In faith whereof, the undersigned, duly authorised by their
respective Governments, have signed this Agreement, and have
affixed thereto their seals.

20

Done in duplicate at London, the 12th day of August, 1905.

    (L. S.) LANSDOWNE, His Britannic Majesty's Principal Secretary of State for Foreign Affairs.

    (L. S.) TADASU HAYASHI, Envoy Extraordinary and Minister Plenipotentiary of His Majesty the Emperor of Japan at the Court of St. James.

APPENDIX C [1]

GREAT BRITAIN AND JAPAN

AGREEMENT RESPECTING THE INTEGRITY OF CHINA, THE
GENERAL PEACE OF EASTERN ASIA AND INDIA, AND
THE TERRITORIAL RIGHTS AND SPECIAL INTERESTS OF
THE PARTIES IN THOSE REGIONS, JULY 13, 1911

Preamble

The Government of Japan and the Government
of Great Britain having in view the important
changes which have taken place in the situation since
the conclusion of the Anglo-Japanese Agreement of
August 12, 1905, and believing that the revision of
that Agreement responding to such changes would
contribute to general stability and repose, have
agreed upon the following stipulations to replace the
Agreement above mentioned, such stipulations having the same object as the said Agreement, namely:

A.—The consolidation and maintenance of the general peace
in the regions of Eastern Asia and India.

B.—The preservation of the common interests of all the
Powers in China by insuring the independence and integrity
of the Chinese Empire and the principle of equal opportunities
for the commerce and industry of all nations in China.

C.—The maintenance of the territorial rights of the High
Contracting Parties in the regions of Eastern Asia and of
India and the defence of their special interests in those
regions:

[1] MacMurray, I, 900-901.

ARTICLE I

It is agreed that whenever, in the opinion of either Japan or Great Britain, any of the rights and interests referred to in the preamble of this Agreement are in jeopardy, the two Governments will communicate with one another fully and frankly, and will consider in common the measures which should be taken to safeguard those menaced rights and interests.

ARTICLE II

If by reason of an unprovoked attack or aggressive action, wherever arising, on the part of any other Power or Powers, either of the High Contracting Parties should be involved in war in defence of its territorial rights or special interests mentioned in the preamble of this Agreement, the other High Contracting Party will at once come to the assistance of its Ally and will conduct the war in common and make peace in mutual agreement with it.

ARTICLE III

The High Contracting Parties agree that neither of them will, without consulting the other, enter into a separate agreement with another Power to the prejudice of the objects described in the preamble of this Agreement.

ARTICLE IV

Should either of the High Contracting Parties conclude a treaty of general arbitration with a third Power, it is agreed that nothing in this Agreement shall impose on such contracting party an obligation to go to war with the Power with whom such an arbitration treaty is in force.

ARTICLE V

The conditions under which armed assistance shall be afforded by either Power to the other in circumstances entered into the present Agreement, and the means by which such assistance is to be made available, will be arranged by the military and naval authorities of the High Contracting Parties, who will from time to time consult one another fully and frankly upon all questions of mutual interests.

ARTICLE VI

The present Agreement shall come into effect immediately after the date of its signature, and remain in force for ten years from that date. In case neither of the High Contracting Parties should have notified twelve months before the expiration the intention of terminating it, it shall remain binding until the expiration of one year from the day on which either of the High Contracting Parties shall have denounced it. But if, when the date fixed for its expiration arrives, either ally is actually engaged in war, the Alliance shall, *ipso facto,* continue until peace is concluded.

In faith whereof the undersigned, duly authorised by their respective Governments, have signed this Agreement and have affixed their seals thereto. Done at London July 13, 1911.

> (L. S.) T. KATO, the Ambassador of His Majesty the Emperor of Japan at the Court of St. James.
>
> (L. S.) EDWARD GREY, H. B. M.'s Secretary of State for Foreign Affairs.

APPENDIX D [1]

(1) A TREATY BETWEEN THE UNITED STATES OF AMERICA, THE BRITISH EMPIRE, FRANCE, AND JAPAN, SIGNED DECEMBER 13, 1921, RELATING TO THEIR INSULAR POSSESSIONS AND INSULAR DOMINIONS IN THE PACIFIC OCEAN

The United States of America, the British Empire, France and Japan,

With a view to the preservation of the general peace and the maintenance of their rights in relation to their insular possessions and insular dominions in the region of the Pacific Ocean,

Have determined to conclude a Treaty to this effect and have appointed as their Plenipotentiaries:

(Names omitted.)

Who, having communicated their full powers, found in good and due form, have agreed as follows:

I

The High Contracting Parties agree as between themselves to respect their rights in relation to their insular possessions and insular dominions in the region of the Pacific Ocean.

If there should develop between any of the High Contracting Parties a controversy arising out of any Pacific question and involving their said rights which is not satis-

[1] U. S. Congress, Senate Doc. No. 126, 67th Congress, 2d Session. *Conference on the Limitation of Armament.* Washington, 1922, pp. 889-893.

factorily settled by diplomacy and is likely to affect the harmonious accord now happily subsisting between them, they shall invite the other High Contracting Parties to a joint conference to which the whole subject will be referred for consideration and adjustment.

II

If the said rights are threatened by the aggressive action of any other Power, the High Contracting Parties shall communicate with one another fully and frankly in order to arrive at an understanding as to the most efficient measures to be taken, jointly or separately, to meet the exigencies of the particular situation.

III

This Treaty shall remain in force for ten years from the time it shall take effect, and after the expiration of said period it shall continue to be in force subject to the right of any of the High Contracting Parties to terminate it upon twelve months' notice.

IV

This Treaty shall be ratified as soon as possible in accordance with the constitutional methods of the High Contracting Parties and shall take effect on the deposit of ratifications, which shall take place at Washington, and thereupon the agreement between Great Britain and Japan, which was concluded at London on July 13, 1911, shall terminate. The Government of the United States will transmit to all the Signatory Powers a certified copy of the *proces-verbal* of the deposit of ratifications.

The present Treaty, in French and in English, shall remain deposited in the Archives of the Government of the United States, and duly certified copies thereof will be transmitted by that Government to each of the Signatory Powers.

In faith whereof the above named Plenipotentiaries have signed the present Treaty.

Done at the City of Washington, the thirteenth day of December, One Thousand Nine Hundred and Twenty-One.

(Signatures omitted.)

(2) DECLARATION ACCOMPANYING THE ABOVE FOUR-POWER TREATY.

In signing the Treaty this day between The United States of America, The British Empire, France, and Japan, it is declared to be the understanding and intent of the Signatory Powers:

1. That the Treaty shall apply to the Mandated Islands in the Pacific Ocean; provided, however, that the making of the Treaty shall not be deemed to be an assent on the part of The United States of America to the mandates and shall not preclude agreements between The United States of America and the Mandatory Powers respectively in relation to the mandated islands.

2. That the controversies to which the second paragraph of Article I refers shall not be taken to embrace questions which according to principles of international law lie exclusively within the domestic jurisdiction of the respective Powers.

Washington, D. C., December 13, 1921.

(Signatures omitted.)

(3) A TREATY BETWEEN THE SAME FOUR POWERS, SUPPLEMENTARY TO THE ABOVE, SIGNED FEBRUARY 6, 1922.

The United States of America, the British Empire, France and Japan have, through their respective Plenipotentiaries, agreed upon the following stipulations supplementary to the Quadruple Treaty signed at Washington on December 13, 1921:

The term "insular possessions and insular dominions" used in the aforesaid Treaty shall, in its application to Japan, include only Karafuto (or the Southern portion of the island of Sakhalin), Formosa and the Pescadores, and the islands under the mandate of Japan.

The present agreement shall have the same force and effect as the said Treaty to which it is supplementary.

The provisions of Article IV of the aforesaid Treaty of December 13, 1921, relating to ratification shall be applicable to the present Agreement, which in French and English shall remain deposited in the Archives of the Government of the United States, and duly certified copies thereof shall be transmitted by that Government to each of the other Contracting Powers.

In faith whereof the respective Plenipotentiaries have signed the present Agreement.

Done at the City of Washington, the sixth day of February, One Thousand Nine Hundred and Twenty-two.

(Signatures omitted.)

APPENDIX E [1]

A TREATY BETWEEN ALL NINE POWERS RELATING TO PRINCIPLES AND POLICIES TO BE FOLLOWED IN MATTERS CONCERNING CHINA.

The United States of America, Belgium, the British Empire, China, France, Italy, Japan, the Netherlands and Portugal,

Desiring to adopt a policy designed to stabilize conditions in the Far East, to safeguard the rights and interests of China, and to promote intercourse between China and the other Powers upon the basis of equality of opportunity;

Have resolved to conclude a treaty for that purpose and to that end have appointed as their respective Plenipotentiaries;

(Names omitted.)

Who, having communicated to each other their full powers, found to be in good and due form, have agreed as follows:

ARTICLE I

The Contracting Powers, other than China, agree:

(1) To respect the sovereignty, the independence, and the territorial and administrative integrity of China;

[1] U. S. Congress, Senate Doc. No. 162, 67th Congress, 2d Session. *Conference on the Limitation of Armament,* Washington, 1922, pp. 893-897.

(2) To provide the fullest and most unembarrassed opportunity to China to develop and maintain for herself an effective and stable government;

(3) To use their influence for the purpose of effectually establishing and maintaining the principle of equal opportunity for the commerce and industry of all nations throughout the territory of China;

(4) To refrain from taking advantage of conditions in China in order to seek special rights or privileges which would abridge the rights of subjects or citizens of friendly States, and from countenancing action inimical to the security of such States.

ARTICLE II

The Contracting Powers agree not to enter into any treaty, agreement, arrangement, or understanding, either with one another, or, individually or collectively, with any Power or Powers, which infringe or impair the principles stated in Article I.

ARTICLE III

With a view to applying more effectually the principles of the Open Door or equality of opportunity in China for the trade and industry of all nations, the Contracting Powers, other than China, agree that they will not seek, nor support their respective nationals in seeking:

(a) any arrangement which might purport to establish in favour of their interests any general superiority of rights with respect to commercial or economic development in any designated region of China;

(b) any such monopoly or preference as would deprive the nationals of any other Power of the right of undertaking any legitimate trade or industry in China, or of participating with the Chinese Government, or with any local authority, in any category of public enterprise, or which by reason of its scope, duration or geographical extent is calculated to frustrate the practical application of the principle of equal opportunity.

It is understood that the foregoing stipulations of this Article are not to be so construed as to prohibit the acquisition of such properties or rights as may be necessary to the conduct of a particular commercial, industrial, or financial undertaking or to the encouragement of invention and research.

China undertakes to be guided by the principles stated in the foregoing stipulations of this Article in dealing with applications for economic rights and privileges from Governments and nationals of all foreign countries, whether parties to the present Treaty or not.

Article IV

The Contracting Powers agree not to support any agreements by their respective nationals with each other designed to create Spheres of Influence or to provide for the enjoyment of mutually exclusive opportunities in designated parts of Chinese territory.

Article V

China agrees that, throughout the whole of the railways in China, she will not exercise or permit unfair discrimination of any kind. In particular there shall be no discrimination whatever, direct or indirect, in respect of charges or of facilities on the ground of the nationality of passengers or the countries from which or to which they are proceeding, or the origin or ownership of goods or the country from which they are consigned, or the nationality or ownership of the ship or other means of conveying such passengers or goods before or after their transport on the Chinese Railways.

The Contracting Powers, other than China, assume a corresponding obligation in respect of any of the aforesaid railways over which they or their nationals are in a position to exercise any control in virtue of any concession, special agreement or otherwise.

Article VI

The Contracting Powers, other than China, agree fully to respect China's rights as a neutral in time of war to which China is not a party; and China declares that when she is a neutral she will observe the obligations of neutrality.

Article VII

The Contracting Powers agree that, whenever a situation arises which in the opinion of any one of them involves the application of the stipulations of the present Treaty, and renders desirable discussion of such application, there shall be full and frank communication between the Contracting Powers concerned.

Article VIII

Powers not signatory to the present Treaty, which have Governments recognized by the Signatory Powers and which have treaty relations with China, shall be invited to adhere to the present Treaty. To this end the Government of the United States will make the necessary communications to nonsignatory Powers and will inform the Contracting Powers of the replies received. Adherence by any Power shall become effective on receipt of notice thereof by the Government of the United States.

Article IX

The present Treaty shall be ratified by the Contracting Powers in accordance with their respective constitutional methods and shall take effect on the date of the deposit of all the ratifications, which shall take place at Washington as soon as possible. The Government of the United States will transmit to the other Contracting Powers a certified copy of the procès-verbal of the deposit of ratifications.

The present Treaty, of which the French and English texts are both authentic, shall remain deposited in the archives of the Government of the United States, and duly certified copies thereof shall be transmitted by that Government to the other Contracting Powers.

In faith whereof the above named Plenipotentiaries have signed the present Treaty.

Done at the City of Washington the Sixth day of February One Thousand Nine Hundred and Twenty-Two.

(Signatures omitted.)

BIBLIOGRAPHY

DOCUMENTS

British Documents on the Origins of the War, 1898-1914, ed. by G. P. Gooch and Harold Temperley.

British Foreign and State Papers.

British Parliamentary Debates.

British Parliamentary Papers.

Die Grosse Politik der Europäischen Kabinette, 1871-1914, Berlin, 1924.

Foreign Relations of the United States.

Livre Noir, Diplomatie d'avant-Guerre d'Apres les documents des Archives Russes, Novembre, 1910, Juillet, 1914.

The United States House Documents.

The United States Senate Documents.

COLLECTION OF TREATIES, ETC.

Aitchison, C. U. A collection of Treaties, Engagements and Sanads relating to India and neighboring countries, Calcutta, 1892.

Chung, Henry. Korean Treaties, New York, 1919.

Customs: Treaties, Conventions, etc., between China and Foreign States.

Hertslet, Sir Edward. Treaties, etc., between Great Britain and China; and between China and Foreign Powers, London, 1908.

League of Nations Treaties Series.

MacMurray, John V. A. Treaties and Agreements with and concerning China, New York, 2 vols., 1921.

Malloy, William M. Treaties, Conventions, International Acts, Protocols, and Agreements between the United States of America and other Powers, Washington, 1910.

Rockhill, William W. Treaties and Conventions with or concerning China and Korea, 1894-1904. Washington, 1904.

LETTERS, MEMOIRS AND OTHER SIMILAR SOURCES

Correspondence of Li Hung Chang (Li Wen Chung Kung Chuan Shu).

Eckardstein, Herman freiherr von. Lebenserinnerungen und politische denkwürdigkeiten, Leipzig, 1921.

301

Gérard, Auguste. Ma Mission au Japan, 1907-1914, Paris, 1919.
—— —— Ma Mission en Chine, 1893-97, Paris, 1918.
Hayashi, Count Tadasu. Secret Memoirs, ed. by Andrew M. Pooley, London, 1915.
Hsieuh, Foo Chen. The Diary of a Diplomat (Chu Shih er Chi).
Izwolsky, Alexander. Memoirs, London, 1920.
Levine, Isaac Don. Letters from the Kaiser to the Czar, New York, 1920.
Rosen, Baron Ramon R. Forty years of Diplomacy, New York, 1922.
Siebert, B. de. Entente Diplomacy and the World, New York, 1921.
The Statesmen of the Ching Dynasty (Kuo Chou Min Chen Yen Hsin Lou).
Thayer, W. R. Life and Letters of John Hay, 2 vols., Boston and New York, 1915.
The Willy-Nicky Correspondence, ed. by H. Berstein.
Witte, Count S. I. Memoirs, New York, 1921.

NEWSPAPERS

Japan Advertiser.
Japan Chronicle.
Japan Daily Herald.
Korean Daily News.
London Times.
New York Times.
North China Herald. New Series.

MAGAZINES AND REVIEWS

American Journal of International Law.
American Political Science Review.
Arena, Boston.
Asia, New York.
Blackwood's Edinburgh Magazine.
Booklover's Magazine, New York.
China Weekly Review, The (formerly Millard's Review of the Far East), Shanghai, China.
Contemporary Review, London.
Cosmopolitan Magazine, New York.
Current History, New York.
Current Opinion, New York.
Everybody's Magazine, New York.
Foreign Affairs.

Fortnightly Review, London.
Forum, New York.
Independent, New York.
Japanese Journal of International Law and Diplomacy (in Japanese).
Literary Digest, New York.
Littell's Living Age, Boston.
Macmillan's Magazine, London.
Monthly Review, London.
Nation, New York.
National Review, London.
Nineteenth Century, London.
North American Review, New York.
Outlook, New York.
Political Science Quarterly, New York.
Putnam's Monthly, New York.
Quarterly Review, London.
Review of Reviews, New York.
Saturday Review, London.
Scribner's Magazine, New York.
World To-day, Chicago.
World's Work, New York.
Yale Review, New Haven.

GENERAL WORKS AND OTHER SECONDARY SOURCES

Abbott, James F. Japanese Expansion and American Policies, New
    York, 1916.
Anethan, Eleanora M. Fourteen Years of Diplomatic Life in Japan,
    London, 1912.
Arbitration and the United States, World Peace Foundation, Boston,
    1926, IX, Nos. 6-7.
Asakawa, Kanichi. The Russo-Japanese Conflict, Boston and New
    York, 1904.
Bancroft, H. H. The New Pacific, New York, 1900.
Bau, M. C. China and World Peace, New York, 1928.
────── ────── The Foreign Relations of China, New York, 1922.
────── ────── The Open Door Doctrine in Relation to China, New
    York, 1923.
Beresford, Lord Charles. The Break-up of China, London, 1899.
Beveridge, A. J. Russian Advance, New York and London, 1903.
Blakeslee, George H. Japan and Japanese-American Relations, New
    York, 1912.

Brown, Arthur. Japan in the World of To-day, New York, 1928.

Buell, R. L. Japanese Immigration, World Peace Foundation, 1924, VII, Nos. 5-6.

Bülow, Prince von. Imperial Germany.

——— ——— The Washington Conference, New York, 1922.

Bywater, Hector C. Sea-Power in the Pacific, Boston and New York, 1921.

Cassell's History of the Russo-Japanese War, 4 vols., London, 1906.

Chirol, V. The Far East Question, London, 1896.

Crisis in China, The. Reprinted from the North American Review. New York and London, 1900.

Chung, Henry. The Case of Korea, New York, 1921.

——— ——— The Oriental Policy of the United States, New York. 1919.

Colquhoun, Archibald R. English Policy in the Far East, London, 1895. (Author was the *Times* Special Correspondent.)

——— ——— The Mastery of the Pacific, New York, 1902.

——— ——— Problem in China and British Policy, London, 1900.

——— ——— Russia against India, London, 1900.

Cordier, Henri. Histoire des relations de la Chine avec les puissances occidentales, 3 vols., Paris, 1901-02.

Crow, Carl. Japan and America; a Contrast, New York, 1916.

Curzon, George N. Problems of the Far East, Westminster, 1896.

Davis, Colonel Warren J. Japan, the Air Menace of the Pacific, Boston, 1928.

De Forest, John H. Is Japan a Menace to the United States? Washington, 1908.

Dennett, Tyler. Roosevelt and the Russo-Japanese War, New York, 1925.

Dennis, Alfred L. P. Adventures in American Diplomacy, New York, 1928.

——— ——— The Anglo-Japanese Alliance, Berkeley, California, 1923.

——— ——— The Foreign Policy of Soviet Russia, New York, 1924.

Dillon, Emile J. The Eclipse of Russia. New York, 1918.

Dunning, William A. The British Empire and the United States, New York, 1914.

Dyer, H. Japan in World Politics, London, 1909.

Farjeuel, tr. by Vivian, M. Through the Chinese Revolution, New York, 1916.

Foster, John W. American Diplomacy in the Orient, Boston, 1903.

Fox, Sir Frank. The Mastery of the Pacific; Can the British Empire and the United States Agree? London, 1928.

Gallagher, D. America's Aim and Asia's Aspirations, New York, 1920.

Gannett, L. S. Young China, New York, 1926.

Gardiner, Charles A. The Proposed Anglo-American Alliance (an address delivered before the American Social Science Association), New York, and London, 1898.

Gérard, A. La Triple Entente et la Guerre, Paris, 1918.

Gooch, George P. History of Modern Europe, London, 1878-1919.

Gooch, G. P., and Masterman, J. H. B. A Century of British Foreign Policy, London, 1917.

Green, Thomas E. War with Japan? Washington, 1916.

Gulick, Sidney L. Anti-Japanese War Scare Stories, Chicago, 1917.

Hall, William E. International Law, Oxford, 8th ed., 1924.

Hammann, Otto. Zur Vorgeschichte des Weltkrieges, Berlin, 1919.

Hishida, Seiji C. The International Position of Japan as a Great Power, New York, 1905.

Hershey, A. S. International Law and Diplomacy of the Russo-Japanese War, New York, 1906.

Hippistery, A. E. The Chinese Revolution, London, 1912.

Hodgkin, H. T. China in the Family of Nations, London, 1923.

Hornbeck, Stanley K. Contemporary Politics in the Far East, New York, 1916.

Hsu, S. China and her Political Entity, New York, 1926.

Hulbert, Homer B. The Passing of Korea, New York, 1906.

Hutchinson, Paul. What and Why in China, Chicago, 1928.

Iyenaga, T. Japan's Real Attitude toward America, New York and London, 1916.

Joseph, P. Foreign Diplomacy in China, 1894-1900, London, 1928.

Kawakami, K. K. American-Japanese Relations; An Inside View of Japan's Policies and Purposes, New York, 1912.

—— —— Japan and World Peace, New York, 1919.

—— —— Japan's Pacific Policy, New York, 1922.

King-Hall, S. The China of To-day, London, 1927.

Kuno, Y. S. What Japan Wants, New York, 1921.

Latané John H. From Isolation to Leadership, New York, 1918.

—— —— A History of American Foreign Policy, New York, 1927.

McClatchy, Valentine S. The Germany of Asia, Sacramento, 1919.

McCormick, Frederick. The Menace of Japan, Boston, 1917.

McKenzie, F. A. The Tragedy of Korea, London, 1908.

——— ——— The Unveiled East, New York, 1907.

Millard, Thomas F. American and Far Eastern Question, New York, 1919.

——— ——— China, Where It is Today and Why, New York, 1928.

——— ——— Conflict of Policies in Asia, New York, 1924.

——— ——— Democracy and the Eastern Question, New York, 1919.

——— ——— The Great War in the Far East, Shanghai, 1915.

——— ——— The New Far East, New York, 1906.

——— ——— Our Eastern Question, New York, 1916.

——— ——— The Shantung Case at the Conference, Shanghai, 1921.

Morse, Hosea B. The International Relations of the Chinese Empire, 3 vols., London, 1918.

Mowat, H. B. The Diplomatic Relations of Great Britain and the United States, New York, 1925.

Murray, Arthur M. Imperial Outposts from a Strategical and Commercial Aspect, with Special Reference to the Japanese Alliance, New York, 1907.

Norton, Henry K. China and the Powers, New York, 1927.

Okuma, Count Shigenolu. Fifty Years of New Japan (Kaikaku Gojanenshi), English Version, ed. by Marcus B. Huish. 2 vols., London, 1910.

Oppenheim, Lassa F. L. International Law, London, 1906.

Osborne, Sidney. The Isolation of Japan, Amsterdam, Rotterdam, 1919.

——— ——— The New Japanese Peril, New York, 1921.

——— ——— The Problem of Japan, Amsterdam, Rotterdam, 1918.

Overlach, T. W. Foreign Financial Control in China, New York, 1919.

Pasvolsky, Leo. Russia in the Far East, New York, 1922.

Pitkin, Walter B. Must We Fight Japan? New York, 1921.

Pooley, Andrew M. Japan's Foreign Policies, London, 1920.

——— Japan at the Cross Road, London, 1917.

Ransome, Arthur. The Chinese Puzzle, London, 1927.

Rea, George B. Japan's Place in the Sun; the Menace to America, Washington, 1915.

Redesdale, Lord Algernon Bertram F. The Garter Mission to Japan, London, 1906.

Reid, G. China, Captive or Free? New York, 1921.

Reinsch, Paul S. An American Diplomat in China, New York, 1923.

——— ——— World Politics at the End of the Nineteenth Century, as Influenced by the Oriental Situation, New York, 1900.

Sargent, A. J. Anglo-Chinese Commerce and Diplomacy, Oxford, 1907.

Sato, K. If Japan and America Fight, Tokio, 1921.

Satow, Sir Ernest. A Guide to Diplomatic Practice, London 1917.

Scholefield, G. H. The Pacific: Its Past and Future, London, 1919.

Sears, Louis M. History of American Foreign Relations, New York, 1927.

Seibold, Louis. Japan, Her Plans and Purposes, New York, 1921.

——— ——— Japan: Her Vast Undertakings and World Expansion. New York, 1921.

Sick, Park-In. The Tragic History of Korea, Chinese Edition, Shanghai, 1915.

Soothill, W. E. China and England. London, 1928.

Sorrel, Albert. L'Europe et la revolution française, Paris, 1904.

Stuart, Graham H. French Foreign Policy, 1898-1914, New York, 1921.

Sullivan, Mark. The Great Adventure at Washington, New York, 1922.

Szilassy. Der untergang der donau-monarchie, Berlin, 1921.

Taft, Henry W. Japan and the Far East Conference, New York, 1921.

Tardieu, Andre. La France et les Alliances, 3rd ed., Paris, 1910.

Treat, Payson J. The Far East: a Political and Diplomatic History, New York and London, 1928.

——— ——— Japan, American and the Great War, World Peace Foundation Pamphlet, Dec., 1918, I, No. 8.

——— ——— Japan and the United States, 1853-1921, Boston, 1921.

Tominas, Shutaro. The Open-door Policy and the Territorial Integrity of China, New York, 1919.

Tyau, M. T. Z. China Awakened, Shanghai, 1919.

Usher, Roland G. The Challenge of the Future, Boston and New York, 1916.

Vladimir (pseud. for Zenone Valpecelli). Russia on the Pacific and the Siberian Railway, London, 1899.

Vrooman, Frank B. British Columbia and Her Imperial Outlook, (A paper read before the Royal Colonial Institute), London, 1912.

Walker, Guy M. Can We Escape War with Japan? New York, 1921.

Ward, A. W., and Gooch, G. P. The Cambridge History of British Foreign Policy, 1783 to 1919, Cambridge, 1922-23.

Weale, B. L. Putnam (pseud. for Simpson, Bertram L.). The Coming Struggle in East Asia, London, 1908.

——— ——— The Fight for the Republic in China, New York, 1917.

——— ——— An Indiscreet Chronicle from the Pacific, New York, 1922.

——— ——— The Re-Shaping of the Far East, 2 vols., New York, 1905.

——— ——— The Truce in the Far East and its Aftermath, New York, 1907.

——— ——— The Truth about China and Japan, New York, 1919.

——— ——— The Vanished Empire, London, 1926.

——— ——— Why China Sees Red, New York, 1925.

Weyl, Walter E. American World Policies, New York, 1917.

Wheeler, W. R. China and the World War, New York, 1919.

Whyte, F. China and Foreign Powers, London, 1927.

Willoughby, W. W. China at the Conference, Baltimore, 1922.

——— ——— Foreign Rights and Interests in China, Baltimore, 1927, 2 vols.

Yoshitomi, M. Les Conflits nippo-américains et le problème du Pacific, Paris, 1926.

INDEX

Afghanistan, 2, 3; frontier of, 4

Aigon, treaty of, 25

Alexiev, Admiral, agreement with Tartar General of Mukden, 240

Alsace-Lorraine, 130

American fleet well received in Japan, 160

Anglo-American arbitration Treaty, 155-156, 157

Anglo-German Agreement as understood by Germany, excluding Manchuria, 73, 94

Anglo-German Alliance failed, 68

Anglo-German Alliance, impossible, 75

Anglo - German - American - Japanese Alliance, possibility of the, 268-269

Anglo-German relations darkened, 65

Anglo-German Syndicate, loan of, to China, 67

Anglo-Japanese Alliance, 49; favored by Japan, 49-50, 79; difficulties of, 51-52, 64-65; public opinion in England toward, 63-64; advantage of, 76-77; negotiation for, 81; suggestion by Eckardstein, 80; opposition by Ito and Inouye, 81-82; terms of, 83-84; reception of, 84-88; comment on, 88-91; aimed at Russia, 91; *status quo* explained, 93-94; real purport of, 96; offensive as well as defensive, 96; renewed, 118-120; praised by British Liberal Party, 120; second Anglo-Japanese Alliance compared with the first one, 122-124; results of the new, 124-128; renewed in 1911, 147; opposition of the Dominions, 149-150; Japan's reasons for renewing the, 151-152; Third version of the, 153-156; welcomed by the London *Times*, 156; oppo-

sitions to the, in 1921, 189-190; termination of Anglo-Japanese Alliance, 196-198; China's objection to renewal of, 213-216

Anglo-Russian Agreement of 1899, 143

Anglo-Russian Agreement on railway zones in China, 69-70, 94

Anglo-Russian Convention of 1909, 133

Anglo-Russian Entente of 1907, 155

Anglo-Russian rapprochement reached an *impasse*, 68

Ashmead-Bartlett, Sir Ellis, advocated Anglo-Japanese Entente, 63-64

Asquith praise of second Anglo-Japanese Alliance, 120

Australia, Japanese immigration in, 149; bad treatment of Japanese in, 150; in favor of modified Anglo-Japanese Alliance, 190-191

Austria annexed Bosnia-Herzegovina, 145

Balfour, A. J., 60; quoted, 187; opposed China's third point, 220

Beresford, Lord Charles, 232; letter to Hay, 233-234; the break-up of China, 234

Bertie's view on Anglo-Japanese Alliance, 76-77, 268

Björko, Alliance at, between Germany and Russia, 132; denounced by Witte, 133

Boers, war with England, 71

Borah, Senator, introduced disarmament resolution, 255

Boxer uprising, 70; Russian aggression in Manchuria, 75; suppression, 238-239; Britain and Germany on the, 265